FROM LIFE TO SURVIVAL

From Life to Survival

DERRIDA, FREUD, AND THE FUTURE OF DECONSTRUCTION

Robert Trumbull

FORDHAM UNIVERSITY PRESS   NEW YORK 2022

Copyright © 2022 Fordham University Press

All rights reserved. No part of this publication may be reproduced, stored in a retrieval system, or transmitted in any form or by any means—electronic, mechanical, photocopy, recording, or any other—except for brief quotations in printed reviews, without the prior permission of the publisher.

Fordham University Press has no responsibility for the persistence or accuracy of URLs for external or third-party Internet websites referred to in this publication and does not guarantee that any content on such websites is, or will remain, accurate or appropriate.

Fordham University Press also publishes its books in a variety of electronic formats. Some content that appears in print may not be available in electronic books.

Visit us online at www.fordhampress.com.

Library of Congress Cataloging-in-Publication Data available online at https://catalog.loc.gov.

Printed in the United States of America

24 23 22   5 4 3 2 1
First edition

For Eli Trumbull, my everything

Contents

LIST OF ABBREVIATIONS ix

Introduction: Derrida, Freud, and the Future of Deconstruction 1

1 From Grammatology to Life Death 11

2 Interrogating the Death Drive 35

3 Survival as Autoimmunity 68

4 Mortality and Normativity 97

5 Sovereignty, Cruelty, and the Death Penalty 127

ACKNOWLEDGMENTS 155

NOTES 157

BIBLIOGRAPHY 185

INDEX 195

Abbreviations

A	*Aporias*
AF	*Archive Fever*
ARSS	"Autoimmunity: Real and Symbolic Suicides"
BS	*The Beast and the Sovereign*, vols. 1 and 2
D	*Dissemination*
DP	*The Death Penalty*, vols. 1 and 2
FK	"Faith and Knowledge"
FWT	*For What Tomorrow . . .*
LD	*Life Death*
LLF	*Learning to Live Finally*
M	*Margins of Philosophy*
N	*Negotiations*
OG	*Of Grammatology*
P	*Psyche: Inventions of the Other*, vol. 1
PC	*The Post Card*
PF	*The Politics of Friendship*
PM	*Paper Machine*
POS	*Positions*
R	*Rogues*
RP	*Resistances of Psychoanalysis*
SM	*Specters of Marx*
VP	*Voice and Phenomenon*
WA	*Without Alibi*
WD	*Writing and Difference*

Citations in text list the source of the English translation followed by the French original (e.g., OG, 70/103).

FROM LIFE TO SURVIVAL

Introduction
Derrida, Freud, and the Future of Deconstruction

Contemporary Continental thought has been marked by a turn away from the concerns of the so-called linguistic turn in twentieth-century European philosophy. New materialisms, posthumanism, speculative realism, and object-oriented ontology all seek to leave behind the thought of language at the heart of poststructuralism as it has been traditionally understood. What these new forms of thought share is the attempt to think beyond the human, whether this is to grasp materiality, ontology, or to think other types of beings. At the same time, biopolitical philosophy, in its diverse forms, has brought critical attention to the question of life, examining new formations of life and death. Within this broader turn, deconstruction, with its apparent focus on language, writing, and textuality, is generally set aside.

This book argues unequivocally for the continued relevance of Derridean deconstruction in contemporary Continental thought by showing that deconstruction does speak to resolutely material issues, and to life and the basic structure of the living. To this extent, in making the case for what deconstruction offers today, the book makes the case for why deconstruction should have a future, why it can and should live on, taking on new problems and new projects.

We will not understand Derrida's vital contributions to these issues, however, without a full grasp of his thinking of life in particular. It is the argument of this book that Derrida's deep engagement with Freud, a critical interlocutor for Derrida across the full trajectory of his work, supplies *the* key to this problematic and its consequential implications. The book shows that in the diverse, at times conflicted and contradictory body of work attributed to Freud, deconstruction finds powerful conceptual resources for developing a remarkably generative thinking of life as constitutively exposed to death, one that I show follows directly from the crucial early deconstructive notions of arche-writing and the trace. The traditional notion of life *versus* death, life thought as what is opposed to death, contaminated by it only secondarily from the outside, is transformed in Derrida's hands, into *la vie la mort*, "life death," and then ultimately, into the thought of what he calls survival (*survivance*). On this view, the life of a living being, in accordance with what Derrida describes as the "ultra-transcendental" logic of *différance* and the trace (OG, 61/90), has to be originarily exposed to its other in order to be at all. Such exposure or opening up to heterogeneity within the structure of what is supposedly selfsame is here revealed to be its very condition of possibility.

Life, then, has to welcome and repeat a certain exposure to death, has to transact with it in what Derrida will characterize as a certain "economy," in order to be what it is in the first place. Viewed from this perspective, absolute closure, the purity of a living being untouched by death at the level of its originary constitution (formed *first* in its purity and touched or contaminated by its other only *secondarily*) would make life impossible, would be its extinction, a kind of asphyxiation. By the same token, total, aneconomic opening to the other in the same, the absolute exposure of life to its other, would equally be the condition of impossibility of life as it is lived. As we will see, life death thus bespeaks neither the simple opposition of life and death nor their total conjuncture or overlapping, but rather the *différantial* structure whereby life necessarily comes into being and persists via the "economy of death" just named. This logic comes to be reelaborated, I go on to show, in the thought of survival in Derrida's later work, the thought of life as structurally, originarily living on, in the sense of living on for some indeterminate time to come or living on and surviving in the wake of a trauma. While legible to various degrees in other areas of Derrida's work, the chapters that follow show that the thought of life death—and in turn survival—in deconstruction emerges most forcefully in Derrida's engagement with Freud, where Derrida is able to think through a set of problematics central to the deconstructive project *in toto*.[1]

The project of tracking this trajectory in Derrida has been made possible by a renewed vitality in Derrida studies, following the publication of Derrida's late seminars, *The Death Penalty* and *The Beast and the Sovereign,* and the strategically important 1975–76 seminar, *La vie la mort (Life Death)* The late 1999–2001 and 2001–2003 seminars have allowed scholars to revisit the earliest insights of deconstruction from the vantage point of their later development, while the publication of the full text of *La vie la mort*—which takes up Freud alongside Nietzsche, Heidegger, and the life sciences—enriches our understanding of the broader trajectory in Derrida's work extending from the thought of life as an economy of death to life death, and ultimately to the logic of survival. Thus, scholars such as Geoffrey Bennington, Vicky Kirby, Martin Hägglund and, most recently, Francesco Vitale and Dawne McCance have called attention to the thought of life in Derrida.[2] But they have not allowed us to grasp it in its full extent, insofar as they have not taken up how thoroughly and deeply Derrida is engaged with Freud in his development of this problematic and how the notion of life death is reconfigured in Derrida's work after 1980, including in his work on ethics, politics, democracy, and sovereignty. Elizabeth Rottenberg, for her part, has recently provided a study of the Derrida-Freud nexus.[3] Yet her account is ultimately focused elsewhere, on the thought of contingency and, in turn, the event that emerges in deconstruction and psychoanalysis.

The present account goes beyond these treatments in two ways. First, the book lays out precisely how Derrida mobilizes Freud to develop a thinking of life death and in turn survival and autoimmunity. Within this elaboration, it shows how the 1975–76 seminar serves to illuminate the major engagements with Freud—in the crucial texts "Freud and the Scene of Writing" (1967) and "To Speculate—on 'Freud'" (1980)—Derrida himself saw as important enough to publish in his lifetime, expanding on the more limited discussion of Freud found in *La vie la mort*, and to which he returned repeatedly in his later work. Moreover, it demonstrates how Derrida's deep engagement with Freud's theory of the drives in this period allows us to grasp key features of the logic of life death central to the line of thought in Derrida running from some of the earliest developments of deconstruction to the late activation of the logic of survival. Indeed, the present account shows how the conception of life death Derrida finds in Freud—and which he subsequently reelaborates after 1975–76—enables him to think a set of consequences that the framework of the life sciences and even the Nietzschean will to power do not allow. Above all, it allows him to think the active installation, in life, of an opening to destruction and violation not simply reducible to exposure to whatever comes from the future.

The second way the account offered in this book differs from earlier treatments of Derrida on Freud and life and death is that it demonstrates clearly the decisive consequences of Derrida's rethinking of life in terms of life death and ultimately survival for our understanding of deconstruction's ethical and political purchase.[4] Indeed, the recasting of life as survival legible in Derrida's dealings with Freud is shown to bear directly on the question of deconstruction's normative possibilities, and specifically its capacity to destabilize and put into question, to "shake up," certain inherited understandings of life, death, and the political (understood in Derrida as the theologico-political).[5] The absence of a proper account of these implications has to this point limited an understanding of deconstruction's critical potential and what it offers today.

While the engagement with Freud is not the only point of entry into the thought of life death and *survivance* in Derrida, it nonetheless provides Derrida with crucial reserves across the full sweep of his work spanning nearly four decades. Yet it is vital, here at the outset, to spell out just what is meant by the statement that Derrida's dealings with Freud supply the key to the deconstructive thought of life recast as survival examined in this book. What the book shows is that in putting Freud to work, Derrida does not simply take over Freud's concepts, deploying them "as is," in order to, say, diagnose the repression of writing in the philosophical tradition since Plato. Rather, in Derrida's hands, Freud's concepts—beginning with the concepts of the memory trace and *Nachträglichkeit*, the strange retroactive temporality of the unconscious—are *transformed*, so that it is better to speak of Derrida's rearticulation of Freud than it is to speak of Derrida "applying" Freud's concepts in a different context (say, within the history of philosophy).[6]

In rearticulating Freud, Derrida mobilizes not just what Freud himself thinks he is doing but also the various impasses, contradictions, and blind spots haunting Freud's work. Indeed, Derrida does not just take inspiration from Freud, he submits his discourse to rigorous critique, questioning its basic assumptions, implicit axiomatics, and limits. We could even go a step further and say that Derrida is only able to develop the deconstructive thought of life death, and in turn survival, by submitting Freud's discourse to scrutiny in this way, via a form of critique that, for the deepest philosophical reasons, takes the form not of a challenge to Freud's concepts and methods from the outside, pointing out what they miss or what has come to overtake them (in the life sciences and elsewhere), but rather of a shaking up of Freud's discourse from the inside, showing how it is internally fraught. It is this procedure that ultimately defines Derrida's sustained engagement with Freud.

This double gesture of taking inspiration from a thinker while submitting his or her discourse to rigorous critique, by itself, is not unique to Derrida's relation to Freud. We could equally say the same of Derrida's engagements with Husserl, Heidegger, Levinas, or even Marx. The chief reason for this has to do with what deconstruction, after Heidegger, sought to do from the very beginning: it set out to disrupt the tradition of Western metaphysics by rereading it, developing a new conceptuality by rearticulating so many metaphysical concepts and discourses.

But as Derrida liked to say, not everyone belongs to the tradition in exactly the same way, and this insight is critical to understanding the particular relation Derrida maintains with Freud across the entirety of his work. All of Freud's concepts, Derrida argues, without exception, belong to the history of metaphysics, and in this respect he is like everyone else, Derrida included. Yet, the way Freud deploys these concepts—the way he uses them, trying to take account of their constructedness, their fragility, and their limits—gestures toward the possibility of something else. Freud himself did not reflect on the precise necessity and direction of this gesture and this opening, however. In this way, Freud's discourse is divided and there remains a dimension of Freud's thought he himself does not think. It contains overlooked or suspended resources to be put to work by deconstruction. Those elements and resources that Freud makes available without fully pursuing or explicitly reflecting on, the lines of inquiry he opens up and turns back on, might even be what is most promising in Freud from a deconstructive standpoint.

If, as I have said, Derrida puts Freud to work in a new way for his own purposes, he does so on the basis of a detailed, rigorous understanding of Freud on his own terms. Moreover, his interrogation of Freud's discourse is not limited to, for instance, the notion of the memory trace, which seems to prefigure, in certain respects, Derrida's own understanding of the trace, nor even to Freud's account of the unconscious, the structure of the psyche, and sexuality. Rather, Derrida engages the full scope of Freud's thought: not just what Freud called his theoretical "metapsychology" but also his thinking on sociocultural issues, on the formation of culture and community, history, religion, ethics, law, and politics.[7] In fact, Derrida's discussions of Freud deploy an especially keen grasp of the nuances and intricacies of Freud's thought, particularly his speculative metapsychology, and the way it changes over time, across the different phases of his thinking. The moves Derrida ultimately makes using Freud are reliant on an understanding that goes well beyond a basic familiarity with Freudian terms and concepts.

The issue is that Derrida does not instruct his readers in the basic terms needed to understand Freud as he goes along, as he does quite often in his readings of Husserl, Levinas, or Heidegger. That is, he does not walk readers through how to understand what Freud is doing in Freud's own terms first before moving on to a deconstructive rearticulation of Freud's discourse. In order to truly see what Derrida is doing with Freud, in order to properly grasp how Derrida transforms his thinking, one needs this crucial background at hand. In fact, given how Derrida works, very often in order to follow his engagement with Freud, one needs a fairly deep grasp not just of Freud's discourse in its complexity and how it changes over time, but also of its fraught, conflicting, and contradictory aspects. At key points in the chapters that follow, this book provides this necessary background. Nonetheless, throughout, the focus is squarely on Derrida's Freud, a Freud who does not look like everyone else's.

Tracing in detail how deconstruction puts the resources it finds in Freud to work, chapter 1 elaborates the powerful, yet frequently overlooked thinking of life as *an economy of death* emerging out of Derrida's early work. Looking at Derrida's output from the crucial period of 1967–68, I show how, already at this early stage, deconstruction offers a powerful way of thinking not just the structure of all materiality in the form of what Derrida calls the trace but also the basic structure of the living, a thought that follows directly from the seminal Derridean notion of arche-writing. This demonstration necessarily draws on Derrida's early engagement with Husserl on temporalization in *Voice and Phenomenon* and the conception of arche-writing offered in *Of Grammatology*, but the chapter's distinctive contribution consists in showing how Derrida's early treatment of Freud in the crucial text "Freud and the Scene of Writing" (published in *Writing and Difference* in 1967 but first delivered as a lecture a year earlier) allows us to understand this thinking of life as an economy of death in terms of a radical conception of finitude. In particular, the chapter delineates how, on the basis of his early reading of Freud, Derrida theorizes the basic conditions of life in terms of a process of internal division and exposure to heterogeneity or exteriority, a process shown to be both constitutive and necessary.

Chapter 2 examines how the logic of life as an economy of death elaborated in Derrida's early work is fleshed out in his subsequent dealings with Freud in the ten or so years following 1967–68, most notably in the crucial extended treatment of Freud in "To Speculate—on 'Freud'" (in *The Post Card*). A careful study of this portion of Derrida's work is especially important insofar as, as the subsequent chapters make clear, the Freudian theory of the drives examined in "To Speculate"—and especially Freud's later conception of the life and death drives, outlined in *Beyond the Pleasure Principle* (1920)—comes to form the most consistent point of reference for Derrida in his later engagements with Freud. In order to elucidate "To Speculate," the chapter situates its core arguments, initially sketched in the final four sessions of the 1975–76 seminar, *La vie la mort*, within the overall context of the seminar and in relation to its main concerns. While the discussion of modern biology found in the seminar, carried out via a reading of François Jacob's *La Logique du vivant*, has attracted substantial critical attention, this is not the only portion of the seminar to shed light on the logic of life death developed in Derrida's rearticulation of Freud. On the contrary, the chapter demonstrates that the analysis of Nietzsche and Heidegger contained in the seminar—Derrida's extended treatment of Nietzsche as a thinker of life, even in certain "autobiographical" texts, and his critique of Heidegger on the question of Nietzsche's alleged biologism—enriches our understanding of what is at stake in "To Speculate." Above all, it clarifies how and why the key line of thinking on life death developed there is elaborated by means of a reading of Freud aimed not simply at treating his concepts but rather the relation between his concepts and his writing. In this way, *La vie la mort* illuminates the manner in which Derrida interrogates a certain nonclassical "autobiographical" dimension in Freud. Offering the necessary background Derrida assumes but does not supply in "To Speculate," chapter 2 also situates Freud's *Beyond the Pleasure Principle* within his long, complex inquiry into the drives.[8] Providing this context enables us to better grasp what the chapter shows is Derrida's unique activation of Freud's theory, and in particular the enigmatic notion of the death drive: what Freud views as an unshakeable, unwavering force, present in the living organism from the very first, yet fundamentally inhospitable to life, silently pushing toward destruction.

Ultimately, chapter 2 demonstrates how Derrida rearticulates the notion of the death drive via a thinking of *stricture* or binding, a move that proves crucial to the thought of life death and, in turn, survival, understood as a radical thinking of finitude and mortality outlined across the rest of the book. What Derrida conceptualizes under the heading of binding, it demonstrates, can best be understood as a certain tension internal to the structure of life, but one which is not, for all that, purely and simply internal, insofar as it bespeaks the arche-originary exposure to exteriority in the same traced in the seminal Derridean notion of arche-writing. The chapter concludes by showing how Derrida's rearticulation of Freud furnishes the deep structure of his contemporaneous critique of Lacan around the question of the letter, one of the most widely cited, and misunderstood, portions of Derrida's output in this period.

While chapters 1 and 2 track the thought of life death as it is developed in Derrida's readings of Freud from the 1960s and 1970s, chapter 3 tracks the implications in Derrida's work after 1990, exploring how Derrida's engagement with Freud allows us to fully understand the crucial notions of survival and the autoimmunity of life. From *Specters of Marx* (1993) on, I argue, we begin to see a shift in Derrida's thought: the logic of life death is rearticulated into a thinking of *survival*; or, as Derrida often writes it, *sur-vivance*, understood as a form of "living on." Crucially, the chapter shows how Derrida's continued engagement with Freud in this later period—and in particular, the figure of the death drive—sheds vital light on the thought of survival in deconstruction. In this way, the chapter brings forward elements of Derrida's later thought at times overlooked by Derrida's readers. In order to properly flesh out the thought of survival in the later Derrida, the chapter looks at the link between this term and the notion of autoimmunity. While Derrida applied this notion to a range of phenomena, from religion to media to democracy (even to Freudian psychoanalysis), the chapter shows that the Derridean logic of autoimmunity has its most forceful potential in the thought of life as autoimmune, where the basic conditions of the living are thought in terms of processes of internal division and contamination as well as originary exposure to destruction, a feature of Derrida's thinking that frequently gets lost in discussions of Derridean autoimmunity. Chapter 3 concludes by addressing a competing interpretation of Derrida and Freud with respect to these issues advanced by Martin Hägglund. My account shows that the exposure to radical destruction figured in Derrida's activation of the death drive stems from a structure more primordial than simply an opening to the unpredictable future, as Hägglund conceptualizes it.

With an explanation of how survival is to be understood firmly in place, chapter 4 undertakes a study of the ethical and political implications, the full scope of which are explored across the book's final two chapters. More specifically, chapter 4 intervenes in recent discussions of the question of normativity in deconstruction by showing how the opening to heterogeneity proper to mortal finitude articulated via the thought of survival allows deconstruction to effect a critical rethinking of the ground for ethics and politics. But it is not just the opening to heterogeneous exteriority that matters here. It is also the opening to destruction implied in the radical notion of mortality at the center of the discussion of *survivance* in chapter 3. It is this thought in Derrida that ultimately allows deconstruction to shake up, disturb, or destabilize what he will diagnose as a certain uncritical "phantasm" of life and death informing our inherited ethico-political concepts, one that most often takes the form of what Derrida characterizes as a fundamentally theological notion of life beyond mortal life, a kind of superlife. Having laid out exactly how this deconstructive destabilization challenges the fantasy of superlife, the chapter ends by bringing the thought of *survivance* and the deconstruction of the phantasm of something beyond life and mortal finitude to bear on Derrida's more well-known discussions of justice, the opening to an unpredictable future, and the *to-come*, themes that have been the subject of considerable scholarship and debate in recent years. I show how the apparently merely negative deconstructive procedure of taking on the phantasm simultaneously carries a certain positive, affirmative purchase: it tells us that it would be *better* to keep the conventions, practices, and institutions through which we necessarily navigate our ethical and political responsibilities open to the incalculable coming of the future, to keep them from calcifying, and that this is something that we *should* do. The inclusion of this discussion of deconstruction's future—understood in the sense of *the future deconstruction theorizes*—provides an additional justification for the book's title.

Chapter 5 explores the implications of the thought of survival for rethinking political practice, looking at Derrida's very late work from the late 1990s and early 2000s on sovereignty and the death penalty. The chapter maps out the deconstructive contestation of the death penalty undertaken in this period, one which, it shows, proceeds by mobilizing *survivance* as a critical alternative logic. This thought comes to serve as *the* key lever used to shake up the fundamentally theological phantasm of something "worth more than life" deconstruction finds at the heart of the political theology of the death penalty. Once again, Freud provides key resources for this project, via his thinking of a continually recurring tendency toward cruelty and an indomitable drive for mastery and domination in living beings. Having demonstrated how the thought of *survivance* destabilizes the death penalty, chapter 5, and the book, concludes by showing why this demonstration is anything but a mere case or example of deconstruction's normative purchase. It shows that the death penalty in fact represents the crucial point of entry for a deconstruction of the political generally, insofar as its dominant configurations can be shown to be still fundamentally theological, bound up with the fantasy of superlife. The book ends, therefore, by pointing to what lies ahead for deconstruction: a broader transformation of the political opened up by Derrida in his treatment of the supposedly circumscribed issue of the death penalty. This transformation is to be carried out, I argue, via new deconstructive engagements with contemporary political concepts and practices well beyond those Derrida himself took up in his lifetime and beyond those practices commonly associated with the logic of sovereignty, from biopolitics to the seemingly ironclad link between law, the putative right to life, and an uncritical humanism.

My hope is that what ultimately emerges from this book is a new understanding of what deconstruction offers today and what it can bring to contemporary debates in Continental thought. In this way, this study aims to open up a new future for deconstruction. Having indicated where I think the key resources lie, I leave it to others to put them to use in analyzing and rethinking twenty-first-century concepts and practices. While I can imagine some of the ways in which they could be put to use in the future, there are likely to be other ways I could never envision. The future to come for deconstruction thus necessarily remains open—as any genuine future always is—to the unpredictable and to rearticulation and reformulation by others.

1
From Grammatology to Life Death

Derrida's early work would seem, by now, fairly well understood. As scholars such as Geoffrey Bennington, Michael Naas, Penelope Deutscher, and Martin Hägglund have helped us see, in his now famous treatment of Husserl in *Voice and Phenomenon* (1967), Derrida was able to show that the supposedly immediate experience of "the living present" in Husserl's transcendental phenomenology is in fact more radically split in its structure than Husserl thinks. At the center of this demonstration was Derrida's foundational treatment of the issue of temporalization, where he would show that the form of the living present Husserl seeks to think in terms of synthesis instead has the structure of an internally differentiated trace.[1] Derrida then simultaneously showed in *Of Grammatology* how this trace structure can perhaps best be thought and described by means of a certain thinking of *arche-trace* or *arche-writing*.

Yet frequently overlooked in Derrida's seminal early works is the particular thought of life that emerges there. Looking back over Derrida's output in this period, one begins to see that, already at this early stage, deconstruction offers a powerful thinking not just of everything subject to time, and thus all forms of materiality, but also of life itself (understood in terms of what Derrida will call *life death*) and the basic structure of the living.

This line of thinking in Derrida is, no doubt, more visible today than it was previously, as scholars return to the major early works of deconstruction in light of the late work. Indeed, the invocation of a certain thinking of life as fundamental to the very project of deconstruction found in texts such as *Learning to Live Finally*, *Rogues*, and *The Beast and the Sovereign* and *The Death Penalty* seminars, has led to renewed interest in this problematic. Yet a full accounting of this issue in Derrida's early work, and the precise way we are to understand it, has to this point been lacking.

In this chapter, I provide this account by demonstrating precisely how the thought of life death follows from the key notion of arche-writing developed in Derrida's early work. Crucially, however, I show that it does so in a way that cannot be construed in terms of a fundamental ontology, and that this in fact constitutes one of deconstruction's most vital interventions in this area. My account will in turn enable us to see how life death opens onto the thought of life as survival elaborated in the later texts just cited.

I begin by retracing Derrida's engagement with temporalization in Husserl and the conception of arche-writing offered in *Of Grammatology*. I do so in order to bring out certain features of arche-writing that, despite Derrida's point of departure in Husserl, have to be thought not merely in temporal terms. At stake is a line of thought at times overlooked in the recent scholarship on Derrida, which has largely focused on the conception of time and in particular the thinking of the future found there.[2] Next, I elaborate how the crucial early text of "Freud and the Scene of Writing" allows us to understand the notion of arche-writing (now grasped in a slightly different way) as opening up the deconstructive thought of life understood as life death.[3] I then show how this text enables us to see this deconstructive thought of life as a radical thinking of mortality and finitude, whereby the basic, enabling conditions of life are understood in terms of a process of internal division and exposure to heterogeneity and death, a process shown to be both constitutive and necessary.

Arche-Writing and Life Death

The thought of life in deconstruction first emerges out of the seminal notion of arche-writing as it is articulated in Derrida's major early works. There we find Derrida conceptualizing the basic structure of the living as constituted in the relation to death. A brief look back at Derrida's works from 1967 allows us to outline the essential terms of this logic.

In his engagement with Husserl's treatment of temporalization in *Voice and Phenomenon*, Derrida is able to show that the supposedly immediate experience of the "living present" in Husserl is in fact more deeply differentiated in its structure than Husserl realizes. What Husserl is unable to think, Derrida shows, is that the supposedly indivisible "now" presupposed by Husserl's notion of the living present is necessarily split and extended by protention and retention, and in a more radical fashion than Husserl himself acknowledges. On the one hand, in order for the living present to be at all, it has to be already originally retained within temporal flow, in which every now immediately passes away.

On the other hand, for the same reason (i.e., in this flow every now disappears and is overtaken by another now as soon it comes to be), it equally has to be constitutively open to the coming of the next now. Derrida's charge is that while Husserl acknowledges the necessity of retention and protention in the moment of the *Augenblick*, he does not adequately think through the implications, ultimately conceiving of retention and protention as mere modifications of a temporal present, such that, in the end, the indivisible point of the now is still conceived as the true, ultimate form of lived experience.

Insofar as it is in fact fundamentally divided between retention and protention, Derrida argues, the structure of the living present has to be understood in an altogether different way, in terms of a specific set of characteristics. To begin with, it should be understood as intrinsically marked not by simple selfsameness but by difference. Divided between retention and protention, the now is, in its very identity, split. It is fundamentally and originarily *differentiated*, and this just is its basic ontological structure. Here we glimpse what Derrida calls the insertion of "the other in the same" in temporalization, the "non-belonging of the living present to itself" (*VP*, 6/5). But protention and retention also imply repetition. Repeatability is the minimal condition for something to be retained from one instant to the next, just as it is the minimal condition of a futural orientation, the condition of something lasting long enough to be exposed to what comes. Crucially, repeatability here is not a secondary, acquired characteristic of the now; rather, it is constitutive of it from the very beginning insofar as repeatability is necessary for the now to come into being in the first place. Here we have the difficult thought—and Derrida is well aware of the aporetic quality of the concept and the formulation—of originary repetition, "a non-originarity that cannot be eradicated" (*VP*, 6/5). Since repeatability has to be originary rather than secondary for any retention to take place, the living present has to be understood as something that is not currently, and never has been, present in any simple sense. But because the now has to be not just retained but also repeated in a process of futural persistence—and this process is strictly necessary for it to be a now minimally differentiated from the next now—it follows that it will never be fully present at any point in the future either. Taken together, these features ensure that the now is always "never finished arriving" in Marie-Eve Morin's words.[4] Its full presence and its identity are thus always originarily and continually *deferred*. At issue here is the "non-presence of the living present" (*VP*, 6/5) in temporalization. We then begin to see that the supposed unity of the "living present" in fact has the structure not of something present in itself but rather of something that can best be thought in terms of the retained, iterative trace.[5] Marked by both difference and deferral, the present lives off of what Derrida would come to call *différance*.[6]

Derrida simultaneously showed in *Of Grammatology* how this quasi-temporal structure can be understood as a certain thinking of *arche-trace* or *arche-writing*. Thus it is conceptualized in terms of a thinking of writing approached in a resolutely nontraditional way. At issue here, Derrida is clear, is an absolutely primary trace structure, the notion of which captures, in a single term, the dual necessity of originary nonpresence (divided between protention and retention) and iterability. While it was perhaps not immediately clear to many of Derrida's early readers, what is by now quite well established is that the project described by Derrida as a thinking of grammatology is an exploration not of the empirical, traditional notion of writing but of a more general, and in fact logically prior, originary trace structure that must be thought as forming the condition of anything at all.[7] Indeed, Derrida refers to arche-writing and the trace as "ultra-transcendental" concepts (OG, 61/90).

That the generalized notion of the trace, or *différance*, is to be thought as an absolutely general condition—and not as secondary in relation to "the living present" and everything that is—is *the* central insight of Derrida's early work, and it allows a general reorientation of thought. In fact, it effects a far-ranging destabilization of the tradition of metaphysics that Derrida sees, following Heidegger, as having dominated the history of philosophy from the ancient Greeks on. More specifically, it alters our conception of what a trace is. If, as Derrida put it in his now infamous formulation in *Of Grammatology*, "there is nothing outside the text" (OG, 158/227), this is not because there is no world or history outside of the literary or philosophical text, as so many of Derrida's early readers thought, but rather because all this too, like everything else, is "text" or trace in the specific sense deconstruction lends this term. Thus, from the very beginning, deconstruction was aimed at allowing us to think the textuality or writing inhabiting everything that is, including all forms of materiality. Indeed, Derrida is clear in *Of Grammatology* that the trace articulates the possibility of all "being" at a primordial level: "There we have all *history*, from what metaphysics has defined as 'non-living' up to 'consciousness,' passing through all levels of animal organization. The trace, where the relationship to the other is marked, articulates its possibility in the entire field of being, which metaphysics has defined as the being-present starting from the occulted movement of the trace" (OG, 47/69, trans. mod.).[8]

Yet, what is often not fully grasped is the precise way the trace makes possible a new thinking not only of materiality in general, but more specifically, of life, "passing through all levels of animal organization." Crucially, however, Derrida also describes arche-writing not just in terms of a thinking of life, but in terms of "the subject's relationship with its own death. . . . On all levels of life's organization" (OG, 69/100). Life, here, is thought in terms of what Derrida calls *"the economy of death"* (OG, 69/100). The question, then, is how exactly to understand these claims.

The key is what Derrida conceptualizes as the opening to exteriority or heterogeneity at stake in the difference and deferral of the living present. As we have now seen, with the term *arche-writing*, Derrida is describing something like an absolutely originary, ultra-transcendental form of articulation always already at work, and this process of articulation insinuates an outside on the inside of the living present, inserts heterogeneity into apparent selfsameness. Arche-writing thus names "the opening of the first exteriority in general" (OG, 70/103). Derrida here describes how the living present, as trace, is necessarily opened up, in its very structure, to an intimate form of alterity, which can be understood as exteriority (the originary relation to the outside already on the inside) or *as death*. A certain type of "relation to death" (VP, 46/44), a "non-life or a non-presence of the living present" (VP, 6/5) which Derrida had already named in his treatment of Husserl, is here thought as inscribed within the supposed unity of the living present, and originally, not merely as what comes to it secondarily. But this holds not just for the living present but also at the level of the living itself, Derrida suggests. In the passage from *Of Grammatology* just cited, arche-writing is in fact described as "the opening of the first exteriority in general, the enigmatic relationship *of the living to its other*" (OG, 70/103, my emphasis). The very possibility of the living, Derrida continues, cannot be thought apart from "differance as temporalization, without the nonpresence of the other inscribed within the sense of the present, *without the relationship with death as the concrete structure of the living present*" (OG, 71/103, my emphasis). Even more emphatically, the form of articulation at stake in temporalization—according to which the living entity is always already put in contact with its other—is even said here to *"put into play* the presence of the present and the life of the living" (OG, 167/237). A certain relation to death, however this is ultimately to be understood, is thus thought as a necessary, constitutive condition of life.

We begin to glimpse here how Derrida can claim, as he will in "Freud and the Scene of Writing," that there is "already death at the origin of a life which can defend itself against death only through an *economy* of death, through deferment, repetition, reserve" (WD, 202/300–301). Or then again, how the thought of arche-writing opens up a thinking of what he describes as "the originary possibility, within life . . . of deferral and the original possibility of the economy of death" (WD, 198/295). In truth, Derrida writes here, "We must be wary of this formulation: there is no life present *at first* which would *then* come to protect, postpone, or reserve itself in *différance*. The latter constitutes the essence of life. Or rather: as *différance* is not an essence, as it is not anything, it *is not* life, if Being is determined as *ousia*, presence, essence/existence, substance or subject.... This is the only condition on which we can say that life *is* death" (WD, 203/302). We begin to see here the necessity of thinking the intrusion of death not as something that supervenes on a form of life already constituted and present to itself but rather as its very condition of possibility. It is this logic, following from the thought of arche-writing, that Derrida will name the thought of life death.

We can only grasp this thought, however, by thinking the opening to exteriority at stake in Derrida's conception of arche-writing. It is my argument, building on the insight of Marie-Eve Morin, that we need to think opening to exteriority as *the* critical component in Derrida's theorization of the trace as the structure of the living present.[9] We need to think it as a kind of excess, or insinuation of heterogeneity, rather than simply as temporal opening (the temporal opening of the trace to the next now and the future to come), the way it has largely been understood in the secondary literature. In fact, Derrida points to just this thought in the famous lecture on *"Différance"* in his description of *espacement* or spacing. There he makes plain that *différance* as difference and deferral is to be understood both in terms of temporization and spacing, the inscription of a kind of hiatus, division, or cleavage in the here and now.[10] In this precise way, he underlines, the living present is constituted "by means of this very relation to what it is not" (M, 13/13). This is a crucial line of thought in Derrida to be further developed. Thinking the opening to exteriority in this way allows us to see it as the insertion of heterogeneity, one at work in everything that is, including the basic structure of the living.

Deconstruction and Psychoanalysis in Relation

If this line of thought has often been overlooked, it is because readers have not pursued it in the context of Derrida's treatment of Freud in the crucial early essay "Freud and the Scene of Writing" (1967). This essay in fact offers *the* way into this problematic as it is articulated in Derrida's early work. Stated succinctly, the thought of life understood in terms of arche-writing, while initially articulated in the reading of Husserl and in *Of Grammatology*, is developed in Derrida's early engagement with Freud. To see this, however, we need to revisit, and resituate, Derrida's stated project in this text.

To begin, we would do well to recall the precise relation between deconstruction and psychoanalysis Derrida assumes in the essay, one that, as we shall see in later chapters, stretches across his entire corpus. This relation is more complicated than it might initially appear. In *Of Grammatology* we find a handful of apparently approving references to Freud: at one point Derrida suggests that perhaps the best chance of a genuine "breakthrough" in rethinking metaphysics as the thought of presence, the very project of deconstruction, is to be found in psychoanalysis (OG, 21/35); and then, somewhat later on, Derrida closely associates the deconstructive thought of time with the Freudian concept of the *aprés coup* (OG, 67–68/97–98). Yet Derrida is quite clear in "Freud and the Scene of Writing" that deconstruction's relation to psychoanalysis is just as fraught as its relation to metaphysics. The reason is that even as psychoanalysis effects a kind of break within the tradition of Western metaphysics, it remains beholden to it.

We can bring more precision to bear on this point by looking at the opening remarks summarized at the outset of "Freud and the Scene of Writing." There Derrida describes the relation between deconstruction and psychoanalysis as one that, despite appearances (for instance, how the deconstruction of logocentrism often appears as a psychoanalysis of philosophy, and its repression of writing since Plato), is anything but straightforward. The issue, as he describes it, is that despite certain appearances, psychoanalysis, beginning with Freud himself, remains enmeshed with the tradition of metaphysics deconstruction seeks to disrupt. Derrida then goes a step further: Freudian concepts *"without exception*, belong to the history of metaphysics" (WD, 197/294, my emphasis), he states.

As Geoffrey Bennington points out, what Derrida then goes on to say about psychoanalysis's mode of belonging in fact complicates matters further.[11] Indeed, Derrida amends this initial statement on psychoanalysis and metaphysics almost immediately: "Certainly, Freudian discourse—in its syntax, or, if you will, its labor—is not to be confused with these necessarily metaphysical and traditional concepts. Certainly it is not exhausted by belonging to them. Witness the precautions and 'nominalism' with which Freud manipulates what he calls conventions and conceptual hypotheses. And a conception of difference is attached less to concepts than to discourse" (WD, 197–98/294). Psychoanalysis does not belong completely within the tradition of metaphysics, Derrida argues, is not fully "exhausted" by its belonging to this history, insofar as while Freud takes over a series of metaphysical concepts, he uses them in a particular way. He deploys them in an original way (he develops a new "syntax" for discussing them) in that he tries to take account of their limitations. In taking so many precautions with metaphysical concepts, we could then say, Freud does not simply take over and inherit elements of the tradition but rather gestures toward the fact that these concepts have limits, that they close off certain avenues for thought. This would remain true even if Freud, Derrida seems to suggest, is not himself able to think beyond these limits.

The problem, however, Derrida specifies, is that "Freud never reflected upon the historical and theoretical sense of these precautions," and this then necessitates "an immense labor of deconstruction of the metaphysical concepts and phrases that are condensed and sedimented within Freud's precautions" (WD, 198/294). Here, we begin to get a better sense of what Derrida calls "the metaphysical complicities of psychoanalysis" (WD, 198/294, trans. mod.). The issue is not that psychoanalysis, and Freud's discourse, simply belong to metaphysics and deconstruction does not. We have just seen Derrida noting that psychoanalysis is not reducible to the metaphysics of presence. Moreover, Derrida's descriptions of deconstruction in *Of Grammatology* make clear that deconstruction itself belongs to the history of metaphysics (the only history and tradition we have at our disposal, and thus the only one to inherit) and must therefore attempt to "solicit" it, or shake it up, from within (OG, 24/39). Rather, the issue is that Freud did not analyze, did not think through, the "sense"—the import, and the necessity—of its rearticulation of metaphysical concepts.[12] And thus he did not reflect on psychoanalysis's own complex relationship of belonging vis-à-vis the metaphysical tradition. This is what differentiates psychoanalysis and deconstruction: while deconstruction reflects explicitly on its relationship to metaphysics, psychoanalysis does not take up its own "metaphysical complicities." It is precisely insofar as these complicities remain unthought, Derrida suggests, that psychoanalysis is not deconstruction, which ensures that "Despite appearances, the deconstruction of logocentrism is not a psychoanalysis of philosophy" (WD, 196/293). And this despite the fact that the two share a common inheritance with respect to the concept of analysis, as Derrida would put it two decades later in "Resistances" (1991).[13]

The strategy Derrida employs in "Freud and the Scene of Writing" thus comes into view here. He will elaborate how Freud's discourse remains within metaphysics, yet manages to effect something like an opening or disruption within the enclosure. But crucially, as we have just seen, this opening or disruption will be thought in Freud without being explicitly recognized and theorized as such. Stated somewhat differently, we could say that this opening or disruption will be initiated in Freud but without his having reflected on the necessity, conditions of possibility, and implications of what he is doing. Hence, the deconstructive task is "to isolate, on the threshold of a systematic examination, those elements of psychoanalysis which can only uneasily be contained within logocentric closure" (WD, 198/296). Yet Derrida then refers to the challenge Freud mounts to classical metaphysics as a movement "somewhere between the implicit and the explicit" (WD, 199/296). Thus, to a certain measurable extent, we will see, Freud remains bound to a pre-deconstructive conception of writing, trace, and indeed, life, even as he opens up new possibilities.

The First Derridean Reading of Freud

With this schema in place, we can turn to the articulation of life death at stake in "Freud and the Scene of Writing." To glimpse it, it is necessary to revisit Derrida's reading of Freud there. At the most general level, Derrida's project is to track the metaphors of writing in Freud across the various stages of his thought, beginning with the very early work of the abandoned *Project for a Scientific Psychology* (1895)—in which Freud is still wedded to a physiological, biologistic model of the psyche grounded in "natural science"—through the *Interpretation of Dreams* (1900) and all the way up to the late "Note on the 'Mystic Writing Pad'" (1925).[14] Yet Derrida, displaying an admirable exactitude in his reading of Freud, sees quickly that if he is interested in Freud's various invocations of writing, there is a complication he will need to account for: namely, that there are two different metaphorical "investments" (WD, 199/297) with respect to writing in Freud. On the one hand, Freud uses metaphors of writing to describe specific elements within the psyche: the memory trace stored in the unconscious is described via the image of psychical inscription, the manifest content of the dream is said to be written in a kind of pictographic script, the relation between the manifest and latent content is likened to that of two different languages in need of translation, and so on.[15] On the other hand, as his thinking develops, Freud increasingly begins to conceptualize the structure of the psyche as a whole in terms of a writing machine. It is this second movement, stillborn in the *Project*, that culminates in his essay on the mystic writing pad, where Freud settles on the child's toy as the most suitable model for describing how the psyche itself works.

What Derrida shows is that these two metaphorical activations of writing remain for a long time "out of phase," but eventually come to overlap (WD, 221/327–28). What's more, what happens when they finally do overlap tells us something about how exactly Freud remains bound to, and potentially challenges, a classical thinking of writing and thus, on the horizon, the tradition of metaphysics. The key question, throughout, is not the intra-psychoanalytic question of whether the metaphor of writing or the writing machine is a good model for understanding the memory trace or the structure of the psyche more generally, but rather the extra-psychoanalytic—in fact, deconstructive—question, "What is a text, and what must the psyche be if it can be represented by a text?" (WD, 199/297).

In fact, once Derrida begins tracking the activation of writing in Freud's work, he uncovers a radical thinking of arche-writing and the trace. It emerges first in the notion of the memory trace and then in the Freudian conception of time as *Nachträglichkeit* (rendered as "deferred action" in the English

Standard Edition), notions Derrida will affirm pose one of the most powerful challenges to metaphysics found in the tradition. While there is a general understanding in the secondary literature of Derrida's treatment of these two motifs, the question consistently left unanswered is how exactly they open up what we have seen Derrida calling, right away in the essay's prefatory remarks, "the originary possibility, within life . . . of deferral and the original possibility of the economy of death" (WD, 198/295). This is the crucial question to address.

The answer lies in Derrida's activation of the problematic of "breaching" or "pathbreaking" (*frayage*) at stake in Freud's very early thought—the material process by which a memory trace is formed by being inscribed. The problematic of breaching is crucial to the *Project* and it plays a key role in the description of the psychic apparatus offered in chapter 7 of *The Interpretation of Dreams*. Indeed, there is a marked continuity between Freud's early theorization of pathbreaking and his thinking after 1900, all the way to *Beyond the Pleasure Principle* in 1920 and the essay on the mystic writing pad. From 1895 on, Freud has to deal with a problem that he glimpses at the very beginning and forces him to try out a number of different ways of representing the psychic apparatus. The problem, in short, is that the psyche operates in a way absolutely unlike any kind of writing system available to us in the world, because it has to be able to meet two seemingly incompatible requirements: it has to have an inexhaustible capacity to retain memory traces permanently, without their ever being destroyed or overwritten, while at the same time remaining continually open to receiving fresh impressions, as the apparatus takes in new stimuli. Freud ultimately solves this problem by positing the existence of two different systems with two different functions. Yet the problem Derrida sees Freud continually wrestling with is how to unite these two functions in a single apparatus, how to think these two requirements within a single technical model. Indeed, it is this problem, Derrida rightly argues, that dictates the way Freud repeatedly turns to different models for thinking the psychic apparatus, none of which will prove entirely adequate prior to the mystic pad.

In order to grasp how Derrida mobilizes the problematic of pathbreaking in Freud, it is necessary to discuss in more detail how Freud understands the memory trace. From beginning to end, Freud always thought the psychic apparatus in terms of energetics, and in the *Project*, Freud posits that physical "neurones" likely form the basic physiological unit of the psyche, speculating that memories are stored in a process of breaching or pathbreaking whereby a path is carved out, in the neurones themselves, by an influx of energy, the influx that comes with a given perceptual stimulus. Once laid down, memory traces are available permanently. This furnishes an account of how the memory trace can be reactivated: under certain conditions, energy once again follows along a specific pathway. If this were the only mode available to the apparatus, however, Freud reasons, it would quickly fill up, making it impossible for it to take in fresh impressions. His solution is to suggest that there must be two different classes of neurones in the psyche, each with different attributes. On the one hand, some of the neurones must be permeable, perpetually open to the influx of stimulus from the outside or the inside, in which no trace of their traversal is left behind. On the other hand, in order for there to be memory, there must be a separate class of impermeable neurones that are "loaded with resistance," such that they mount what Freud calls a "contact barrier" in the face of an influx of energy (SE, 1:300). If the influx of stimulus is sufficiently powerful, it breaks through this barrier and carves a path in the subset of impermeable neurones. In this way, the class of resistant neurones retains the trace left behind by the breaching of the contact barriers. These originally impermeable neurones are those that ultimately comprise the system "Ucs." in Freud's model. The other class of permeable neurones conduct energy, via "facilitations" that act as channels of passage, but do not retain any impression, since they offer no resistance (SE, 1:300). Thus, the permeable neurones comprise the system of perception continuously open to the outside world and to endogenous influxes of stimulus. The preconscious and conscious systems are then situated between the system of impermeable neurones and the perception system (later, the "Ucs." and "Pcpt." systems), since consciousness must be able to register both sensation deriving from perception and activated memory traces, which, we have seen, are not stored there.

This division of the psychic apparatus into different systems prefigures the approach Freud will take, and increasingly refine, throughout his thinking, but these two capabilities will not come together in one ideal machine until 1925, when Freud turns to the mystic writing pad. First, in the account of how memory traces are formed in *The Interpretation of Dreams* (1900), Freud retains the notions of resistance and facilitation articulated in the *Project*, but he now conceptualizes the psychic apparatus itself in completely other terms, dropping the earlier biologistic model. Thus, while he invokes writing in describing the peculiar form of the dream, the dream-thoughts and so on, he describes the structure of the psychic apparatus via the image of a compound microscope, telescope, or photographic apparatus. Speaking of the memory trace and perception and different psychical systems lends itself to the idea that there are actual physical localities in the psyche, Freud notes, but we should not give in to this temptation, he says. Rather, these psychical systems are to be thought of in terms of a purely "ideal" or virtual place, akin to the point in a telescope where the image coalesces, an ideal point located *between* the lenses that refract the rays of light (SE, 5:536). But even the comparison to these optical machines carries "imperfections," Freud is quick to point out (SE, 5:536), given the difficulty of conceiving of one that, like the psyche, can remain perpetually open to registering new images while retaining the imprint of every prior image (SE, 5:538). A telescope or a microscope allows for there to be an image, but it has no capacity to hold onto it; the photographic negative, on the other hand, registers and retains an imprint, but once it has been exposed and developed, it is unable to receive any new impressions (see SE, 2:188–89n1, cited approvingly by Freud at SE, 18:25).

In the end, it is only the mystic pad that provides a suitable model for Freud for the precise mode of functioning of the psyche. This is because it is fundamentally different than other machines for writing in his view. Writing with chalk on a handheld slate, he writes in 1925, can be periodically erased, such that new markings can always be recorded on it, but in the process, the traces of any previous markings are irrevocably lost and destroyed. Writing on a sheet of paper records indefinitely the traces that are inscribed on it, but the sheet quickly fills up and cannot receive fresh impressions (SE, 19:227). But the mystic pad does not have these limitations. As Freud describes it, the toy consists of a receptive wax tablet beneath a translucent sheet of paper upon which one writes. The upper sheet is attached loosely to the wax tablet beneath by means of an intermediary layer of waxed paper, so that the contact between the top and bottom layers can be periodically broken—thus "erasing" the marks visible on its surface, while the trace of those marks remain on the tablet below. By raising the translucent sheet, one can always refresh its capacity for new impressions, while the tablet below retains the contours of each and every inscription permanently. The dual requirement Freud recognizes as early as the *Project* is captured years later with the example of the mystic pad.

Yet the key point for Derrida is that from very early on Freud mobilizes, with the notion of pathbreaking, a radical understanding of the principle of difference. This is because the memory trace produced by the breaching of contact barriers is not reducible to a simple positivity. Indeed, it is never purely and simply present as a locatable entity. Rather, in the model of inscription Freud offers, "it is the difference between breaches which is the true origin of memory, and thus of the psyche" (WD, 201/299). That is, since Freud has said resistance is the key determinant in pathbreaking, it must necessarily be the case, Derrida notes, that the memory trace is, in a strong sense, constituted in and through a relation of difference: in this case, the difference in resistances *between* pathways. Without this principle of difference, there would be no way to account for what separates one memory trace from another; there would be no possibility of certain pathways being carved out and not others. There would be no way to explain how it is possible for "a pathway to be preferred," in Freud's words (SE, 1:300, trans. mod.). Hence, "trace as memory is not a pure breaching that might be reappropriated at any time as simple presence; it is rather the ungraspable and invisible difference between breaches" (WD, 201/299).[16]

Moreover, a similar logic is at work in how Freud thinks the relation between memory, perception, and the preconscious-conscious systems at this stage. Since it is the quantity of the stimulus that is responsible for pathbreaking in the production of the memory trace in the system of the unconscious, Freud posits that consciousness of a given stimulus must be of something else. This other thing must be quality, he suggests (of the type of perception it is or was, whether it is in a series, shows similarity to others, and so on). The question then becomes how the system *Pcpt.*, through which stimulus reaches the preconscious-conscious system, can register quality. The answer, he theorizes, is that perception registers not the pure quantity of energy associated with a given influx but rather periodicity, its intensity over a given period of time. As Derrida points out, this necessarily presupposes a certain discontinuity, or interval, at work within every influx of excitation, and this ultimately forms the very condition of possibility of quality. Thus, a form of spacing, the insertion of an internal difference in a given quantum of energy, is the key to quality. We begin to see here that much, if not all, of the *Project* "depends in its entirety upon an incessant and increasingly radical invocation of the principle of difference" (WD, 205/305). The essence of the psyche, here, increasingly appears to lie in spacing and the operations of difference, and not in the production of psychical entities that could be simply said to be present. Rather, we have here a much more complex understanding of the trace, and the beginnings of a thought increasingly at odds with metaphysics as the thought of presence.

At the same time, the notion of the memory trace in Freud opens onto a particular thinking of time, thought not as the succession of individual present moments but as irreducible delay or lag. This is the second crucial motif in "Freud and the Scene of Writing."[17] Derrida here picks up on the thinking of *Nachträglichkeit* that emerges quite early on in Freud. Already in the "Preliminary Communication" of *Studies on Hysteria* (1893), Freud posits this mechanism as a key operational principle of the psychic apparatus, one closely alloyed to his conception of the unconscious memory trace working as a "foreign body" lodged in the psyche, capable of producing effects long after its initial implantation (SE, 2:6). As he describes it there with reference to the etiology of hysteria, the memory of a traumatic scene of seduction from childhood can be activated long after the fact, after the onset of puberty and mature sexuality, even though it was not experienced as traumatic, or even registered, originally. With this notion, Derrida suggests, Freud undermines the Husserlian conception of the living present as linked to a past that is a mere modification of the present (a past present moment). Instead, Freud points to the thought of a present moment determined by a trace that, importantly, "has never been *perceived*, whose meaning has never been lived in the present" (WD, 214/317).

It is precisely here, Derrida says, that Freud poses one of the most serious challenges to metaphysics and its conception of time. "That the present in general is not primal, but rather, reconstituted, that it is not the absolute, wholly living form which constitutes experience, that there is no purity of the living present—such is the theme, formidable for metaphysics, which Freud . . . would have us pursue. This pursuit is doubtless *the only one* which is exhausted neither within metaphysics nor within science," he writes (WD, 212/314, my emphasis). Later, in *Archive Fever* (1995), Derrida would revisit this statement, explicitly citing "Freud and the Scene of Writing." There, he puts it this way: "The logic of the after-the-fact (*Nachträglichkeit*), which is at the heart of psychoanalysis . . . turns out to disrupt, disturb, entangle forever the reassuring distinction . . . between the past and the future, that is to say, between the three actual presents, which would be the past present, the present present, and the future present" (AF, 80/127).

We have before us, then, the two lines of thinking in Freud mobilized by deconstruction: a radical thinking of the principle of difference (including a kind of pre-understanding of spacing), and a new conception of time understood in terms of originary deferral or lag. If, as I have said, these two motifs make possible a thinking of life as life death, however, it is because they point to a form of originary repetition at the heart of the living present.

Life Death and Mortality in "Freud and the Scene of Writing"

The crucial element is the thinking of repetition and delay offered in Freud. It surfaces initially in the discussion of pathbreaking in "Freud and the Scene of Writing." There Derrida suggests that the radicalization of the principle of difference I just spoke of is carried even further in Freud in his thinking of originary repetition and deferral in the dynamics of the memory trace. To see this, it is necessary to return to Freud's understanding of memory in the *Project*.

We have seen how memories are formed and retained for Freud. The issue now is given everything he has said about resistance and contact barriers, his model has to assume what he makes a bit clearer later on, in chapter 7 of the *Interpretation of Dreams*: namely, that whenever the apparatus is faced with a fresh influx of energy, this influx will first follow "old facilitations" on the path to discharge (SE, 1:340). Freud's thinking here is that the overall apparatus seeks discharge and return to equilibrium, the energetic state as it existed before the influx of new energy. This aim is the aim of the "primary process" of the psychic apparatus as Freud terms it, its most primitive mode of operating whereby it seeks satisfaction in immediate discharge, the mode of operation characteristic of unconscious processes. The avoidance of influxes of energy is the original reflex of the apparatus, Freud posits, such that an increase is associated with unpleasure and the reduction of energetic tension corresponds with the experience of satisfaction. Thus the psychic apparatus is governed by the functional mechanism of the primary process, what Freud names the pleasure principle (originally the "unpleasure principle"). With respect to pathbreaking and the memory trace, as we can now see, the flow of energy along old facilitations, and the reactivation of an existing memory trace, must be the initial way the apparatus seeks to achieve discharge whenever there is a fresh influx of energy, since this path poses no resistance.

Freud sees right away, however, that a system governed entirely by the primary process would be unable to persist for any time at all. Hunger is one of the primary examples Freud gives of a source of an influx of stimulus, and this example makes fairly clear how the organism, were it to try to meet this need only by following old facilitations (activating only the memory of a satisfaction), would quickly perish (SE, 1:297). The organism functioning in accordance with the primary process alone would never be able to meet what Freud calls simply "the exigencies of life" (SE, 1:297; see also SE, 5:565). He thus postulates the emergence of a kind of subsystem within the class of impermeable neurones that acts to delay the final discharge of energy so that some of it is retained. With this energy, the organism can then produce motor action to pursue forms of satisfaction in line with its "major [somatic] needs: hunger, respiration, sexuality" (SE, 1:297). This subsystem thus obeys not the primary process, but the "secondary process" of retention and deferral of discharge, even though the ultimate aim of the apparatus as a whole remains that of energetic reduction back to the lowest level possible. It operates in accordance with what Freud will call the reality principle.

Derrida's insight is that the form of repetition implied in this conception of memory points to a thinking of *différance* as originary deferral and delay. To see this, we ought to distinguish between two types of repetition—a distinction Derrida himself does not make but which is suggested by his treatment of Freud on this point. The first is the one that Freud thinks explicitly: the repetition of energy moving along a given pathway, the process at the heart of memory. Derrida sees in this process another instance of Freud's activation of the principle of difference. This is because Freud stipulates that memory so understood is not to be thought simply in terms of the quantity of energy following a given old facilitation, but rather in terms of the *magnitude* of the initial impression resulting in a "preferred pathway" and the *frequency* with which the traversal of this pathway is repeated. The essence of memory thus lies not in the simple quantity of energy responsible for carving out a given path but rather, as above, in the difference between the pathways offering up initial resistance, the difference that makes one pathway "preferred" in relation to another. Equally necessary in this model is the *difference between repeated instances of facilitation* along the pathway thus carved out, the difference without which frequency is not possible. The very notion of frequency presupposes "the diastem which maintains [discrete repetitions's] separation" (WD, 201/300).

Yet there is a second type of repetition in this model that speaks even more directly to the thought of *différance* as originary deferral. In truth, we have already glimpsed this second type of repetition in the above discussion of the memory trace. In his treatment of the *Project*, Derrida demonstrates that Freud's model necessarily posits a form of originary repetition at its core. Indeed, for the neurones to exert a resistance to the force of inscription—and they must, if there is to be such a thing as a memory trace—a certain kind of repetition has to be at work from even before the very start. "Repetition," Derrida writes, "does not *happen to* an initial impression; its possibility is already there, in the resistance offered *the first time* by the psychical neurones. Resistance itself is possible only if the opposition lasts and is repeated at the beginning" (WD, 202/301). We see here that the very notion of resistance to inscription implies repeatability: indeed, repetition is the necessary condition of there being any resistance at all. Opposition to a given force is only possible if the exertion of an opposing counterforce is repeated from one instant to the next. And what's more, this must be the case from a moment even prior to the first break-in of energy. Without a form of arche-originary repetition operative already, before this break-in, there would be no resistance to the influx of excitation, and no pathbreaking could take place.

The link between originary repetition and the notion of a delay prior to presence or the living present is to be found here. If this form of repetition is originary and always already repeated, then, as Derrida puts it, "the very idea of a *first time* . . . becomes enigmatic" (WD, 202/301). Hence, a bit later on, Derrida specifies that what Freud discovers with the notion of the pathbreaking is that "It is thus *the delay* which is in the beginning" (WD, 203/302). "To say that *différance* is originary is simultaneously to erase the myth of a present origin. Which is why 'originary' must be understood as having been *crossed out*, without which *différance* would be derived from an original plenitude. It is a non-origin which is originary" (WD, 203/302–3).

The "living present" as it plays itself out in psychic life is here only possible on the basis of repetition, that is, originary delay at the origin. It is predicated on a quasi-aporetic, ultra-transcendental structure of originary deferral operative at its origin. Thus, Derrida will identify "the irreducibility of the 'effect of deferral'" as Freud's singular discovery (WD, 203/303). It is this specific thinking of deferral that Derrida then sees being developed in the notion of *Nachträglichkeit*.

This logic communicates directly with the notion of arche-writing. As we saw in Derrida's treatment of Husserl, in order for the now of the living present to emerge, it has to be, already, the very first time it comes into being, something that is both *retained* and *repeatable*. This is the minimal condition required for it to "be" at all, the minimal condition of its persisting such that it does not immediately pass way in temporal flow, insofar as it is futurally exposed. Originarily retained and repeated, this difficult-to-think structure is that of an iterative mark or trace.

The key question we began with was how exactly this thought entails a relation to death and how this relation is to be understood. "Freud and the Scene of Writing" now allows us to see that it is to be understood in terms of a kind of interruption, or excess, at work in the trace, and thus at work within the very structure of the living. To see this, let us return to Derrida's claim that it is "the irreducibility of the 'effect of deferral'" that constitutes Freud's major discovery. Stated succinctly, Derrida's insight is that this logic of originary delay and deferral is ultimately played out in Freud's thinking of energetics, giving rise to the thought of a radical, originary complication internal to life, the inscription of a form of heterogeneity within the unfolding of the living present. This consequently challenges the traditional notion of life as simple spontaneous unfolding or self-driven persistence.

Derrida is able to make this move on account of how Freud defines life and death. As early as the *Project*, and throughout the entire rest of his output, Freud sees psychic life as essentially consisting in the pursuit of pleasure, understood as the reduction of excitation or tension in the psychic apparatus. The very essence of psychic life lies in "the endeavor of the nervous system, maintained through every modification, to avoid being burdened by a Qn [a quantity of excitation] or to keep the burden as small as possible" (SE, 1:301). But since the avoidance of this burden would quickly result in the absolute expenditure of all excitation, or death, Freud speaks of a necessary deviation right at the very beginning, "under the compulsion of the exigencies of life," such that the system "was obliged to lay up a store of Qn," enabling the organism to persist instead of immediately perishing (WD, 202–3/301). The "economy of death" at the heart of life thus comes into view. On this view, the organism can only sustain itself and defend itself from death (absolute expenditure) by deferring the guiding principle of psychic life, the principle dictating the discharge of excitation. In order to live on for any amount of time at all, the psychic apparatus has to deviate from life plain and simple, welcoming in impurity, a certain amount of death. It thus makes use of a certain "economy of death" in order to live in the first place. Moreover, this process of deferral does not emerge belatedly—even though, as we have seen, Freud refers to the operational mechanism responsible for deferring discharge and storing up excitation as the "secondary process"—but has to be at work in life from the very beginning. This is what Derrida means when he writes that in Freud we see "already death at the origin of a life which can defend itself against death only through an *economy* of death, through deferment, repetition, reserve" (WD, 202/300–301). The deviation of life from its own principle, the process of "dying a little" in order to live as Bennington calls it, does not come secondarily to a life already constituted in itself, in the fullness of a plenitude.[18] Rather, it has to be present within life from the very start, as its necessary condition, in order for life to minimally sustain itself.

There is another aspect to Derrida's activation of Freud here. This is because in Freud's model absolute expenditure is just one of the mortal threats the organism faces. The whole apparatus can only come into being and last if it defends against the influx of too much excitation, if it can close off absolute exposure. This would even appear to be the primary purpose of neuronal resistance to effraction. Resistance, and with it some amount of impermeability, is critical because without it the psyche would be immediately overcome. This means that the influx of excitation that makes memory, "the very essence of the psyche" (WD, 201/299), possible can itself be a mortal threat. And once again, this resistance to effraction has to be operative from the very start, has to be arche-originary, because without it the psyche could never have emerged in the first place. Hence, we see how Derrida can say that here "life is already threatened [from the first moment] by the origin of the memory that constitutes it, and by the breaching which it resists" (WD, 202/301).

Furthermore, given the ground we have covered to this point, we can now see that the laying in reserve of excitation along certain pathways in order to meet the exigencies of life should be understood not just as a process of deferral necessary to life but as a more active installation of an economy of death. Why? Because this laying in reserve introduces into the psychic apparatus a portion of the very increase in tension it seeks to defend itself against. Yet the introduction of this internal threat is absolutely necessary for the system to sustain itself for any amount of time at all. As we have seen, it is necessary for this process to be underway from the very beginning for life to come into being and last. Thus, we begin to see how life is originarily threatened by "the effraction which it can contain *only by repeating it*" (WD, 202/301, my emphasis), and repeating it already at the outset, in the very moment of its emergence.

Here the thought of life death found in Freud comes fully into view. Life only comes into being and persists by means of an arche-originary, iterative process of deferral of absolute life and thus by means of the installation of a certain economy of death that must be operative from the very start. This process is then necessary to life as its enabling condition. One sees here that life, as thought from the perspective of the trace and arche-writing, is constitutively divided and deferred, and from a moment prior to the origin of life understood in terms of simple presence. Here, life requires exposure on the inside to its other, to death, it requires the introduction of the other in the economy of the same, to persist for any time at all. This internal interruption, this exposure to heterogeneity, has to be operative already at the very origin of life. But this also means that life can only persist by introducing within itself a trace of the mortal threat it continually seeks to defend itself against.

This thought makes possible a radical thinking of mortality in Derrida. With the term *mortality*, I am referring to a thinking of life that does not simply posit exposure to death at each and every moment (coming from the future) as life's originary, necessary condition. This is most often how Derrida's reference to the relation to death at stake in the trace is understood. Rather, I am speaking of the more complex notion of life as necessarily constituted via an economy of death in which heterogeneity is introduced into the very heart of life. It is this difficult-to-think, quasi-aporetic structure that ultimately forms the very condition of finitude in the early Derrida.[19] "No doubt," he writes, "life protects itself by repetition, trace, *différance* (deferral)." And yet, he continues:

> We must be wary of this formulation: there is no life present *at first* which would *then* come to protect, postpone, or reserve itself in *différance*. The latter constitutes the essence of life. Or rather: as *différance* is not an essence, as it is not anything, it *is not* life, if Being is determined as *ousia*, presence, essence/existence, substance or subject. Life must be thought of as trace before Being may be determined as presence. This is the only condition on which we can say that life *is* death. (WD, 203/302)

The key point here is that the threat of death does not supervene on a form of life already constituted and present to itself but rather forms the very condition of its possibility (pure, uncompromised life is rendered impossible within this logic). For this to be the case, we have to think life death not simply in terms of life's intrinsic exposure to the threat of what comes from the future but in terms of its internal exposure to heterogeneity. We have to think life, approached via the notion of arche-writing, other than in strictly temporal terms.[20]

Life thought in this way entails thinking the basic structure of the living as constitutively divided and differentiated and thus opened up to an outside. To put it in terms of Derrida's account of temporalization, life here requires exposure on the inside to what is heterogeneous to it, to death—it requires the introduction of the other in the same—for the most minimal form of retention or futural extension to take place; indeed, for the living entity to come into being and persist for any time at all. Life thus exposes itself, from the very start, to an internal hollowing-out, to an internal disruption, in order to sustain itself and defend against death *tout court*, the mortal threat that can come at any time from the future. Once again we see here that the living present, or life in its basic structure, has to be not just constitutively *exposed* on a temporal plane to an unpredictable future but rather, more radically, constitutively rent open, originarily, by a disruptive excess that introduces into it its own outside. In this way, life has to welcome and repeat the irruption of the other, death as what is other than life. Such is the thought of life Derrida claims to find in Freud.

Indeed, it is precisely this dimension of Freud's thought that Derrida highlights in *"Différance"* (1968), where the whole problematic of *différance* is explicitly described as a thinking of "the tomb of the proper in which is produced, by *différance*, the *economy of death*" (M, 4/4). There, the sole thinkers who resist the language of metaphysics according to Derrida are, aside from Heidegger, Nietzsche and Freud; so much so that *"différance* appears almost by name in their texts, and in those places where everything is at stake" (M, 17/18). In the case of Freud, Derrida argues, this is because the two motifs of *différance*—temporization and spacing—come together, as we have already seen, in the thematics of breaching and resistance (*différance* as the articulation of difference, interval, or spacing) and of *Nachträglichkeit* (temporization and the originary delay) (M, 21/21–22). But what he ultimately underscores here is how these themes communicate with a certain thinking of life. "According to a schema that never ceased to guide Freud's thought," he writes, "the movement of the trace is described as an effort of life to protect itself by *deferring* the dangerous investment, by constituting a reserve" (M, 18/19). Referring explicitly to a certain notion of energetics, Derrida notes the following:

> Here we are touching on the point of greatest obscurity, on the very enigma of *différance*, on that which divides precisely its concept by

means of a strange sharing. We must not hasten to decide. How to think *at the same time*, on the one hand, *différance* as the economic detour which, in the element of the same, always aims at finding again the pleasure or presence deferred through calculation (conscious or unconscious), and, on the other hand, *différance* as the relation to impossible presence, expenditure without reserve, as the irreparable loss of presence, the irreversible wearing down of energy, indeed as . . . the relation to the absolutely other that, to all appearances, interrupt every economy? (M, 19/20, trans. mod.)[21]

While this passage is not as clear as it could be, and not as clear as other formulations of this problematic in Derrida, it can be understood on the basis of the logic I have just outlined. *Différantial* deferral, he suggests here, has to be thought as the deferral of, or deviation from, pure life that makes possible finite life as it is lived. It is this very process that staves off the death that would accompany the attainment of absolute pleasure, the full discharge of energy that would spell the end of the living organism. Yet at the same time, in this process of deferral, the living entity actively welcomes a form of death into the operations of life, a form of the death promised in the absolute wearing down of all energy. This is because it now not only deviates from its primary aim (the pursuit of pleasure or discharge) but invites within itself the absolutely other life must resist.

Moreover, immediately after the passage just cited, Derrida spells out why the thematics of pathbreaking and the economy of death found in Freud are necessary resources for deconstruction. They are necessary because they indicate a thought—the thought of *différance* itself—unthinkable within the classical logic of philosophy, which always begins with the principle of identity, unthinkable "in the philosophical element of evidentiality which would make short work of dissipating the mirage and illogicalness of *différance*" (M, 19/20). Psychoanalysis is thus said to be a strategic place where a genuine thinking of *différance* in completely other terms is possible, but without simply renouncing the language of reason.[22] A new, productive line of deconstructive questioning, we begin to see, follows on the opening found in Freud in its attempt to think the arche-originary form of tracing at the heart of life.

Freud's Turn Away from Life Death

There is one final complication to take account of here, however. This is because deconstruction pursues this line of questioning concerning the form of tracing at the heart of life by taking up what is not fully explicit in Freud, what he thinks without fully realizing what he is doing. This is what Derrida's treatment of the "Note on the Mystic Writing Pad" (1925) in the final sections of "Freud of the Scene of Writing" comes to confirm, and it tells us something about the precise relation between Derrida and Freud.

Indeed, looking at this portion of the text, we find Derrida underscoring how Freud remains firmly within the metaphysical enclosure at the very moment he traces an opening in it. This is because Derrida finds in the "Note" Freud ultimately disavowing what all the various figures of writing in his own thinking suggest: namely, that it is necessary to think the form of temporality and tracing he envisions starting from a conception of writing that does not reduce it to a mere metaphor. More importantly, Derrida sees Freud here disavowing the thought of life death he himself inaugurates.

On the one hand, Derrida argues, in the "Note on the Mystic Writing Pad" Freud consolidates the logic of originary deferral glimpsed earlier. Indeed, one of the primary reasons Freud is drawn to the child's toy is that its top layer (the celluloid sheet) mimics what he had increasingly seen as the essential protective function of the *Pcpt.* system. In the case of the toy, the celluloid sheet ensures that the wax paper beneath it is not torn in the process of writing. Crucially, Freud observes that the capacity of the toy to receive fresh impressions is only possible when contact between the top layers and the underlying slab is occasionally broken, so that the uppermost writing surface can be refreshed. In the essay, Freud admits to being particularly struck by this feature, in that it seems to him the perfect metaphor for a feature of the psychic apparatus he had postulated five years earlier, in *Beyond the Pleasure Principle* (1920), as the only possible way to understand how the psychic apparatus could be continually open to fresh impressions. The psychic apparatus would likely be quickly overwhelmed, Freud had speculated there, by continual influxes of stimuli from the outside. Thus the exposure to stimulus at the site of the system's outermost protective shield must be *periodic*. In *Beyond the Pleasure Principle*, Freud described this mechanism via the memorable image of the system *Pcpt.* periodically putting out and retracting "feelers" sensitive to stimulus, as a primitive organism might do (*SE*, 18:28). Freud had even gone so far as to suggest that this discontinuous process is the very source of our concept of time (*SE*, 18:27).[23]

Here Freud seems to posit the priority of a certain trace structure. Why? Because this periodicity, it quickly becomes clear, is the name Freud gives to the thought of what deconstruction calls spacing, inherent in the structure of the trace. "Temporality as spacing," Derrida writes, appears here "as the interruption and restoration of contact between the various depths of psychical levels" (WD, 225/333). Put differently, Freud seems to at least glimpse here that there has to be a diastem, a primary form of spacing, for psychic life to emerge and be minimally sustained. In this way, he sees that "traces thus produce the space of their inscription only by acceding to the period of their erasure," such that psychic life itself is in fact "constituted by the double force of repetition and erasure" (WD, 226/334). The vision of psychic life Freud offers here is one that entails an absolutely primary complication at the heart of what we have called the living present: "an originary spacing, deferring, and erasure of the simple origin," which is here nothing other than *"the first relation of life to its other, the origin of life"* (WD, 226/334, my emphasis).

Yet Freud ultimately disavows the pathbreaking gesture he himself opens up. This is because just as he begins to think the structure just named, Freud turns back on it. That is, he rejects the mystic writing pad as ultimately inadequate to what he wants to describe in the psychic apparatus because it doesn't run by itself. As a machine that requires a living user, it lacks the supposedly pure spontaneity of auto-propelling life. Derrida's reading of Freud is quite precise on this point. Indeed, after Freud notes the various ways in which the mystic pad fulfills the dual requirements he had long sought, he remarks on its singular "limitation" (WD, 227/336): it does not operate automatically, by itself. "Once the writing has been erased, the Mystic Pad cannot 'reproduce' it from within," he writes; "it would be a mystic pad indeed if, like our memory, it could accomplish that" (SE, 19:230). The apparatus of the mystic pad is thus ultimately opposed here to the "alleged spontaneity" of the living psyche (WD, 227/336).

Derrida rightly reads this comment as an attempt on Freud's part to exclude what his own thinking suggests; namely, that the apparent spontaneity and purity of auto-propelling life, of the living psyche, is in fact dependent on a form of tracing that introduces into it repetition, automaticity, and the relation to death from the very beginning. Freud, we begin to see, in the end wants to banish from the living psyche not just all the attributes of automaticity normally associated with the machine. He also wants to exclude the presence, within life, of the economy of death. What Freud cannot think is, precisely, the way "the machine . . . is death and finitude *within* the psyche" (WD, 228/336). Emphasizing this point, Derrida writes "all that Freud had thought about the unity of life and death . . . should have led him to ask other questions here. And to ask them explicitly" (WD, 227/336). Freud ultimately remains blind to the necessity of thinking life on the basis of writing (rather than the other way around) and the dynamics of tracing, which "did not happen to memory from without, any more than death surprises life" (WD, 228/337). This problematic is what "Freud failed to make explicit, at the very moment when he had brought this question to the threshold of being thematic and urgent" (WD, 228/337).

Freud thus turns back on the thinking of life death he himself had opened up. This is, in the end, why Derrida will say that "Freud performs for us the scene of writing" (WD, 229/338), without this being something that Freud himself ever fully thinks through, without this being the explicit theme of Freud's thought. "In that moment of world history 'subsumed' by the name Freud, by means of an unbelievable mythology (be it neurological or metapsychological: for we never dreamed of taking it seriously . . .) a relationship to itself of the historico-transcendental stage of writing was spoken without being said, thought without being thought: was written and simultaneously erased" (WD, 228–29/337–38). We begin to see here how exactly Derrida's reading of Freud leads to deconstructive questioning. Derrida's rearticulation of Freud seeks to think explicitly what is thought in Freud with respect to "the unity of life and death" but which remains only implicit there, ultimately refused even. Deconstruction does not simply take over Freudian concepts—all of which, without exception, are said to belong to the tradition of metaphysics—but rather submits them to rigorous questioning and, through this process, transforms them. As we begin to see more clearly, then, at stake in the thought of life death, and in turn survival, in Derrida is a certain *activation* of Freud: a certain mode of inheriting from Freud that not only reinscribes his thinking in new contexts but seeks to rearticulate it.

2
Interrogating the Death Drive

Chapter 1 showed that the thought of life death that emerges in Derrida's early work is powerfully developed in Derrida's engagement with Freud during this period. Looking beyond Derrida's early work from the 1960s, it is the task of this chapter to show how the logic of life death in deconstruction is fleshed out in Derrida's engagement with the Freudian theory of the drives beginning in the 1970s. This subsequent engagement with Freud is key insofar as the theory of the drives—especially Freud's conception of life and death drives—will ultimately come to form the most consistent point of reference in Derrida's subsequent dealings with Freud.

There were hints that this would be an important area of inquiry for deconstruction already in the earlier works. As revealed in chapter 1, in his work from the mid- to late 1960s, Derrida explicitly identifies a certain thinking of life in terms of "an economy of death" as one of the key places where Freudian psychoanalysis resists metaphysics. Following the development of this thought in "Freud and the Scene of Writing," Derrida, in the lecture on *"Différance,"* argues that it forms, alongside a certain thinking of time, one of Freud's most revolutionary insights. Indeed, he explicitly names Freud's *"pulsion de mort"* as close to the very enigma of *différance* (M, 19/20).[1] Yet it is only in *The Post Card* (1980), in material developed out of Derrida's 1975–76 *La vie la mort* seminar, that the problematic of life and death in Freudian psychoanalysis truly comes to the fore.

That Derrida would engage substantively with the theory of the drives was inevitable given his concerns. Derrida is led to the Freudian theory of the drives because it is precisely there that Freud treats head on the problematic of "the unity of life and death" identified in "Freud and the Scene of Writing"

(*WD*, 227/336), the problematic discussed in chapter 1. The portion of *The Post Card* devoted to Freud, "To Speculate—on 'Freud,'" thus comes to focus on Freud's major later work *Beyond the Pleasure Principle* (1920), in which the notion of fundamental life and death instincts is first introduced (a notion that increasingly occupies a major place in Freud's thought in the years after 1920). Indeed, the enigmatic notion of a "death instinct" first broached in *Beyond the Pleasure Principle*—Freud's name for a force present in the living but antithetical to life (one of the most difficult, and most frequently misunderstood, concepts in Freud's thought)—then becomes a key figure for Derrida.[2] After *The Post Card*, the notion of the death drive would subsequently mark for Derrida the place where "Freudian psychoanalysis found both its resource and its limit" (*RP*, 32/46), where it opens onto another thinking of "what is most alive in life" (*RP*, 118/146).

"To Speculate" is thus absolutely key to this trajectory in Derrida. Consequently, to understand Derrida's activation of the death drive, it is necessary to examine the complex treatment of the drives found in this text. This, in turn, will allow us to grasp how the logic of life death mutates, in Derrida's later works, into the thought of life as survival. It will also shed light on the reasons for Derrida's continued recourse to Freud after *The Post Card* (which forms the focus of chapter 3).

We are in a better position today to approach the arguments of "To Speculate" from the point of view of its thinking of life insofar as we now have at our disposal the full text of the 1975–76 seminar Derrida gave at the École normale supérieure.[3] "To Speculate," we can now see, is based on the final four sessions of the seminar but was substantially expanded for publication. As its title indicates, the 1975–76 seminar is a strategically important piece in the broader trajectory in Derrida I am tracing in that it pursues the thought initially opened up in the major works from 1967 to 1968.[4] Indeed, Derrida makes clear right away in the first session that the project of the seminar is to develop another thinking of life called *la vie la mort*, beyond the opposition life and death *and* their coincidence (in the thought that life *is* death, that life essentially consists in overcoming the threat of death) (*LD*, 3–4/22–23). To this end, traversing what Derrida describes as three linked loops or rings (*LD*, 140/184; see also *PC*, 259n1/277n1), the seminar engages not just Freud but Nietzsche and modern biology and the life sciences. The latter is then carried out via an examination of Canguilhem and a sustained reading of François Jacob's *La Logique du vivant*—in particular, Jacob's notion of an encoded program for reproduction as the essential feature of living beings—and, to a lesser extent, Hegel's vitalist metaphysics.[5] Consequently, our understanding of Derrida's engagement with

Freud's thinking on life and death is enhanced by viewing it within the overall context of the seminar.

In particular, the seminar enriches our understanding of how and why the crucial line of thinking we are following in "To Speculate" is elaborated via a detailed reading of Freud aimed not simply at treating his concepts but rather at treating *the relation between his concepts and his writing*. Derrida underscores this approach early on in the portions of the seminar that would become "To Speculate," and emphasizes it repeatedly throughout. That is, Derrida's reading of Freud in these texts attempts to weigh a certain "autobiographical" dimension in *Beyond the Pleasure Principle*, understood not in the classical sense of weighing the connection between the "life" and "thought" of the author but in a rigorously nonclassical sense. Coming under scrutiny will be the intertwining of "the scene of the writing" of *Beyond the Pleasure Principle* and its concepts, the interlacing of what Freud *does* in his writing and what he speaks about.[6] This is the explicit focus of the section of "To Speculate" most frequently cited and discussed in the commentary, the portion that probes the mirrored relation between, on the one side, the famous scene of the child's game of *fort/da* relayed by Freud (played by his grandson, Ernst) and, on the other side, Freud's relation to the boy's mother, his daughter Sophie, and his desire to dictate a legacy for the psychoanalytic movement. Much of the secondary literature on "To Speculate" has focused on this "autobiographical" reading of *Beyond the Pleasure Principle*, yet the originality and radicality of what exactly Derrida is doing under the heading of autobiography in this reading has often been missed.[7]

Recently, the thinking of *la vie la mort* at stake in Derrida's treatment of Freud in the seminar has received some attention. Building on the work of Bennington in particular, scholars such as Dawne McCance and Francesco Vitale have opened up new lines of inquiry.[8] Indeed, because of this recent work, we now have a better sense of the seminar's engagement with Jacob and the discourse of the life sciences. Both Vitale and McCance have discussed the analysis of Jacob in considerable detail. Vitale, for his part, shows how Derrida takes up the question of the reproducibility of life from a deconstructive perspective. This in turn clarifies the material stakes of the major engagement with Freud in the seminar, the one Derrida himself saw as important enough to publish in his lifetime, even expanding on it, and to which he returned repeatedly (by contrast, Derrida never returned to Jacob over the course of thirty years). Yet still, the ultimate significance of the Derridean logic of life death—and how exactly Derrida's engagement with Freud allows us to understand key features of this logic central to the broader move from life versus death to survival in Derrida—remains unaccounted for.[9]

Ultimately, we will see, once we hold the final four sessions of the 1975–76 seminar and "To Speculate" alongside "Freud and the Scene of Writing," it becomes clear that, embedded within Derrida's project, there is a powerful new formulation of the deconstructive logic of life death. Crucially, "To Speculate" articulates this logic in terms of a thinking of "the band" or binding. This move will prove crucial to the thought of life death, and in turn *survivance*, outlined across the rest of this book.

In particular, the conception of binding I elaborate in this chapter enables us to see just how mortality, as the radical thought of finitude in deconstruction, is to be understood. *The Post Card* in effect shows how the deconstructive logic that dictates the insertion of heterogeneity within the economy of the same is to be thought not in terms of energetics, nor in terms of a drive or tendency operative in the living being, but in terms of a kind of *tension* internal to life. Yet this tension will not be purely or simply internal because it bespeaks the arche-originary presence of the other in the same.

This demonstration provides the basis for understanding what exactly is at stake in Derrida's contemporaneous engagement with Lacan in *The Post Card*, one which, for all the attention it has received, has remained somewhat obscured in the secondary literature. In fact, as I show in the final section of this chapter, the debate with Lacan in this period sheds further light on how the problematic of binding I elaborate is to be distinguished from pre-deconstructive modes of thinking the general structure subtending the thought of life death: the structure whereby the condition of possibility of life (*différance* as originary difference and deferral) is revealed to be the condition of impossibility of its closure or purity.

The argument on binding pursued in this chapter will seem to bring me close to Martin Hägglund's recent articulation of deconstructive survival in terms of what he calls a more fundamental "bindinal economy" of life and desire. However, I forgo a full accounting of Hägglund's work in this chapter so that I can take it up in further detail in chapter 3, having by then fleshed out what exactly is at stake in the general thinking of life death in Derrida and the subsequent notion of *survivance*. With this trajectory in place, we will be in a better position to see where and how the present account differs from Hägglund's.

To see all this, however, we first need to situate the treatment of Freud in *La vie la mort* and "To Speculate" within the overall context of the seminar and in relation to its main concerns. As I have indicated, Derrida indicates that the overarching project of the seminar is to develop an altogether other thinking of life beyond the opposition life and death and their coincidence in the thought that life *is* death. This second thought, Derrida argues in the seminar, is found in Hegel, where the imperishable life of the Spirit comes into itself by traversing and overcoming natural death (LD, 3–4/22–23). If the notion of life death is to be beyond the thought of life conceived on the basis of a logic of opposition, however, it will itself not be opposed to life/death, but rather will answer to an altogether different logic. It will attest, Derrida says, to a nonoppositional logic offering itself to be read "concealed . . . beneath a positional (oppositional, juxtapositional, or dialectical) schema" (LD, 2/20).

It is in order to develop this thought that Derrida takes on the then-current biological model of life via the reading of Jacob. In particular, Derrida takes aim at Jacob's conception of self-reproduction as "the very essence or essential property of the living" (LD, 86/120), Jacob having claimed to overcome a teleological-metaphysical understanding of life, replacing the vitalist notion of an essence of life with the notion of the program in the living (LD, 84/117). Derrida then further critiques Jacob's precritical understanding of text, message, and a certain kind of writing as the model for the very structure of the living being, both of these motifs ultimately registering the appearance of "a kind of clandestine metaphysics" (LD, 17/38) at work in Jacob's theorization of the living.

Further, *La vie la mort* allows us to better grasp Derrida's treatment of the "autobiographical" dimension of *Beyond the Pleasure Principle* in "To Speculate" insofar as it also includes an extensive engagement with life as "the thing or object of bio-ology and bio-graphy" in Nietzsche (LD, 27/49). While some of this material on autobiography in Nietzsche had been available previously, we are now able to consider this thread in the context of Derrida's treatment of Nietzsche in the seminar as a thinker of life.[10] In particular, he takes up the Nietzsche of *The Gay Science* and *The Will to Power*, who alternately claims that life is but a special case of death ("Let us beware of saying that death is the opposite of life; the living creature is simply a kind of dead creature, and a very rare kind" [*Gay Science* §109, quoted in LD, 155/200]), and that to be dead is unthinkable, since we have no representation of "being" other than "living" (LD, 5/23). The thought that life is nothing but will to power, in which health and sickness are just differences of degree within a relation of forces, is equally one, Derrida claims, "for which the usual logic of relations between life and death will have difficulty providing an explanation" (LD, 66/95).

In particular, Derrida's focus falls on the Nietzsche interrogated by Heidegger with respect to the question of biologism, whether the thought of will to power and eternal return ultimately bespeak a biological determination of life. Heidegger will answer this question in the negative, but as Derrida shows, via a reading of Nietzsche that just as problematically places him at "the peak, the crest, at the summit" of Western metaphysics (*LD*, 157/202). Nietzsche, according to Heidegger, does not think *bios* biologistically, such that everything that *is* is thought on the basis of the biological simply understood. Rather, he determines the essence of the living in terms of the will to power. But this then entails a metaphysical anthropology of the human, conceived in terms of its freedom and its capacity to have a perspective (*LD*, 201–2/253). On this view, Nietzsche's thought is thus a "thinking of beings as a totality, a thinking riveted to a thought of beings as a totality, closed off to the question of the being of beings" (*LD*, 178/226). For Heidegger, Nietzsche's status as metaphysician is subsequently confirmed in the thought of life and world as subject to eternal return (see *LD*, 198/250). This is because, Heidegger claims, Nietzsche thinks eternal return as a kind of eternal present; he determines what he calls life "on the basis of an implicit determination of time that privileges the present, eternity as present . . . which would be that which allows one to conceive of the totality of beings as present, on the basis of the present" (*LD*, 190/239). Ultimately, Heidegger "saves Nietzsche from biologism only in order to confine him to a metaphysics of life" (*LD*, 215/270). He saves Nietzsche from biologism by arguing that, in determining the totality of beings as life, Nietzsche is "not borrowing his concepts from a regional science called biology" (*LD*, 218/273). He is not borrowing his concepts from biology because he is trying to think the metaphysical foundation of every regional science. He is trying to think "both life and the conditions of life as the totality of beings" (*LD*, 218/273). But in so doing, while escaping biologism, Nietzsche consummates Western metaphysics.

Yet what Heidegger overlooks, Derrida demonstrates, is the complex scene at work in Nietzsche's quasi-autobiographical writings (*Ecce Homo*, but also select unpublished fragments and *The Will to Power*) and visible across his entire oeuvre. The scene of writing ultimately undermines or overdetermines any attempt to make Nietzsche a univocal thinker of whatever kind, whether of biologism or metaphysics. In particular, Heidegger overlooks how Nietzsche advances his thinking behind so many masks and pseudonyms, "plural masks or plural names . . . wherein the ruse of life can be seen at work" (*LD*, 28/51). *Contra* Heidegger, this produces a state of affairs, Derrida argues in the later sessions of the seminar, in which it is as if what "Nietzsche had called for, without calling himself a single time unique, were this festival of names, this multiplicity of names which disturbs that whole schema" (*LD*, 174/222). In Nietzsche's gestures of writing, Derrida finds not a unity of thought, as does Heidegger, but rather a unity "put into question, broken up into pieces or into plural masks by the feast of the nietzsches" (*LD*, 176/223, trans. mod.). What

Heidegger fails to take account of is "what happens when Nietzsche says or writes I, Nietzsche, the undersigned, *ecce homo*" (*LD*, 157/202). In a previously published revised extract of the seminar, Derrida writes explicitly (inserting a phrase absent in the seminar text) that this gesture and scene puts into question "the *gathering* of this logic" concerning life and beings presupposed by Heidegger.[11] What's more, Derrida underscores, it is actually "in the name of life death" that Nietzsche offers the thought in which "the value of totality comes to lose its privileged position once the whole becomes, in accordance with eternal return, both more and less than itself" (*LD*, 180/228).[12] The treatment of Nietzsche in the seminar then equally casts in relief how a certain "autobiographical" dimension is at work in Jacob's text, problematizing Jacob's conclusions. This is because once the essence of the living is thought as text, "what we then claim to take as a model, comparison, or analogy in order to understand the living at its most elementary level is itself a complex product of life, of the living, and the alleged model is external neither to the knowing subject nor to the known object" (*LD*, 81/114).[13]

The more limited engagement with Jacob and Nietzsche (on his own and via Heidegger) in the 1975–76 seminar thus enriches our understanding of the "autobiographical" analysis of the relation between Freud's writing and concepts proposed in "To Speculate" by showing how Freud's contribution to the thinking of life death is unique. It illuminates how the problematic of autobiography understood in a new sense opens onto the deconstructive thought of life death in Freud. Further and more importantly, it serves to demonstrate why, for Derrida, Freud offers the most powerful thinking of life death. As we will see, the engagement with Freud and the death drive forms the major articulation of life death Derrida returns to repeatedly after 1976, because the thought of life death Derrida finds in Freud enables him to think a set of consequences—glimpsed in the seminar and elaborated further in "To Speculate"—that Jacob's biological model and the thought of life as a special case of death in Nietzsche do not allow us to think.

The "Third Step" in the Theory of the Drives

The task now is to see how Derrida redeploys and refines the notion of life as an economy of death after 1967–68 in "To Speculate," with the recently published 1975–76 seminar providing additional background for understanding this text. Having reserved a discussion of the Freudian theory of the drives and the issues around it until now, it can be instructive, as a first step, to briefly situate *Beyond the Pleasure Principle* in the broader context of Freud's theorization of the drives insofar as it is presupposed by Derrida in his treatment of this text.

Crucial to Derrida's reading will be Freud's description of *Beyond the Pleasure Principle* as taking the "third step" in the theory of the drives (SE, 18:59). Freud refers to *Beyond the Pleasure Principle* this way insofar as it offers a significant revision of his earlier thinking on the basic structure of the psychic apparatus and its relation to the somatic, thinking that had already undergone a previous alteration. At each step, Freud is concerned with one of the most speculative and most fundamental portions of his metapsychology, a crucial component, alongside the notions of the unconscious and repression, in the conceptual infrastructure underlying everything psychoanalysis advances at the level of theory (its theory of the psyche, sexuality, psychopathology, and of culture and religion) and clinical practice. *Beyond the Pleasure Principle* constitutes a major revision to Freudian metapsychology insofar as it offers a new structural model of the drives substantially different from the theory of the drives Freud had first advanced in the *Three Essays on the Theory of Sexuality* (1905) and then subsequently reworked in the papers "On Narcissism" and "Instincts and Their Vicissitudes" (1914–15).

In order to approach Freud's project in *Beyond the Pleasure Principle*, we can briefly recap Freud's thinking on the drive as it is formulated in these earlier works, prior to 1920.[14] In truth, we have already seen certain features of his thinking in this area coming into view in the portions of Freud's corpus examined in the previous chapter. This is because Freud's first major formulations in the chapter on metapsychology in *The Interpretation of Dreams* (1900) are prefigured in the *Project*, in the latter's discussion of how the psychic apparatus must deal with the "exigencies of life," which will lead directly to the problematic of the drive. While Freud endeavors to think how the psychic apparatus deals with excitation in these texts via a kind of reflex function (see SE, 5:565), it is a bit later, in the *Three Essays on the Theory of Sexuality* (1905), that Freud offers a specific term for describing the source of the endogenous excitation or pressure the psychic apparatus has to work to discharge (hunger, for instance, and then, thought on this model, sexuality).[15] The term he chooses is drive (*Trieb*), what James Strachey in the English *Standard Edition of the Complete Psychological Works of Sigmund Freud* translates as "instinct." The notion of the drive is then meant to articulate the relation between the psyche and the somatic-material body in which it is necessarily situated. This relation, however, is far from simple and direct in Freud, a fact that makes it eternally difficult to reduce Freudian metapsychology to a biologism. It is for this reason that many contemporary readers of Freud choose the word *drive* for *Trieb* over Strachey's *instinct* (indeed, the term *Instinkt* is readily available to Freud, and does appear in his writing from time to time, but almost always when he is speaking of animals or a similarly bodily instinct dictating a response to danger).

Fleshing out Freud's thinking in this area in full is beyond the scope of this book, but since my focus is on Derrida, I can briefly indicate: from the beginning and throughout his work, Freud understands the drive as something that is not simply material but is nonetheless an expression of material, somatic processes. Freud thus describes the drive in 1905 as a borderline concept, "lying on the frontier between the mental and the physical" (SE, 7:168). The drive is therefore the name for something located *between* the bodily-material and the psychic-virtual.[16] Moreover, this concept formulates a relation between the body and the psyche, but it does so in a fundamentally mediated way. Freud is absolutely clear already in 1900 that, from a metapsychological perspective, when we deal with the question of endogenous energy in the psyche—and thus, on the horizon, the drive—we are only ever dealing with representatives. This means that what he calls drive is never directly present "in person" in the psyche; it can gain admittance only by being translated, as it were, in the form of a psychic representative, ideas that can carry a certain charge of excitation (Freud's "*Besetzung*," which Strachey translates as "cathexis") or affect. Freud's definition of the drive in the *Three Essays* underlines this fact: he defines it as "*the psychical representative* of an endosomatic, continuously flowing source of stimulation, as contrasted with a 'stimulus,' which is set up by single excitations coming from without" (SE, 7:168, my emphasis). The psychical representative acts as a kind of delegate, but we have no access whatsoever to the somatic source of the drive outside of its representatives.

Having defined the drive in this way, from 1905 to 1914 Freud maintains an essentially dualistic theory. Initially, in the *Three Essays*, Freud begins by distinguishing the sexual drives from basic vital needs, what we have seen Freud thinking quite early on under the heading of "the exigencies of life." Beginning in 1910, however, Freud formalizes this approach by ascribing the fulfillment of these vital needs to a separate set of "self-preservative" drives (SE, 11:214). The only partially domesticatible sexual drives are here set on one side, and the self-preservative drives, designated by Freud with the term *ego instincts*, are set on the other. This model begins to undergo a shift, however, in the paper "On Narcissism" (1914). There, Freud substantially revises the basic opposition between the sexual drives and the ego instincts and complicates the picture of the psyche he had employed to that point. His innovation is to suggest that the internal psychical structure of the ego—the broader structural model of three different agencies (the ego, id, and the superego) will not come until *The Ego and the Id* (1923)—can itself be an object of the sexual drive, while the self-preservative instincts are now said to be aimed solely at external objects.[17]

Approaching the Death Drive

Such is the state of the theory of the drives in 1920 when Freud begins to revise, once again, this basic dualism of the drives. Moving away from the opposition between the sexual drives and self-preservative drives, Freud will now posit a new dualism of life and death drives. While *Beyond the Pleasure Principle* is famous for introducing the notion of the death drive—working silently in opposition to both the sexual drives *and* the self-preservative drives—it is particularly important in the present context to understand how and why Freud arrives at this hypothesis.

In brief, Freud revises the theory of the drives in *Beyond the Pleasure Principle* in order to better account for certain phenomena he had observed in psychoanalytic practice (each of which are touchstones, in their own way, in a vast psychoanalytic literature after Freud): forms of repetition that seem to him to operate under the force of a compulsion, and the so-called "war neuroses." In the first case, Freud observes analysands continually haunted by and returned to scarring psychic material. In the case of the war neuroses, Freud encounters analysands who repeatedly replay traumatic material in dreams, in a way that fundamentally seems to challenge the inaugural insight of psychoanalysis that every dream is the fulfillment of a wish. In both cases, there is a form of repetition, the "perpetual recurrence of the same thing" (SE, 18:22), and this repetition evidences something that Freud's existing model of the psyche, regulated from start to finish by the pleasure principle, simply cannot account for: the recurring repetition of psychic experiences of *unpleasure*. According to Freud's original model, the repetition of unpleasurable psychic material would produce an increase of tension in the psychic apparatus, and this is impossible to square with the postulate that the apparatus continually seeks, via the pleasure principle, to discharge energy and return to the lowest level possible (the pleasure principle defined, as we have seen, as a principle of constancy).

Freud is clear in *Beyond the Pleasure Principle* that there are certain forms of repetition that appear disruptive but are nevertheless consistent with the pleasure principle. For instance, some types of repetition seem to him to constitute an attempt to master traumatic psychic material so that it can be worked through and discharged later on, via the mechanism of what he calls binding. In this process, excitation freely circulating at the level of the primary process is brought under the control of the secondary process by being "bound," held up in certain pathways before ultimate discharge. This form of repetition aimed at mastering certain material and preparing it for discharge thus contributes to the overall goal of lessening the amount of tension in the apparatus as a whole.

Not all repetition seems to him to operate in this way, however, and this leads him to speculate that there is perhaps a separate "compulsion to repeat" at work in certain instances, producing forms of repetition driven as if by "some 'daemonic' power" (SE, 18:35). It is this suspicion that puts him on the track of something "beyond the pleasure principle," another drive, or tendency, apparently operating independently of the pleasure principle. The reason is that such compulsive forms of repetition seem to him to "exhibit to a high degree an instinctual character": they are not governed by the secondary process, but rather, seem to belong solely to the primary process, the earliest, most fundamental mode of functioning of the apparatus, the mode of functioning characteristic of unconscious processes (SE, 18:35). Yet if this is the case, the compulsion to repeat would reflect the operations of an "instinctual" process present alongside and working counter to the principle thought at this point to hold sway at the level of the primary process, in fact ruling the psychic apparatus *in toto*.

The hypothesis of another drive operating beyond the pleasure principle leads Freud to offer a new definition of the drive: it is a tendency to return to an earlier state. Stated succinctly, the *regressive* character of the forms of repetition he observes in traumatic dreams and in the analytic treatment—the repetition of "purely infantile" material or the repeated return to a past trauma (SE, 18:36)—leads Freud to rethink what a drive in general is, the previously identified ones and any drive operating independently of the pleasure principle. If the regressive character of the drive is fundamental, Freud posits, then the drive can be redefined as a tendency pushing toward *an earlier state*. Moreover, given that the drive has its source in the material life of the living organism, Freud can go further and state more generally *"an instinct is an urge inherent in organic life to restore an earlier state of things* which the living entity has been obliged to abandon under the pressure of external disturbing forces" (SE, 18:36). The drives operating in accordance with the pleasure principle, Freud theorizes, press toward a return to a previous energetic state of equilibrium (prior, that is, to a given endogenous influx of excitation). But then, if this push to return to an earlier state *"is inherent in organic life"* more generally, Freud realizes, the organism will also be pushed on some level toward a state beyond equilibrium, toward the original energetic state: the state of inanimate quiescence, the "initial state from which the living entity has at one time or other departed and to which it is striving to return" (SE, 18:38). This push would be a tendency to reduce excitation within the psychic apparatus beyond the threshold maintained by the pleasure principle to absolute zero, the energetic state of death.[18] On the basis of this hypothesis, Freud speculates that the previously mentioned negative phenomena, if they exhibit "a highly instinctual character," are in fact instances of a radically disruptive drive that undoes every form of psychical organization—it appears, then, as a radical force of unbinding—in view of returning the living organism to its original state of quiescence, pushing toward absolute zero. They are thus instances of what Freud will begin to call *Todestriebe*, a drive toward death.

But he quickly realizes that if such a drive exists and the living organism lives for any sustained amount of time, this can only be because something opposes this drive toward death right away. Otherwise, life would cease, would short-circuit, the very moment it had begun. In fact, in the most speculative portion of *Beyond the Pleasure Principle*, Freud, holding fast to the postulate that the death drive is fundamentally a primary process phenomenon, postulates that something like this was actually the case with the emergence of the first single-cell organism. Thus, the first emergence of life that is sustained for any amount of time at all, he speculates, must have been the result of accidental, "external disturbing influences"—presumably environmental factors—that cause the entity to abandon this primary mode, to stray from its original aim and pursue a new one (SE, 18:37–38).

This leads Freud to speculate that if the living organism lasts once it has emerged, even though an originary drive toward death is present in it, this drive tends not toward any form of death but rather pushes toward a *return* to the prior state of quiescence from which the organism originally departed. It thus seeks the death that the living organism reaches "only in its own fashion" (SE, 18:39) and not by means of some external accident: it tends toward a death that is the organism's own, its proper death. The life drives, Freud then has to acknowledge, must be thought of as collaborating with the death drive in its pursuit of this aim, insofar as, in seeking to prolong life, they support the endeavor of the death drive in seeking to guide the organism to its own proper death. On this most "extreme," speculative line of thinking (SE, 18:37), the self-preservative drives, "the guardians of life," now appear as "myrmidons of death," ensuring the organism follows only "its own path to death, [warding] off any possible ways of returning to inorganic existence other than those which are immanent in the organism itself" (SE, 18:39). If the self-preservative drives ultimately serve the death drive, Freud concludes, we are left with the "paradoxical" image of the living organism struggling vigorously against mortal threats that would end its life prematurely, in order to pursue its own path to death. Nevertheless, he avers, "such behavior is . . . precisely what characterizes purely instinctual as contrasted with intelligent efforts" (SE, 18:39).

Setting aside this most speculative line of thinking, Freud ultimately posits that, if life is able to get going and last at all, there must be two groups of drives militating against one another "from the very first" (SE, 18:61). According to this new model, there is, on the one hand, a "death drive" that seeks the absolute dissolution of excitation, beyond the state of equilibrium sought by the pleasure principle, and on the other hand, the "life drives," which seek to prolong life by binding and holding organic substance together. This latter group now includes both the self-preservative drives and the sexual drives, which serve the broader purpose of the life drives, Freud speculates, by ensuring the joining together of the seeds of reproduction, making possible the continuation of living matter and greater unities of cells. Thus, Freud names this second set of drives Eros, "the true life instincts" (SE, 18:48–49), conceived now as an elemental force opposed to the death drive. Viewed from this broader perspective, the death drive is a radical force of unbinding that not only undoes individual psychical organization, seeking the disintegration of the living organism, but actually seeks the dissolution of every form of life-enabling binding together, all the way up to the level of the social group.[19]

There is one last complication Freud has to address before *Beyond the Pleasure Principle* comes to a close, however. This is the complication introduced by the fact that, given the definition of pleasure he maintains (the reduction of tension to a minimal but constant level), it is impossible not to conclude that the two groups of drives, Eros and the death drive, are in fact opposed only *at a certain point*. Stated somewhat differently, the speculative theory of the death drive as a tendency to push to absolute zero ultimately produces a model in which the drives are not in fact distinguished by a hard and fast opposition. Rather, as Freud has to acknowledge in the final chapters of *Beyond the Pleasure Principle*, if the pleasure principle seeks any reduction of excitation at all—even if it does not aim toward the reduction of all tension, but rather a return to equilibrium—the life drives operating in accordance with it necessarily sometimes *collaborate* with the death drive. As Freud writes, at times "the pleasure principle seems actually to serve the death instincts" (SE, 18:63). Furthermore, this conclusion is inevitable once we are reminded of the distinction between endogenous and external sources of excitation. The pleasure principle works to ensure the discharge of external excitation, Freud notes, but, as the basic mode of operation of the life drives, it is even "more especially on guard against increases of stimulation from within, which would make the task of living more difficult" (SE, 18:63). What the pleasure principle in actuality concerns itself with, then, is the very excess of excitation that gets in the way of the path back to the original inorganic state, death. In pursuing the reduction of internal excitation, the pleasure principle actually works on behalf of the tendency toward the total dissolution of all tension in the apparatus. Thus, we have no choice but to conclude that, within the larger trajectory of Eros pursuing its aim of creating ever greater unities, the operations of the life drives and the pleasure principle in effect support the tendency toward absolute dissolution at the very moment they are supposedly struggling against it.

Freud is not put off by this apparent undoing of the strict dualism of the drives, however. Rather, he takes it as one last clue as to how the death drive operates. The fact that the two sets of drives are not always strictly opposed but rather frequently intermingled suggests that the death drive does not work in quite the same way as the sexual drives and the drives toward self-preservation, he concludes. The life drives are "noisy" insofar as they make themselves known in various easily perceptible ways: sexuality, and the basic tendencies of nourishment and respiration. But the death drive, he surmises, is fundamentally different. Unlike the life drives, the death drive is "by its nature mute" as he will put it three years later in *The Ego and the Id* (SE, 19:46)—this same description of the death drive as "mute" (*stumm*) is rendered as "operating silently" later still in *Civilization and Its Discontents* (SE, 21:119).[20] In *Beyond the Pleasure Principle*, Freud simply says that "the death instincts seem to do their work unobtrusively" (SE, 18:63). In the terms of Freud's metapsychology, this means that the death drive has no psychical representatives. It is always operative in the psyche and in the living organism, but it itself will never be perceptible, Freud seems to suggest. Its presence in mental life can only be deduced from the fact of its effects, from the disruptive disturbances it produces.

Hence the essentially speculative character of the theory of the death drive according to Freud. It cannot be pursued without "diverging widely from empirical observation" (SE, 18:59). We should therefore not be surprised, Freud writes at the close of *Beyond the Pleasure Principle*, adopting a consoling tone, that the third step in the theory of the drives will be extremely difficult to verify through observation insofar as the death drive will always be hidden from every possible viewpoint. It is speculative, in the end, on Freud's view, in the sense that psychoanalytic theory has no choice but to postulate, or hypothesize, the existence of such a drive. Yet, classical thinker that Freud is, he nevertheless seems to retain the possibility that the life sciences will someday come to confirm, in their own way, the veracity of this new theoretical claim.[21]

The Project of "To Speculate—on 'Freud'"

At this point, we can situate the expanded project of "To Speculate—on 'Freud'" with greater precision. As I indicated above, Derrida's "autobiographical" reading of *Beyond the Pleasure Principle* takes as its point of departure the relation between Freud's writing and Freud's thinking. Bearing Freud's broader project in mind, we can now see why Derrida came to be interested in exploring this question via a reading of *Beyond the Pleasure Principle* initially in the 1975–76 seminar. This is because we ourselves can now see how Freud's text continually labors to identify, to speculate on, a beyond of the pleasure principle—"the totally-other (*than* the pleasure principle)" (*PC*, 283/303)—but fails in this task. Hence Derrida, picking up on this odd feature, will refer to Freud's writing as "a-thetic" or "non-thetic" (*PC*, 261/27; *LD*, 219/275):[22] never quite arriving at its stated thesis, never quite taking the step it purports to take.[23] As we have seen, it continually fails to make any progress on a beyond or other of pleasure distinct from the pleasure principle. Indeed, a "beyond" that is not simply opposed to pleasure is the very thing Freud ultimately winds up formulating. Viewed from this perspective, in its very failure, Freud's text enacts or performs what it is attempting to theorize.

If this is the case, it is not possible to simply set aside the issue of Freud's writing and focus on Freud's concepts. Rather, the two are necessarily conjoined. Even a purely "internal" (*LD*, 227/284) reading of Freud's writings on life death ultimately opens onto the question of writing and "*bios* in its autobiographical import," Derrida argues in "To Speculate," and this register directly touches on, he continues, "*bios* in its biological or biologistic register" (*PC*, 273/291; see also *LD*, 227/284).[24]

Consequently, in order for us to treat Derrida's philosophical thought as it comes to be articulated in his dealings with Freud, it is necessary to take account of this engagement with the question of Freud's writing. To do so, we ought to circle back to the interpretive schema sketched earlier for understanding Derrida's engagement with Freud. In chapter 1, I demonstrate that the chief means by which Derrida differentiates deconstruction from psychoanalysis is by arguing that while psychoanalysis opens up certain pathways for thought that militate against metaphysics—while Freud opens up (along with a few others) the very space in which deconstruction operates—the crucial difference is that Freud never reflected explicitly on the necessity and conditions of possibility of this breakthrough. The first consequence of this move is that it allows Derrida to bring out certain aspects of Freudian thought to which Freud himself remains blind. A further consequence is that it furnishes Derrida with a means of showing how it is that Freud is able to transmit this thought even though he does not think it explicitly: showing that, unlike Nietzsche, Freud *performs* a challenge to metaphysics less than he formulates it.

"To Speculate" is thus equally focused on a certain "unconscious" performance at the level of Freud's writing.[25] This performance has to do, first and foremost, with Freud's repeated attempts in *Beyond the Pleasure Principle* to track down, to make progress on, some other tendency beyond the pleasure principle. But what Derrida shows is that if Freud fails in this regard, he "succeeds in failing." The failed demonstration succeeds in putting forward, or putting on display, how what is other than the pleasure principle is not to be thought in accordance with the logic of opposition. As we saw, on Freud's own terms, he cannot avoid the consequence—one that he seems to remain, if not blind to, at least reluctant to admit has definitive consequences for any attempt to maintain firm distinctions between the aims of the pleasure principle and the death drive—whereby the pleasure principle is not strictly opposed to its contrary, but rather finds itself sometimes in conflict with the death drive, and sometimes already working on its behalf. Thus, the speculative attempt to think the so-called death drive performs the nonclassical logic of life death—beyond the oppositional logic of life *and* death, "but not in a relation of opposition but in another relation with that which it goes beyond or breaks free from" [*LD*, 219/275; see also *PC*, 260/278]—Freud continually labors to grasp, but ultimately cannot think.

This, then, is the chief aim of Derrida's demonstration in "To Speculate," building on the text of his seminar: to show how Freud thinks life death without thinking it, without saying it explicitly, without taking on this problematic frontally. In the course of this demonstration, the strict dualism of life and death found in Freud "mutates," to borrow a term from Bennington, into Derridean life death.[26] But this mutation is *staged* more than it is theorized. What *Beyond the Pleasure Principle*, and Freud's thinking on the death drive more generally, brings forward, on Derrida's view, will be nothing other than the resolutely nonclassical logic of *différance* as self-differing, as irreducible nonselfsameness, constitutive of the very structure of life.

Before turning to this logic, it is worth looking at how Derrida advances this argument concerning Freud's performance. Derrida articulates it most forcefully in the most frequently cited portion of "To Speculate," his reading of the famous account of the child's game of *fort/da* described in chapter 2 of *Beyond of the Pleasure Principle*, an extensive expansion of the twelfth session of the 1975–76 seminar. There Freud recounts the scene of "the first game played by a little boy of one and a half and invented by himself" (SE, 18:14), a game played by his grandson, Ernst. The game is noteworthy because Ernst had developed "an occasional disturbing habit" (SE, 18:13): He did not disturb his parents at night, but he did disturb them in his play, by throwing away his toys and other small objects:

> The child had a wooden spool with a piece of string tied round it. It never occurred to him to pull it along the floor behind him, for instance, and play at its being a carriage. What he did was to hold the spool by the string and very skillfully throw it over the edge of his curtained cot, so that it disappeared into it, at the same time uttering his expressive "o-o-o-o" [which Freud and the boy's mother "were agreed in thinking ... represented the German word '*fort*' ('gone'—trans.)"]. He then pulled the spool out of the cot again by the string and hailed its reappearance with a joyful "*da*" ["there"]. This, then was the complete game—disappearance and return. (SE, 18:15, trans. mod.) [27]

The remainder of the chapter is devoted to the problem of interpreting this scene, in which Freud attempts to provide an account of its "*economic* motive, the consideration of the yield of pleasure involved" (SE, 18:14). Nowhere, however, does Freud suggest that there might be at work here a compulsion to repeat beyond the pleasure principle. Rather, he chalks up the game to the boy's attempt to master the disturbing experience of unpleasure associated with his mother's absence, referring somewhat enigmatically to the possibility of a separate drive for mastery (*Bemächtigungstrieb*) acting more or less "independently" of the pleasure principle (SE, 18:16). Thus, at the conclusion of the chapter, no progress has been made on "the operation of tendencies *beyond* the pleasure principle ... tendencies more primitive than it and independent of it" (SE, 18:17).

Derrida picks up right away on this fact. Indeed, he is right to state that this lack of progress is often missed in the vast secondary literature on *Beyond the Pleasure Principle*. As he writes, "since one connects the repetition compulsion (*Wiederholungszwang*) to the death drive, and since in effect a repetition compulsion seems to dominate the scene of the spool, it is believed that this story can be tied to the exhibition, that is, the demonstration, of the so-called death drive" (PC, 294/315, trans. mod.; see also LD, 241/299). On the contrary, the scene of the *fort/da* actually serves to confirm the dominance of the pleasure principle. For Derrida, then, if the game of the *fort/da* is to be ascribed any significance at all, he makes clear, "its import is perhaps not inscribed in the register of the *demonstration* whose most apparent and continuous thread is held in the question: are we correct, we psychoanalysts, to *believe* in the absolute domination of the PP [Derrida's abbreviation for the pleasure principle]?" (PC, 294/315). (It might be helpful to recall here that this is the precise question with which *Beyond the Pleasure Principle* opens, and which Derrida glosses at some length in the first seminar session on Freud and in the opening send-off of "To Speculate"). While most readings of "To Speculate" have focused on how Derrida reads the scene in terms of its distinct autobiographical resonances—a kind of identification with Freud and a desire to establish a legacy in the psychoanalytic movement on Freud's part—more important to Derrida's overall project is what he identifies as a certain abyssal structure at work in Freud's writing here.

This abyssal structure emerges once we take account of what Freud is doing at this moment at the level of his metapsychological theory. That is, Freud's interpretation of the game attempts to think the absolutely other than the pleasure principle only to ultimately confirm it as the regulating mechanism of psychic life. Freud's text, in other words, "makes as if . . . it puts at a distance, pleasure," makes as if it does away with the pleasure principle only "to bring it back untiringly" (*PC*, 302/323, trans. mod.; *LD*, 246/305), only to return it to its rightful place by means of an interpretation in which the game "is, taken as a whole, going to be placed under the authority of the pleasure principle" (*PC*, 317/338, trans. mod.; *LD*, 251/311). Freud, at the level of the writing, plays *fort/da* with the pleasure principle. What we encounter here is a "double *fort/da*" (*PC*, 303/323).[28] The structure of the writing is, in Derrida's words, one of "abyssal mirroring [*le rapporté abyssal*]" (*PC*, 320/334, trans. mod.; *LD*, 253/312): the mirroring of "the object or content of *Beyond* . . . , of what Freud is supposedly writing, describing, analyzing, questioning, treating, etc., and, on the other hand, the system of his writing gestures, the scene of writing that he is playing or that plays itself" (*PC*, 320/341; see also *LD*, 253/312). The relation between content and writing here is one of repetition: the writing repeats the content. But crucially, it can be demonstrated that this procedure does not adhere to a classical logic wherein there is *first* some original and *then* a repetition. Rather, as each side of the structure mirrors the other, what is original and what is secondary is put into question.

One of the primary reasons for this abyss is the fact that the content Freud's writing repeats is not an object like any other; it is ceaseless, recurrent repetition. Indeed, the form of repetition Freud observes is only "complete" (as we saw Freud saying of Ernst's game) insofar as it continues to indefinitely recur. Hence we have an exceedingly complex situation. Derrida spells this out in "To Speculate," glossing a point left implicit in the seminar: "Freud does with (without) the object of his text exactly what Ernst does with (without) his spool. And if the game is called complete on one side and the other, we have to envisage an eminently symbolic completion which itself would be formed by these two completions, and which therefore would be incomplete in each of its pieces, and consequently would be completely incomplete when the two incompletions, related and joined the one to the other, start to multiply themselves, supplementing each other without completing each other" (PC, 320/341).[29]

The first consequence of this situation is that the theoretical coherence of Freud's account of the child's game is rendered unstable by repeating what it relates: repetition without end (this then unleashing further, repeated attempts to do away with and bring back the pleasure principle). Recall, however, that Derrida sees in Freud's failure a kind of success. Consequently, a kind of success is to be found here too. It makes legible a general structure of hollowing out that then repeats throughout *Beyond the Pleasure Principle* in its theorization of the death drive, one that opens onto the thought of life death.

Derrida's crucial intervention is to show that the abyssal structure on display in the scene of the *fort/da* actually furnishes the structural model for the relation between the death drive and the pleasure principle, a relation, we have seen, that cannot be understood in terms of the logic of opposition. That is, the abyssal structure just identified ultimately comes to be installed within Freud's conception of the death drive: "The value of a repetition '*en abyme*' of Freud's writing has a relation of structural *mimesis* with the relation between the PP and 'its' death drive. The latter, once again, is not opposed to the former, but hollows it out with a testamentary writing '*en abyme*' originally, at the origin of the origin" (PC, 304/325, trans. mod.; see also LD, 246/305). This is perhaps *the* key move in Derrida's reading of *Beyond the Pleasure Principle*, identifying the abyssal structure that shapes the relation between the pleasure principle and the death drive.[30] At stake in Freud's thought here, Derrida shows, is a general, nonclassical structure of originary hollowing out. And if this is also operative in the relation between the pleasure principle and the death drive, then Freud will have glimpsed in his own way that life and death are not simply opposed. Rather, as we shall see, the pleasure principle, and in turn life, will have to be understood as *already*, originally undermined from within, in its very functioning.

Life Death in "To Speculate—on 'Freud'"

We have arrived at the point where Derrida's reading of *Beyond the Pleasure Principle* begins to give rise to a thinking of life death. The key was seeing Derrida's argument on how the logic of opposition is suspended in Freud's thinking. This suspension is critical to what Derrida wants to bring out in Freud's thinking on the death drive.

The first place we see this is in Derrida's treatment of the relation between the pleasure principle and the reality principle in "To Speculate."[31] In fact, Derrida argues that everything Freud tries to think under the heading of the death drive is in fact already present in this relation. The pleasure principle, recall, holds sway as the governing mechanism of psychic life. It is operative at the level of the primary process, the most fundamental and first mode of functioning of the psychic apparatus, which seeks satisfaction through the immediate discharge of influxes of excitation. Yet, given that the organism needs to negotiate with the external world to meet its basic somatic needs, the secondary process, governed by the reality principle intervenes, deferring immediate discharge so that some amount of energy can be put to work in meeting the organism's vital needs. So defined, the distinction between the pleasure principle and the reality principle is not a hard and fast opposition, however. Because the reality principle still operates in view of ultimate discharge (discharge delayed and deferred, yes, but discharge, and therefore pleasure, nonetheless), it is not actually opposed to the pleasure principle. Rather, as Freud maintains from quite early on, it should in fact be viewed as a particular *modification* of it (*SE*, 18:11; see also *SE*, 12:223).[32]

The functioning of the reality principle is thus the imposition of "a detour in order to defer satisfaction, the waystation of a *différance*" (*PC*, 282/301, trans. mod.; *LD*, 234/291), Derrida suggests.[33] Freud speaks of it as a kind of indirect detour ("*Umwege zur Lust*") (*SE*, 18:10). But insofar as, on Freud's own account, the reality principle is but a modification of the pleasure principle, this can only mean that here the pleasure principle is "in *différance* with itself"; what we have is a situation in which the pleasure principle "*unleashes* in itself the *absolute* other" (*PC*, 283/302). The possibility of the absolutely other than the PP, its beyond, is already present within it. To the extent that the pleasure principle according to Freud rules the operations of life, a form of death is thus already inscribed within life from the very first. "Pure pleasure and pure reality are ideal limits, which is as much to say fictions. The one is as destructive and mortal as the other. Between the two the *différant* detour therefore forms the very actuality of the process, of the 'psychic' process as a 'living' process" (*PC*, 284/204; *LD* 234/291–92). But then, Derrida continues, "whichever *end* one takes this structure . . . it is death. *At the end*, and this death is not opposable, does not differ, in the sense of opposition from the two principles and their *différance*. It is inscribed, although noninscribable, in the process of this structure—which we will call later stricture. If death is not opposable it is, already, *life death*" (*PC*, 285/305; see also *LD* 234/292).

This is what Freud's text gives to be thought, "without ever being given or thought" according to Derrida (*PC*, 285/305). It is this structure that Derrida then uses to rethink life and death as life death in this period.³⁴ The point in the reading of Freud here is to adduce "a structure of alteration without opposition. That which seems, then, to make the belonging—a belonging without interiority—of death to pleasure more continuous, more immanent, and more natural too" (PC, 285/305; LD 234–35/292).

We see what Derrida is after here when we examine more closely the relation between the reality principle and pleasure principle as Freud defines it. On Freud's own terms, the reality principle is a modification of the pleasure principle in the sense that if the former were to function fully, it would cut off all pleasure. "Pure reality," as Derrida puts it, would be "pleasure that, by protecting itself too much, would come to asphyxiate itself in the economy of its own reserves" (PC, 286/306; LD, 235/293). In terms of Freud's energetics, this would mean the organism holds on to all excitation, deferring all discharge, which would quickly overwhelm the whole system and cause its disintegration. In Derridean terms, if the *différantial* detour that describes the movement of alteration from the pleasure principle to the reality principle were not a detour, but all that life is—this is what Derrida describes as "[going] to the end of the transactional compromise that is the *Umweg*" (PC, 286/306; LD, 235/293)—this would be death. Why? Because here there would be no possibility of discharge and "no pleasure would ever present itself" (PC, 286/306; LD, 235/293). There would be nothing whatsoever to defer in the movement of life.

By the same token, if the pleasure principle functions fully, this is also death. If it is unleashed without restraint, "if it follows its 'own' tendential law which leads back to the lowest level of excitation, there is the 'same' *arrêt de mort*" (PC, 286/306; see also LD, 236/293). As we have seen, Freud, in his energetics, seems to have an intimation of this consequence, and this is what leads him to define the pleasure principle as a principle of constancy. But in Derrida's terms, the point is that the *différance* internal to the pleasure principle offered in the form of the reality principle, the *différance* constitutive of life as life death, must be arche-originary. This is because pure pleasure would also be death. The absolutely unleashed pursuit of pleasure would result in the reduction of all excitation and the return to the state of the inorganic.

Moreover, if the psychic apparatus pursues only pleasure from the very beginning, there is no possibility of life getting going in the first place and subsisting. If the detour or compromise were not originary, as we saw in the discussion of the life and death drives in Freud, the life of the organism would cease at the very moment it begins. Crucially, this originary delay and deferral has to be present *already* in the relation between the pleasure principle and the reality principle. Indeed, as Freud seems to grasp at times, there would be no *need* for the reality principle if the pleasure principle did not press toward something beyond what allows the organism to meet "the exigencies of life," and thus to persist. In this way, the living entity "resists its own preservation . . . resists that which protects it from itself, resists its proper, and the proper itself, resists economy" (PC, 286/306, trans. mod.; see also LD 236/293).

Here we glimpse the general structure Derrida's entire reading of Freud in "To Speculate" is meant to bring out. It is this: the condition of possibility of life as it is lived—*différance,* deferral—is at the same time the condition of impossibility of absolute life, pure life (PC, 353/375). The organism "exposes itself to death . . . by making-letting a guard rail be jumped" (PC, 286/306; LD, 236/294), the guard rail that protects its purity. But it does this, exposing itself to a certain death, precisely in order to live. What Freud ultimately offers here is not the thought of two opposed, self-standing principles (a notion he both endorses and struggles with), but rather the thought of a single principle of life that differs from and defers itself. As we have now seen, the pleasure principle regulates life in its absolute "mastery" (Freud invokes this metaphorics in his persistent description of the *Herrschaft,* or dominance, of the pleasure principle), but has to expose itself to its other in order to get going in the first place and persist for any time at all. The *différantial* detour of the pleasure principle in the unfolding of life, "makes or lets the other return in its domestic specter":

> What will come back, in having already come, but not in order to contradict the PP, nor to oppose itself to the PP, but to mine the PP as its proper stranger, to hollow it into an abyss from the vantage point of an origin more original than it and independent of it, older than it within it, will not be, under the name of the death drive or the repetition compulsion, an *other master* or a *counter-master,* but . . . something completely other. In order to be something completely other, it will have to not oppose itself, will have to not enter into a dialectical relation with the mastery (life, the PP *as* life, the living PP, the PP alive). (PC, 317–18/338; see also LD 251/310–11)

Again, this exposure has to be arche-originary and originarily repeated in order for persistence and living for some amount of time to be possible. The opposition of life *and* death, life *versus* death, is here left behind on the way to a thinking of life death on the basis of *différance.*

Death, in this model, is not merely the end of life nor what supervenes on life from the outside, diminishing it or encroaching on it. Rather, a certain relation to death is internal to life from the outset, as the very condition of its possibility. It is present in life as that which simultaneously makes pure life, teleologically unfolding and only secondarily infected or compromised by its other, impossible. There is no first seed of life or of a vitalism that, subsequently, comes to be compromised by its other. Rather, this compromise is the very first condition of the emergence of life as such.

This precise structure reemerges, Derrida shows, in the description of the life and death drives and the living organism found in *Beyond the Pleasure Principle*. He begins by noting that what he finds in the theory of the drives was *"already* at work in the logic we have just recognized"—the logic of the *Umweg* or *différantial* detour (PC, 291/311). But because in the case of the life and death drives what is at issue is the very origin and operations of the organic in general, what Freud is in fact describing is an even more general detour that in fact provides the "foundation" for the one present in the relation between the pleasure principle and the reality principle (PC, 354/377, trans. mod.; LD, 271/333). The detour or deferral at issue now is the one that ultimately defines the life of the living organism itself, as it seeks to return to state of the inorganic. This is the "absolute and unconditional *Umweg*" (PC, 354/377; LD, 271/333). "The end of the living, its goal and its end point, is the return to the inorganic. The evolution of life is but a detour of the inorganic aiming for itself, a race to the death. . . . This death is inscribed as an internal law, and not as an accident of life (what we had called the law of supplementarity in the margins of *La Logique du vivant*). It is life that resembles an accident of death or an excess of death" (PC, 355/377, trans. mod.; see also LD, 271/333). That is, without thinking it explicitly, Freud, in his notion of the life and death drives, offers a *différantial*, deconstructive conception of life as life death. This is because here, in Derrida's words, the "double determination that I had assigned to the 'word' *différance* with an *a*" (PC, 354/377; LD, 271/333) has to be at work from the very beginning in order for life to come into being at all and last. Life, to be at all, has to defer itself, its return to the inorganic. But it also has to differ from itself, deviate from its most proper aim. In fact, life cannot defer itself unless it differs from itself *a priori*. It has to be minimally internally divided, split, rather than a plenitude. Only a divided entity can defer its own functioning.

Freud ultimately tries to bend this thought to a classical logic of opposition and a strict dualism of the drives, as we saw, first by positing that the organism tries to die its *own* death, the death that results from internal reasons. He is then able to reconfigure things such that, as he sees it, the two groups of drives are still fundamentally in conflict. Even in this model, the conservative, preservative drives "are the guardians of life, but by the same token also the sentinels or satellites of death" (PC, 360/383; see also LD, 273/335), insofar as they guard life so that it seeks its own proper death, rather than the one that would bring it to an end too soon. But in fact, the image here is actually one of "the satellites of life death" (PC, 360/383). The reason is that even though Freud seems to insist on the logic of the proper in order to save the dualism of the drives, the dualism cannot be maintained: the very process of "guarding death in order to save one's own death, the death of the living (*safe within it*) dying in its own fashion (*auf seine Weise*) and at its own pace" (*PC*, 361/383 trans. mod.; see also *LD*, 273/335) produces the absolute erasure of the proper. There is something like a *différantial* rhythm here, Derrida notes: "One group of drives rushes forward to reach the final aim of life as quickly as possible. But, division of labor, another group comes back to the start of the same path in order to go over the route and 'so prolong the journey'" (*PC*, 361–62/384).

As we have seen, however, this thought cannot be maintained within the logic of a dualism, the logic of the "sharp distinction" Freud tries to draw between the death drive and the life drives (*SE*, 18:44). Instead, it answers to the logic of what Derrida calls "exappropriation," here understood as the exappropriation of the proper (*LD*, 286/350). The organism tries to achieve its own most proper goal, it tries to appropriate itself, in its deferral of immediate death so as to give itself its own, proper death.[35] But in so doing, it welcomes within itself the guardians not of life but of death. It thus loses itself, exappropriates itself, in pursuing its proper aim as a living organism. This is a key way of thinking the deepest condition of life death, Derrida suggests: via the logic of exappropriation. Here, he writes, "the *exappropriating* structure is irreducible and undecomposable" (*PC*, 362/385). The general condition of life death is here understood on the basis of the deconstructive thought of exappropriation.

The Logic of Stricture

But this is not the only way to understand the structure of life death according to Derrida. In fact, he suggests that it is better thought in terms of the logic of what he calls *stricture*, which describes a kind of internal tension. This notion is developed in its fullest scope in Derrida's engagement with the problematic of binding in *Beyond the Pleasure Principle*.

This discussion in Derrida is critical insofar as it allows us to see the general structure at stake in the treatment of Freud in "To Speculate" taken as a whole. Indeed, arriving at this point, we can now formulate the point this chapter has been driving at for some time: the chief contribution of "To Speculate" is that it fleshes out the thought that the structure of life as it is lived is nonoppositional stricture, a structure dictated by the absolute irreducibility of *différance*.

The key discussion of stricture in "To Speculate" is to be found in Derrida's reading of chapter 7 of *Beyond the Pleasure Principle*, an expansion of the final session of *La vie la mort*. It is there that Freud finally returns to the hypothesis of the repetition compulsion. He had effectively set it aside at the close of chapter 2, recall, in the reference to a possible independent drive for mastery. Instead of pursuing repetition, Freud had gone on to investigate, and ultimately confirm, the hypothesis that a drive in general seeks a return to an earlier state. Thus, the issue in chapter 7 remains how to relate instances of drive repetition to the pleasure principle. Ultimately, as we saw, Freud will come to the realization that even in his strict dualism of the drives, "the pleasure principle seems actually to serve the death instincts" (SE, 18:63). Given the way Freud has defined pleasure and unpleasure to this point, this is the only coherent answer he can give, and it can be stated another way: sometimes repetition confirms the pleasure principle, and sometimes it threatens it. This conclusion essentially confirms Derrida's proposition that the pleasure principle already contains, in its very operations, the principle of its own deferral and a principle of death.

However, what especially interests Derrida in chapter 7 is something else. Because, in order to bring the problematic into clearer focus, Freud takes up what he had earlier described as the mechanism of binding operative in the psychic apparatus. Here Freud speculates, as he had several chapters earlier in his treatment of the war neuroses, that certain instances of drive repetition are to be understood as an effort on the part of the psychic apparatus at binding—rendering less mobile and disturbing—excessive, traumatic influxes of excitation.

Yet in the process, the binding mechanism is subtly reconceptualized. From the beginning of his thinking, Freud had maintained that binding was aligned with the secondary process, characteristic of the preconscious-conscious system, which retains a quantity of excitation in a controlled state in order to allow for the procurement of certain satisfactions. In this way, the secondary process is distinguished from the primary process, characteristic of the unconscious and aimed at immediate discharge. But at the close of *Beyond the Pleasure Principle*, Freud suggests that perhaps, under certain conditions, binding operates at the level of the primary process as well, since the form of repetition he is considering at this point—compulsive repetition—appears to him to be driven by an unconscious drive. In order to bring this thought in line with the existing notion of the pleasure principle, Freud hypothesizes that perhaps the binding mechanism, at this level, does not oppose the pleasure principle but actually contributes to its operations, insofar as binding, here, could serve as a "preparatory act" necessary for the ultimate discharge of excitation (SE, 18:76). Binding now appears as the first step on the overall path toward the reduction of tension, "a preliminary function designed to prepare the excitation for its final elimination in the pleasure of discharge" (SE, 18:76).

Ultimately, Freud does not significantly alter his understanding of the primary and secondary processes in *Beyond the Pleasure Principle*, but he recognizes that in this new model the nature of the difference between the two processes is difficult to account for. Thus, he offers a solution: he suggests that the difference between them perhaps lies in the fact that feelings of pleasure or unpleasure arising out of the primary process are more intense than in the secondary process, just as they were at the beginning of mental life, before the secondary process was in full effect (*SE*, 18:76). The pleasure principle would never have been able to establish its dominance if it had not already been at work at this early stage, however, he surmises—it must be ontogenetically coexistent with this binding mechanism—and thus he is left with what Strachey translates as "no very simple conclusion" (*SE*, 18:76). The conclusion is that "at the beginning . . . the struggle for pleasure was far more intense than later but not so unrestricted" (*SE*, 18:76). On this view, pleasure was originally intense but restricted, not so free as later on, and this in fact forms the very condition of its emergence.

Holding the various threads of Freud's argumentation in *Beyond the Pleasure Principle* together at this point, the picture of the psychic apparatus now includes a binding mechanism that ultimately serves the pleasure principle (without being confused with it), while the pleasure principle in turns serves (without being confused with) the even more general function of the death drive, as it seeks to reduce excitation to absolute zero, in the return to the inorganic.[36] Pleasure, Freud seems to suggest, but without fully grasping the consequences, can only be found between two limits.[37] It can only take place between the absence of pleasure present when freely circulating energy is not yet bound and available for discharge, and the absence of pleasure that results from the absolute reduction of all excitation to zero.

Consequently, the pleasure principle works by exappropriating itself. We can see this in the case of both limits. In the case of the first limit, once Freud suggests that the pursuit of pleasure would have to have been originally restricted, we cannot avoid the conclusion that the pursuit of pleasure can only get underway, or operate, by first limiting pleasure, its overall quantity if not its intensity. The fullest, unleashed force of feelings of pleasure has to be foreclosed, and thus pleasure has to be to some extent restricted, in order for pleasure to be pursued and experienced. The psychic apparatus, here, has to disallow the experience of pleasure in its fullest expression in order for there to be any possible experience of pleasure. In Derrida's words, "such is the mission of the pleasure principle. It is by limiting the possible intensity of pleasure or unpleasure that the PP conquers its mastery. It can fulfill it only by moderating force or intensity, the force or intensity of pleasure as much as that of unpleasure"

(*PC*, 400/427; *LD*, 291/356). The pursuit of pleasure, the fundamental operation of the psyche, is in effect originally interrupted, undermined to a certain degree from within.

In the case of the second limit, if the pleasure principle were to function absolutely, without deferring itself at all, it would serve the ultimate aim of the organism in the reduction of all energy to zero, returning it to death.[38] In order for there to be pleasure for an organism that subsists for any amount of time, the pleasure principle actually has to limit pleasure. On Freud's own terms here, "the pleasure *principle* makes war on pleasure. This hostility resembles, at least, a hostility to itself" (*PC*, 399/426; see also *LD*, 291/355–56). On either end, the "very principle of pleasure would manifest itself as a kind of counter-pleasure . . . which comes to limit pleasure in order to make it possible" (*PC*, 399/426; see also *LD*, 291/355–56).

Thus, in this thinking of pleasure, there is a *différantial* logic of stricture in Freud. This logic allows us to think a kind of internal tension. The thought of pleasure in Freudian psychoanalysis proceeds fully in this direction without knowing it. With respect to pleasure, "Its unleashed intensity would destroy it immediately if it did not submit itself to the moderating stricture. . . . Death threat: no more [*plus de*] principle of pleasure thus no more *modifying différance* in the reality principle" (*PC*, 400/427 trans. mod.; *LD*, 292/357). That is, "if it liberates something as close as possible to the *pp* (a theoretical fiction), thus if *it does not limit itself,* not *at all,* it limits itself absolutely: absolute discharge, disbanding, nothingness or death" (*PC*, 401/428; *LD*, 292/357). Yet, by the same token, "if it limits itself absolutely"—by absolutely limiting discharge, via total, pure deferral—"it disappears" (*PC*, 401/428; *LD*, 292/357). At this point, we see that the quasi-aporetic "irresolution" at stake in the conception of pleasure in Freud is not a failure of Freud's classical logic, but the opening in Freud to the logic of stricture. Here, "there is no more opposition between pleasure and unpleasure, life and death, within and beyond. . . . There is only pleasure which itself, limits itself, only pain which itself limits itself, with all the differences of force, intensity, and quality that a set, a corpus, a 'body' can bear or give 'itself,' let itself be given. A 'set' being *given,* which we are not limiting here to the 'subject,' the individual, and even less to the 'ego,' to consciousness or the unconscious, and no more to the set as a *totality* of parts" (*PC*, 401–2/428–29; see also *LD*, 293/358).

Derrida thus draws an absolutely general implication from Freud here, that the logic of stricture pertains to anything that is at all. But since only a divided entity can have an internal tension, can be in tension with itself, every apparent unity or gathering together includes a kind of hiatus, an opening to heterogeneity, at the most primordial level. Any "set," Derrida argues, any supposed "unity" at all—not just "that of the subject . . . of consciousness, the unconscious, the person, the soul and/or the body, the socius, or a 'system' in general" (*PC*, 402/429)[39]—must, originarily, "*bind itself* to itself in order to constitute itself as such" and "in a *différantial* relation to itself" (*PC*, 402/429).

Critically, as we have now seen, a deconstructive approach shows decisively that such a process of binding always entails exappropriation, in a *différantial* movement without end. At the same time, this movement, like whatever it makes possible, must be understood as necessarily finite, since infinite *différance* would not be a movement of deferral and differing but a plenitude. We have here, then, a picture of the general logic of binding as it emerges in the thought of life death that in many ways gives life to the general principle we have seen at stake in Derrida's discussion of Freud here, and in his earlier engagement with Freud: the logic of binding describes how the condition of possibility of a given entity simultaneously forms the condition of impossibility of its plenitude or purity. But crucially, given that Derrida is discussing the economy of pleasure and life death, this general structure, just as it was in chapter 1, is no less spatial than it is temporal. The structure we are describing is predicated on arche-originary *différance*, but it cannot be understood simply in terms of temporal opening. It is, instead, to be thought in terms of the form of internal tension we saw Derrida trying to capture with the term stricture. The logic of binding here provides the most rigorous way to think the spatial, material structure of everything subject to the movement of *différance* and, thus, of life as life death.

We thus begin to see once again how Derrida rearticulates Freud rather than simply taking over his concepts. Freud, according to the grid for understanding we have laid out, thinks the logic of stricture without thinking it, performs it rather than theorizing it explicitly. While the problematic of binding in Freud provides a window onto the general structure of *différantial* stricture, it should now be clear that Derrida does not simply take over the notion of the drive or Freud's energetics.[40] Indeed, in a somewhat truncated discussion of the drive in "To Speculate," Derrida argues that the necessity of rethinking the drive in other terms is opened up by the very thought of binding in Freud I have just glossed. Insofar as what Freud is describing via the mechanism of binding is what prepares the way for the pleasure principle's "mastery," and insofar as the pleasure principle is not just one psychical process among others but the very ruling principle of life in Freud's model, it is possible to view the problematic of binding as bound up with a form of mastery that is absolutely foundational and prior to mastery understood in the usual sense, that is, in a social or intersubjective sense (*LD*, 286/350). Yet, given that the form of mastery at issue has its origin in stricture, it cannot be thought in terms of an oppositional agon or dialectical process. Rather, it has to be thought in altogether other terms.

To develop this idea, Derrida returns to Freud's fairly discreet reference (earlier in *Beyond the Pleasure Principle*) to the possibility of a "drive for mastery" independent of the pleasure principle in a section of "To Speculate" added to the original seminar text.[41] But he then reworks this notion in a different direction. Derrida sees in this suggestion not some other drive beyond the pleasure principle or even beyond the death drive but, rather, a figure for the logic of stricture Freud's thinking ultimately offers, the thought of which *the drive* is something like the *metaphysical name*.[42] Why? Because if we grant a certain relation of mastery, or tendency toward mastery, "a quasi-transcendental privilege," then the notion of mastery at stake here overflows the metapsychological categories within which it is contained in Freud (PC, 403/430).[43] At this point, it becomes impossible not to begin to think mastery in terms of a relation operative in any entity whatsoever, in accordance with stricture understood as an absolutely general structure. This relation would be "the relation to the other, even in domination *over oneself*" (PC, 403/430). This anterior relation of mastery would also be operative in "the drive's *relation to itself*" (PC, 403/430). There can be no drive at all, neither of life nor death, if it is not "driven to bind itself to itself and to assure itself of mastery over itself as drive" (PC, 403/430). "Mastery" here is the name for the very "drivenness of the drive" (PC, 403/430). A bit further on, Derrida writes that this quasi-transcendental notion of a certain relation of power or mastery defines the "relation to oneself as the relation to the other" of the drive, such that it has an absolutely originary root (PC, 404/431). "The motif of power," he writes, "is more originary and more general than the PP, is independent of it, is its beyond. But it is not to be confused with the death drive or the repetition compulsion, it gives us with what to describe them, and in respect to them, as well as to a 'mastery' of the PP, it plays the role of transcendental predicate. Beyond the pleasure principle—power" (PC, 405/432).

We have arrived at a crucial point then, where the *différantial* logic of stricture allows Derrida to redescribe the Freudian concept of the drive in deconstructive terms. Here, the figure of binding—a figure of stricture—describes the movement of deferral and exposure to heterogeneity necessary to life as life death, a movement no less spatial and material than it is temporal. But crucially, here stricture—an absolutely general condition, and thus the very condition of life—always entails exappropriation. It produces an entity that will never be able to close in on itself in a unity.

This becomes all the more clear when Derrida puts the deconstructive thought of mastery at stake in the thought of binding back into communication with the notion of the death drive and repetition compulsion in Freud. If we follow Freud's suggestion regarding a drive for mastery and posit that the death drive and the repetition compulsion have their root in the motif of power, Derrida suggests, we cannot avoid the conclusion that power, at whatever level (be it at the level of the social or of the quasi-transcendental) undoes itself: "For it is equally the case that everything described under the heading of the death drive or the repetition compulsion, although proceeding from a drive for power, and borrowing all its descriptive traits from this drive, no less overflows power. This is simultaneously the reason and the failure, the origin and the limit of power" (PC, 405/432). This is because, in Freud's own framework, a drive for power at the root of the death drive cancels itself out in the very unfolding of the death drive, since at the moment the organism achieves its own proper death, it perishes, disintegrates, loses itself.[44]

Translating this into Derrida's terms, we could say that the form of mastery at stake in an entity binding itself to itself (in the movement of articulation described by the structure of the trace) would cancel itself out without *différance*, would short-circuit by attaining its goal as soon as it emerges. This is another way of saying that self-mastery without *différance* and exappropriation, unity without stricture, would simply be stasis, asphyxiation, or plenitude; it would provide no condition of possibility for a relation to the other in the same that makes mastery possible in the first place. At the same time, pure *différance* would be the loss of whatever there is to bind. Pure *différance* would be another form of plenitude, and another form of death. What makes this quasi-aporetic structure thinkable is the *différantial* logic of stricture, which is presented here as an absolutely general logic that describes the arche-originary condition of anything at all, and thus the arche-originary condition of life, now understood as life death.

There is another important consequence to take from Derrida's development of this logic, which we will see deployed throughout the remainder of this book. The consequence is that while Derrida will frequently invoke the death drive after *The Post Card*—often appearing to endorse the concept—he never simply takes over Freud's concept. Rather, he submits it to scrutiny and rearticulation. As we have now seen, Derrida displaces the very notion of the drive in general, pushing it in the direction of stricture and binding. Thus, as we will see in subsequent chapters, while Derrida frequently invokes the *figure* of the death drive, and all that it asks us to think, he continually takes his distance from Freudian metapsychology, from a set of concepts—now including the death drive—that remain within the metaphysical enclosure.[45]

In Conclusion, the Question of the Letter

There is one last matter to address, however. This arises out of the fact that the period examined in this chapter on Derrida's engagement with psychoanalytic texts extends beyond Freud to the influential, linguistically oriented theory of Jacques Lacan. But unlike Derrida's treatment of Freud, his treatment of Lacan takes the form of a pointed critique, in the now-famous essay "Le facteur de la verité."[46] Coming under scrutiny in Lacan will be his inscription of the repetition compulsion and the death drive within "the field of the signifier" in his "Seminar on 'The Purloined Letter.'"

In fact, Derrida's treatment of Lacan in this period sheds crucial light on how the thought of life death is to be understood. In particular, it shows how the logic of stricture allows us to avoid an uncritical conception of the opening to heterogeneity traced in the thought of *différance* that ultimately converts it back into a kind of presence. The key is seeing how what we have described thus far as stricture in fact forms an ultra-transcendental structure that impossibilizes alterity and heterogeneity understood as a mere modification of presence. This in turn opens onto a *structural* conception of the constitutive conditions of mortal life distinct from the apparent break with the metaphysics offered by Lacan—one Derrida shows is only apparent. Hence the crucial component of Derrida's treatment of Lacan lies in the not-quite spoken contrast with his own thought Derrida is able to identify in Lacan. This contrast can then be seen working itself out across Derrida's treatment of Lacan in texts published in the ten years or so after "Le facteur de la verité."[47] It then crucially informs, it can be demonstrated, Derrida's critique of Lacan's uncritical humanism in *The Animal That Therefore I Am* (1997) and his late seminars published as *The Beast and Sovereign* (2001–3).[48]

This feature of Derrida's dealings with Lacan—the implicit, and at times explicit, contrast between the Derridean notion of stricture and what can be described as Lacan's conception of pure absence as a constitutive structural condition—nevertheless remains the least considered aspect of the debate. The central problem with the existing analyses is their overreliance on early commentary, and in particular Barbara Johnson's "The Frame of Reference," which argued that Derrida misreads Lacan in "Le facteur de la verité."[49] Johnson's essay in many ways set the terms for subsequent discussions of the debate.[50] But insofar as the relation between Derrida's specific criticisms of Lacan and the broader deconstructive project Derrida outlines in *The Post Card* escapes Johnson, and subsequently others, they miss what exactly is at stake in Derrida's intervention.

To be sure, Johnson correctly identifies the two central movements in Derrida's criticism: his critique of Lacan's notion of the letter in the unconscious, and his treatment of Lacan's reduction of the literary signifier. Her account is on target with respect to the second issue.[51] Yet, this issue—while undoubtedly important[52]—is not the galvanizing issue in the Derrida-Lacan nexus. The more important issue, which Derrida returns to much more frequently in subsequent texts on Lacan (*P*, 127/141–42; *P*, 353–54/362–63; and *RP*, 59–60/78), is the first one: Derrida's criticism of Lacan's conception of the letter and in particular his notion of the letter as oddly resistant to destruction and division.[53] In "Du tout," a dialogue included in *The Post Card*, Derrida describes the argument around the divisibility of the letter as "the argument of last resort in 'Le facteur de la vérité'" (*PC*, 512/540). One can demonstrate, however, that Johnson's account misconstrues Derrida's argument on this issue.

The major point that has been missed is how exactly Derrida critiques Lacan's conception of the letter. Derrida focuses on Lacan's conception of the void or hole at the base of subjectivity, the hole in the subject carved out by the autonomous functioning of the signifier. What he picks up on, however, is that the way Lacan actually conceptualizes the signifier—specifically, what Lacan understands as its particular form of materiality (the materiality of the signifier is precisely what the notion of "the letter" describes in Lacan), whereby it is resistant to all division and can never be lost[54]—is such that the autonomous functioning of the signifier ultimately comes to serve as the stable, transcendental term at the base of the theory of the subject thus constructed. In short, Derrida shows that Lacan conceives of the letter in such a way that his discourse ultimately reduces the play of difference said to be constitutive of the field of the signifier to a determined difference, a given hole or absence that Lacan then identifies as occupying a specific place.

Derrida's point is that Lacan conceives of the empty place of this absence, or lack of being, in such a way that it remains entirely determinable and delimited, and this then ensures that it functions as the ultimate ground of the whole structure thus described. So long as the hole at the center of the subject—the circulation of the letter in its place—remains stable and identifiable in Lacan, he will wind up reinstalling a transcendental signified in the place where there supposedly isn't one. At the core of the radically "de-centered" subject as Lacan describes it, Derrida is saying, there is in fact a centering absence, "a determined place with defined contours" (*PC*, 425/453)—and this is enough for the hole in the subject to be effectively "filled in," as Derrida puts it. To stop a hole, in Derrida's words, "one does have to fill it, but only to see and to delimit its contour" (*PC*, 436/464). And if this is the case, "the existing order will not have been upset: the letter will always find its proper place"

(PC, 425/453).⁵⁵ Lacan's conception of the subject here reveals itself to be actually centered in relation to the hole the signifier carves out in it. If, as Derrida consistently reaffirms, "the lack does not have its place" in deconstruction (PC, 441/470), this is because the form of difference and division at stake in the trace and arche-writing destabilizes not only the thought of a transcendental origin or foundational element, but also the thought of *a simple absence of foundation*, which winds up positioning this absence as a new transcendental term.⁵⁶

The debate with Lacan thus points to how exactly the ultra-transcendental" structures crucial to the thought of life death in deconstruction are to be understood.⁵⁷ As we saw in the discussion of stricture, life death can be understood as the thought of the internal reserve, or deferral, of pure life necessary for life as it is lived, an internal hiatus or opening to heterogeneity. It is this deferral of absolute life that Derrida describes with the term *economy of death*, the specific mode of *différance* at play in the living. Consequently, the thought of life death, what we have seen as the opening to heterogeneity in the economy of the same, is not that of a simple negation or inversion of pure life. It is not to be thought in terms of a simple absence, or lack, in mortal life, something missing in what would otherwise be pure life. Rather, as we have just seen, it bespeaks the more complex logic of an originary deferral of life necessarily at work in its very unfolding in space and time, one that actually allows life, via an economy of death, to persist for any time at all and resist death *tout court*. It is the notion of such an internal tension that Derrida tries to capture with the terms *stricture* and *binding*. Indeed, in the 1975–76 seminar, Derrida underlines that "the strictural logic (a non-dialectical, non-oppositional logic that nonetheless produces dialectical or oppositional effects) . . . is in some sense without lack, without negativity, or at least without oppositional negativity, without desire that comes from lack, without 'without,' if you will" (LD, 293/358).

Thus, we begin to see here that the core logic at work in the thought of life death, the logic of stricture—the logic articulated in *La vie la mort* and solidified in "To Speculate"—is distinct from the logic Lacan activates in his failed attempt to go beyond metaphysics. If Freud is cited more approvingly than Lacan in Derrida, we can now see, it is because Lacan, "so much more the philosopher than Freud" (RP, 47/65), makes the mistake of substantializing the profound challenge to the thought of presence Freud inaugurates.

3
Survival as Autoimmunity

As we have seen in the previous two chapters, a certain thinking of life legible in Derrida's early work is powerfully articulated in his seminal engagement with Freud in the 1960s and 1970s. In this chapter, we will see that this trajectory continues right up through some of the very last texts. It does not remain unchanged in Derrida's work, however. While this change was already discreetly underway in texts such as "Living On—Borderlines" (1979) and "No Apocalypse, Not Now" (1984),[1] the clearest indications are to be found in *Specters of Marx* (1993). While *Specters of Marx*, along with "Force of Law" (1990), is well known for announcing a shift in Derrida's work toward more explicitly political themes—and toward a new rearticulation of concepts privileged by the philosophical tradition (justice, responsibility, law) as opposed to those overlooked or marginalized in this tradition, such as writing—we also find in this text a shift in Derrida's vocabulary with respect to the deconstructive notion of life death.

The key element in this shift is the emergence in Derrida's discourse of the term and the logic of *survivance*, or, as he himself often writes it, *sur-vivance*, to be understood as "living on," in the sense of living on for some indeterminate time to come, or living on and surviving in the wake of a trauma. *Specters* is not the first text in which Derrida would use this term and invoke a certain logic of survival, but it is the first in which survival emerges as a crucial concept within deconstruction.

There, Derrida explicitly links *survival* to *différance* and the relation to death as the arche-originary condition of the living present.[2] He then describes the originary condition of everything that would seem, on the surface, to be simply alive and not dead as that of *survivance*. This is the name for the "beyond present life or its actual being-there" deconstruction tries to think in its thinking of the trace, what in *Specters* Derrida calls the "*non-contemporaneity with itself of the living present*" (SM, xviii–xx/16). Hence, in *Specters*, when Derrida famously states that the possibility of justice is necessarily conjoined to something beyond the living present, it is, he says, because the very idea of justice beyond law actually entails such a notion of life as "*living-on [sur-vie]*, namely, a trace of which life and death would themselves be but traces and traces of traces, a survival whose possibility in advance comes to dis-join or dis-adjust the identity to itself of the living present as well as of any effectivity" (SM, xx/17–18). As soon as there is *différance* and the trace, Derrida thus suggests, there is *survivance*, originally and structurally.

The term survival thus redescribes the notions of life as an economy of death and life death I have tracked to this point. The term describes, in a new way, how a certain contamination on the inside of life by its apparent contrary is necessary for its unfolding and persistence, is necessary to its very living on. Indeed, in *Specters*, Derrida indicates that survival in essence rearticulates the structure of what he had earlier called life death. What the term survival captures quite economically, he suggests, is the way life is always already exposed to death in its most basic structure, via a thought of "life death beyond the opposition between life and death" (SM, 67/94). Derrida spells this out in stating that the whole problematic of the specter necessarily bears on "the question of life death, before being a question of Being, of essence, or of existence. It would open onto a dimension of irreducible *sur-vival* or *surviving* [*survivance*] and onto Being and onto some opposition between living and dying" (SM, 185/235–36). Here, the spectral and the thought of *survivance* is distinguished from "absolute life, fully present life, the one that does not know death and does not want to hear about it" (SM, 220/278). This thought is beyond the opposition life/death insofar as it speaks to a more primary dimension, a prior dimension "before life *as such*, before death *as such*" (SM, 220/278).[3] *Survivance*, Derrida thus suggests, is nothing other than the general condition of living, beyond, and in fact anterior to, the simple opposition life *and* death.

Derrida would develop this line of thinking in later texts such as *The Animal That Therefore I Am, For What Tomorrow*, and "Psychoanalysis Searches the States of Its Soul," but it is most visible in the interview published as *Learning to Live Finally*, the last interview Derrida gave before his death. There, he provides perhaps the most vivid formulation of the logic of survival, speaking powerfully about his longstanding concern with so many figures of death. While expressing a fear that, after his death, there would be nothing left of him or his work (see LLF, 30/30–31), he nonetheless affirms the structural inevitability of survival, saying "it is *not to be added on* to living and dying. It is originary: life *is* living on, life *is* survival" (*LLF*, 26/26). He continues, "All the concepts that have helped me in my work, and notably that of the trace or of the spectral, were related to this 'surviving' as a structural and rigorously originary dimension. It is not derived from either living or dying" (*LLF*, 26/26).[4] Again, what Derrida is describing, he underscores, is a universal structure that harkens back to some of the core concepts of deconstruction. "As I recalled earlier, already from the beginning, and well before the experiences of *survivance* that are at the moment mine, I maintained that survival is an originary concept that constitutes the very structure of what we call existence, *Dasein*, if you will. We are structurally survivors, marked by this structure of the trace and of the testament" (*LLF*, 50/54). Here he describes, in a particularly resonant way, a universal feature of mortality and finitude. He then emphasizes how this notion has a kind of destabilizing effect on traditional notions of life and death, such that by reaffirming a radical thinking of mortality, deconstruction opens onto "the side of the affirmation of life," but in the form of "life beyond life, life more than life," "the affirmation a living being who prefers living and thus surviving to death, because survival is not simply that which remains but the most intense life possible" (*LLF*, 50–51/54–55).

Moreover, throughout his late work, Derrida consistently reaffirms that this thought follows from the earliest insights of deconstruction. In *For What Tomorrow* (2000), Derrida explicitly describes deconstruction as a project of thought that has always taken up the question of life. There, in a brief discussion of the notion of "psychic life" in Freud, Derrida affirms:

> Differ*a*nce means at once *the same* (the living being, but deferred, relayed . . .) and *the other* (absolutely heterogeneous, radically different, irreducible and untranslatable, the aneconomic, the wholly-other or death). An interruption involving differ*a*nce is both reinscribed into the economy of the same and opened to an excess of the wholly other. To return to this word, there is some *psyché*, that is, there is some "life," as soon as this difference appears, or more precisely (for it may not appear *as such*; no doubt it never does) as soon as it leaves a *trace*. (*FWT*, 40/74)

Hence, looking retrospectively, Derrida notes, "Beginning with *Of Grammatology*, the re-elaboration of a new concept of the trace had to be extended to the entire field of the living, or rather to the life/death relation, beyond the anthropological limits of 'spoken' language (or 'written' language, in the ordinary sense)" (*FWT*, 63/106).[5] This line of thought comes to play a key role in late texts such as *Rogues* (2002) and the *Death Penalty* (1999–2001) and *The Beast and the Sovereign* (2001–3) seminars.[6]

While the theme of survival in Derrida has garnered some attention among his readers, it has not, for all this, been systematically put into conversation with his earlier treatment of life death.[7] Moreover, it has not been examined with an eye toward his treatment of this concept via Freud, in which, as we have seen, some of the most crucial dimensions of this thought are developed. The task of this chapter is to fill this void. As I will demonstrate in the remainder of this book, this adds considerably to our understanding of deconstruction's unique contributions to contemporary Continental thought. The aim of this chapter is not just to show how the thought of life death elaborated in chapters 1 and 2 undergoes transformation, however. It also shows how Derrida's continued engagement with Freud after *La vie la mort* and *The Post Card*—and in particular, his engagement with the figure of the death drive—illuminates crucial features of the thought of survival.

In order to develop this argument, it will be necessary to look closely at what Derrida came to call, with a growing emphasis after 1990, "autoimmunity." While Derrida applied this term to a range of phenomena—from religion, to media, to democracy, and to psychoanalysis[8]—it will be necessary to examine precisely how autoimmunity is to be understood in the register where life is thought as *survivance*. In any number of places, Derrida elaborates the thought of life as autoimmune. The task, then, is to examine the precise relation between these two terms, survival and autoimmunity, and to show how the figure of the death drive offers a way of grasping the constellation of issues at stake in Derrida's thinking in this area. Once we come to grips with these issues, we will see that it is actually in the deconstructive thought of life that autoimmunity has its full implications. This is because the understanding of the basic conditions of life at stake in autoimmunity—thought in terms of a process of internal division and contamination, a process shown to be both constitutive and necessary—enables us to reapproach the opening to heterogeneity within the economy of the same implied in the structure of the trace, showing that this opening must be thought in other terms than simply as the opening to what comes from the future. This ultimately allows us to grasp, I argue, the radical conception of finitude and exappropriation at work in autoimmunity and in particular a certain undecidability of chance and threat that can easily get lost in discussions of Derrida. I will argue in chapters 4 and 5 that this radical conception of finitude is crucial to understanding the ethico-political implications of the autoimmunity of life as Derrida conceptualizes it.

Looking at how the activation of the death drive in Derrida's later work rearticulates the notion of life death outlined in chapters 1 and 2 will also allow me to turn my attention, in the final section of the chapter, to a discussion of

Martin Hägglund's competing interpretation of Derrida on this point. While I give Hägglund all due credit for having fleshed out in some detail this very logic—and for providing an account that my own inherits—I take my distance from Hägglund's argument that Derrida in essence goes astray in his activation of the death drive. For Hägglund, the very notion of the drive is inconsistent with Derrida's own thinking. I will show, however, how the figure of the death drive in Derrida allows him to elaborate key features of the logics of life death and survival. In particular, I demonstrate that it enables Derrida to think a form of internal exposure to heterogeneity, and in turn radical destruction, Hägglund's account at times forecloses. Before getting to this, it is necessary to first provide an account of Derrida's use of the death drive in this logic.

Life Death and Autoimmunity

We can begin by articulating the link between the notion of life death and its subsequent development in Derrida's work in the 1990s and 2000s on the deconstructive logic of autoimmunity, most notably in a pair of major works, *Specters of Marx* (1993) and "Faith and Knowledge" (1995), and in later texts such as "Autoimmunity: Real and Symbolic Suicides" (2001) and *Rogues* (2002). A term borrowed from the life sciences but explicitly theorized in a philosophical register in Derrida, the notion of autoimmunity powerfully redescribes the necessity of an originary contamination of life by its apparent contrary.

More specifically, as the existing treatments of autoimmunity in the secondary literature have established, autoimmunity describes the way for Derrida an entity turns back on itself and attacks the very mechanisms originally meant to protect it—in the model of the life sciences, this entity is the living organism. In the model of immune system functioning, the autoimmune response is a pathological response whereby the body's system of defenses, originally aimed at protecting against infection or attack from the outside, is redirected, so that immune functions begin to attack not external, alien elements but the very system of defense itself. On this model, the living thing's efforts at self-protection are not simply short-circuited or shut down but rather extended beyond their usual limits, so that the immune system of defense begins to protect against the organism's own system of self-protection, such that, in the wider view, the organism is now attacking itself.

Deploying this term in an expansive sense, Derrida applies it to a range of phenomena but it is nonetheless initially a way for deconstruction to rearticulate the logic that gives rise to the notion of life death. This is clear in the first real mention of autoimmunity in a major work, *Specters of Marx*. Derrida had previously invoked autoimmunity in the seminar published as *The Politics of Friendship*, but without developing it. There, Derrida speaks somewhat obliquely of "the imminence of a self-destruction by the infinite development of a madness of self-immunity" (*PF*, 76/94). In the first full description of autoimmunity in *Specters of Marx*, however, it is said to bear on the relation between life and death opened up by the thought of the specter. Here, Derrida writes, "life does not go without death, and that death is not beyond, outside of life, unless one inscribes the beyond in the inside, in the essence of the living" (SM, 176–177/224). "The living ego is autoimmune," he continues, "to protect its life, to constitute itself as unique living ego, to relate, as the same, to itself, it is necessarily led to welcome the other within (so many figures of death: differance of the technical apparatus, iterability, non-uniqueness, prosthesis, synthetic image, simulacrum, all of which begins with language, before language), it must therefore take the immune defenses apparently meant for the non-ego, the enemy, the opposite, the adversary and direct them at once *for itself and against itself*" (SM, 177/224).[9] As Derrida makes fairly clear here, this autoimmune process is not a way of describing how something *can* turn back on itself but rather *must automatically*, as it were, turn back on itself. The living entity must open itself to alterity, and to death, in order to constitute itself and persist, and thus it must at least in part attack its own defenses, the forces of self-protection that would keep it hermetically sealed. And it must do so, Derrida suggests here, *in order to live or survive at all*, to "protect its life" from absolute death. Autoimmunity, then, is inevitable because it is necessary, insofar as it describes, from a philosophical perspective, how the living entity has to compromise its self-protection in order to live on in time and space.[10]

Hence, as Michael Naas has shown, already in this passage there are two dimensions to autoimmunity.[11] In the first, the apparently unitary, selfsame structure of the living entity—the structure of identity invoked in the Latin word *autos* embedded in the language of autoimmunity—is put into question. The apparent unity of the entity in question is undone in the attack that sees it turn back against itself. As Derrida puts it succinctly in "Resistances," the very notion of an autoimmune process presupposes a kind of internal tension, but "[since] a purely internal tension is impossible, it is a matter of an absolute inherence of the other or the outside at the heart of the internal" (*RP*, 26/40). Beyond this complication at the level of the identity of the living entity, *life in general* is here conceived as autoimmune. At stake here, Naas writes, is "not only . . . the way in which the life of the ego or the *autos* gets compromised or threatened in its life, but the way in which *life itself*, almost automatically, with the regularity, repeatability, and predictability of a machine admits nonlife . . . and thus the way in which life itself, in order to sustain itself, in order to *live on*, requires the introduction of the nonliving and the foreign body."[12]

The thought of autoimmunity as operative at the level of life itself is central to the argument in "Faith and Knowledge,"[13] and subsequently comes through clearly in the dialogue conducted in the wake of September 11 published as "Autoimmunity: Real and Symbolic Suicides." In the latter text, justifying extending the use of the term autoimmunity to a whole range of phenomena and practices (in this context, predominantly political), Derrida writes, "Despite their apparently biological, genetic, or zoological provenance, these contradictions [he has just spoken of contradiction and 'autoimmunitary overdeterminations'] all concern . . . what is beyond living being pure and simple. If only because they bear death in life" (ARSS, 119).[14] Nevertheless, he affirms, this logic "extends to life *in general*" even though this logic's pertinence "first seemed to be limited to so-called natural life or to life pure and simple, to what is believed to be the purely 'zoological,' 'biological,' or 'genetic'" (ARSS, 187n7). Initially, then, the logic of autoimmunity offers another way of approaching what Derrida had earlier called life death and developing further what was at stake there.

In the texts after *Specters*, however, we see yet another dimension of autoimmunity come into view: that of a radical, internal threat, one that takes the form of self-destruction. In these texts, Derrida emphasizes much more forcefully how an autoimmune process is not just compromising with respect to the integrity of the living entity—a compromise, we have just seen, that is necessary and enabling—but simultaneously *threatening* to the living entity's very living on. This line of thinking plays a key role in *Rogues*, to which I will return, but it is most clear in "Real and Symbolic Suicides." There, Derrida designates the form of compromise at work in autoimmunity as "that strange behavior where a living being, in quasi-*suicidal* fashion, 'itself' works to destroy its own protection, to immunize itself *against* its 'own' immunity" (ARSS, 94); later in the same text he describes this logic explicitly in terms of "self-destructive, quasi-suicidal, autoimmunitary processes" (ARSS, 115). At stake in autoimmunity, then, is a process that threatens not just the entity's sovereignty over itself, but the systems of self-protection that allow it to live in the first place. As we have seen, in this model, to live on and persist, any entity must be simultaneously "self-protecting and self-destroying" (ARSS, 124); but this self-destruction can extend beyond compromising the border between self and other to threaten the life of the living being itself. To return to the model borrowed from the biological sciences, when an autoimmune response is operative, defenses are turned back on the very thing they are meant to protect, a process that can be ruinous. Thus, Derrida is clear in a number of places, most notably in his discussions of the concept of hospitality,[15] that this internal resistance-to-self captured in the term autoimmunity is potentially catastrophic: in the dialogue with Borradori, Derrida affirms that the suppression of protective forces of immunity in an autoimmune response, the suppression of "the immunity that protects me from the other," might very well "be nothing short of life-threatening" (ARSS, 129).

This thought was in fact already signaled, if somewhat discreetly, in "Freud and the Scene of Writing." In an easily overlooked passage, Derrida in essence offers a powerful formulation of autoimmunity.[16] Tracking how the mystic writing pad ultimately meets the various requirements of Freud's psychic apparatus, Derrida alights on Freud's insistence on the "essentially protective nature" of the outermost celluloid sheet (WD, 224/331). In his description of the child's toy, recall, Freud notes the way the external protective layer ensures the wax paper beneath it does not rip or tear when impressions are inscribed on the tablet or when contact with the wax slab that retains traces is periodically broken. Freud even cites *Beyond the Pleasure Principle* explicitly here, remarking on how the requirement of a protective "shield" essential to the living organism and, in turn, to the operations of the psychic apparatus is rather fortuitously modeled by this feature of the toy (SE, 19:230). Yet Derrida draws a different conclusion from this insight than Freud. To Derrida's eye, it suggests, first and foremost, "There is no writing which does not constitute a means of protection, *to protect against itself*, against the writing by which the 'subject' is himself threatened as he lets himself be written: *as he exposes himself*" (WD, 224/331, trans. mod.).

This is a striking formulation of the insight that Freud allows us to see that "life protects itself by means of an economy of death." Only here it is explicitly formulated in terms of the logic of protection essential to the thought of autoimmunity. The living being ensures its living on, sustains itself, only in opening itself to alterity and to death; and it does so via an internal tension, it does so by "protecting itself against itself." Such an autoimmune process menaces the entity at the same time that it forms the essential condition of its survival.[17]

The term autoimmunity then, as Derrida uses it, refers to the way something is threatened with the possibility of destruction from within. But holding this together with what we saw at work in this concept above, this is a process that threatens the life of a living being *at the same moment it makes living on possible*. The question is how exactly the relation between enabling living on and the threat of self-destruction in autoimmunity is to be understood. If the opening to heterogeneity and to its other allows life to persist, in what way exactly is this suicidal and destructive? More specifically, does exposure to the outside only speak to life's *potential* destruction at any moment, or does it speak to something more actively threatening? Again, stated somewhat differently, what requires fleshing out is how exactly the simultaneously destructive and enabling character of autoimmunity is to be thought.

The Autoimmune and the Death Drive

It is my argument that Derrida's use of the death drive as a figure for the autoimmune speaks directly to this question. Indeed, when we look carefully at autoimmunity, we see that Derrida's engagement with Freud allows him to think a crucial feature of this concept: its intrinsically destructive aspect. Following the ways he uses the figure of the death drive in this context in turn sheds important light on just what the thought of survival in Derrida is, insofar as this is his name for the basic autoimmunity of life.

As we saw, the death drive allows Derrida to think the full implications of the co-implication of life and death. As he begins to rearticulate this logic in terms of autoimmunity, he mobilizes just this productive aporia and the figure of the Freudian death drive. The image of a drive toward death that, he had shown, is not opposed to the principle of life because it is part of it, appears as one of the key ways of thinking—before the letter, as it were—the way the living being, in its survival in space and time, perpetually has to differentiate and defer itself in "quasi-suicidal fashion," offering a thinking of internal threat the model borrowed from the life sciences, such as Jacob's, does not furnish.

The stage for this development was set, without being fully developed, in Derrida's later engagement with Foucault in "'To Do Justice to Freud'" (delivered as a lecture in 1991). There, Derrida had spoken of the death drive in a way that prefigures how he describes the compromising of identity at work in an autoimmune process and the autoimmunity of life more generally in *Specters of Marx* (in the crucial passage on the ego cited above). In "'To Do Justice,'" in the midst of a discussion of Freud's notion of a drive for mastery (*Bemächtigungstrieb*) beyond the death drive, Derrida speaks of the ruin of identity in general as the ruin of principled unity and asks, "Is not what Freud was looking for, under the names 'death drive' and 'repetition compulsion,' that which, coming 'before' the principle (of pleasure or reality), would remain forever heterogeneous to the principle of the principle?" (*RP*, 117–18/146). Indeed, it is this very unprincipled thing, according to Derrida, that "Freud tried to oppose to all monisms by speaking of a dual drive and of a death drive, of a death drive that was no doubt not alien to the drive for mastery.... And, thus, to what is most alive in life" (*RP*, 118/146).[18] The key to how Derrida would mobilize the death drive in his later work, however, lies in the specific form of internal opening or exposure the Freudian death drive ultimately allows him to think. In order to see this, we need to look at how Derrida activates this term in the works after *Specters of Marx*. Perhaps the best place to start is the next substantive discussion of autoimmunity to follow *Specters*, "Faith and Knowledge."

In that essay, Derrida makes clear that the opening up to the other at stake in autoimmunity is not simply a pathology, as it is in the life sciences. It is not simply a sickness or mutation some entities would be subject to, but not others, as it is in Jacob.[19] In a move that will prove crucial later on, Derrida here describes the classical, metaphysical notion of life as autopropelling and autopropagating—invaded by death secondarily, from a place external to it—as in fact a fundamentally *theological* notion. It is theological, he argues, insofar as it implicitly mobilizes the thought of the sacred which Derrida, following Benveniste, grounds in the belief in "the safe and the sound" (FK, 61/38). He thus indicates clearly that life as it is traditionally understood is to be radically distinguished from "a general logic of autoimmunity" as it is articulated at the level of the living being. Following the full implications of this distinction, we can say that the opening to heterogeneity at stake in the autoimmunity of life, if it is threatening, is not to be thought as a threat that *can turn out to be either salutary or ruinous* (since this would still be reliant on the notion that compromise comes only secondarily to already-constituted living life), but rather is to be understood as *undecidably both salutary and ruinous*. The two possibilities, their necessary conjunction, are indissociable Derrida thus suggests in "Faith and Knowledge." As he would put it later in *For What Tomorrow*, using a kind of shorthand formula, the task is to think, at the same time, "autoimmunity as survival; invincibility as autoimmunity" (*FWT*, 178/289).

We find further clues as to how this conjunction is to be understood in "Faith and Knowledge." One of the key references is to be found in Derrida's description of autoimmunity as a process that is always at work, even on the desire for the unscathed animating religion. What the notion of the safe and the sound overlooks is that "all self-protection of the unscathed . . . must protect itself against its own protection, its own police, its own power of rejection, in short against its own, which is to say, against its own immunity" (FK, 79–80/67). Derrida calls this logic "terrifying but fatal" (FK, 80/67), where the French *fatale* can mean both ruinous and fated, inevitable, or ineluctable. The stakes of this thought are fleshed out when Derrida links the theological belief in the safe and the sound to a belief in something *worth more than life*, the belief underlying the logic of sacrifice.[20] In a complex move, Derrida suggests this belief in something worth more than life is not only a kind of disavowal of finite, mortal life, but also, at the level of community, unknowingly unleashes "a spectrality without limit" (FK, 87/78). Of this belief Derrida writes:

> This excess above and beyond the living ... this, in short, is what opens the space of death that is linked to the automaton ... to technics, the machine, the prosthesis: in a word, to the dimensions of autoimmune and self-sacrificial supplementarity, to this death-drive that is silently at work in every community, every *auto-co-immunity*, constituting it as such in its iterability, its heritage, its spectral tradition. Community as *com-mon auto-immunity*: no community is possible that would not cultivate its own autoimmunity, a principle of sacrificial self-destruction ruining the principle of self-protection (that of maintaining its self-integrity intact), and this in view of some sort of invisible and spectral sur-vival. This self-contesting attestation keeps the auto-immune community alive, which is to say, open to something other and more than itself: the other, the future, death, freedom, the coming or the love of the other, the space and time of a spectralizing messianicity beyond all messianism. (FK, 87/79)

Here, autoimmunity is not only at work at the heart of life, it is also at work in what Derrida describes as the projection of something of value beyond mortality in the life of the community, supposedly secure in its integrity. Yet this projection is autoimmune, because the spectral dimension at work in this ideal is disavowed or repressed. But the point for us is that the conjunction we are interested in is here described not so much as an opening to what comes from the future, what might potentially threaten the entity in question, but rather, as a *radically threatening compromise* (one that does not pose the *possibility* of "sacrificial self-destruction" but in some sense actually *enacts* it) absolutely necessary for its living on.

The fullest indications of this thought are to be found in *Archive Fever*, written just after "Faith and Knowledge" and very much of a piece with this earlier text. In fact, though it is not often considered as such, *Archive Fever* forms one of the key texts in the nexus of works (*Specters*, "Faith and Knowledge," and *Rogues*) in which the logic of autoimmunity and survival is spelled out. The relevant passages are to be found in Derrida's discussion of Freud's *Civilization and Its Discontents* (1929), in which Freud grapples with the profound implications of the postulate of an ineradicable tendency toward aggression and destruction he associates with the death drive. In *Beyond the Pleasure Principle*, recall, Freud had envisioned the death drive as a tendency that opposes the efforts of the life drives to construct ever greater unities, at the level of organic matter all the way up to the level of the social unit. In *Civilization and Its Discontents*, Freud develops this notion further, suggesting that in the sphere of human relations the death or "destruction" drive, as he now at times calls it, takes the form of a fundamental, ineradicable aggressivity (SE, 21:119).[21]

What is key is the way Derrida mobilizes the death drive in *Archive Fever*. Drawing on Freud's later description of the death drive, Derrida recasts the entirety of Freud's thought—on the structure of the psyche and on personal and historical memory (which Freud somewhat stubbornly never stopped thinking in terms of phylogenesis)—as a theory of the archive. In "Resistances," Derrida had done something similar in approaching psychoanalytic theory, practice, even its social and political position in modernity, from the perspective of resistance. Unlike in "Resistances," however, in *Archive Fever*, Derrida explicitly returns to the metaphors of writing and inscription in Freud explored in "Freud and the Scene of Writing." One of Derrida's central moves in *Archive Fever* is thus to reformulate, in view of this inquiry into the archive, what he had advanced in 1967 on Freud's challenge to traditional notions of consciousness and self-presence.[22]

If Derrida returns here to issues discussed early on, a similar move is at work in his activation of the figure of the death drive in *Archive Fever*. In the book's exergue, describing Freud's claim that the death drive is "mute" (has no psychical representatives), Derrida interprets this as a statement concerning the radical implications of the Freudian death drive. "It never leaves any archives of its own," Derrida writes (AF, 10/24). And if this is possible, it must be because "It destroys in advance its own archive, as if that were in truth the very motivation of its proper movement. It works *to destroy the archive: on condition of effacing* but also *with a view to effacing* its own 'proper' traces—which consequently cannot be called 'proper.' It devours it even before producing it on the outside. This drive, from then on, seems not only to be anarchic.... The death drive is above all anarchivic, one could say, or *archiviolithic*. It will always have been archive-destroying, by silent vocation" (AF, 10/24–25).

But then, with a shift in register, Derrida expands the scope of the death drive's operations considerably. He writes:

> This archiviolithic force leaves nothing of its own behind. As the death drive is also, according to the most striking words of Freud himself, an aggression and a destruction (*Destruktion*) drive, it not only incites forgetfulness, amnesia, the annihilation of memory, as *mnēmē* or *anamenēsis*, but also commands the radical effacement, in truth the eradication, of that which can never be reduced to *mnēmē* or to *anamenēsis*, that is,

the archive, consignation, the documentary or monumental apparatus as *phyomnēma*, mnemotechnical supplement or representative, auxiliary or memorandum. (AF, 11/25–26)

Derrida then remarks that this notion of radical destructiveness will threaten the archive down to its very core, insofar as the very concept of the archive requires "accumulation and capitalization of memory on some substrate and in an exterior place" (AF, 12/27). Indeed, *"There is no archive without a place of consignation, without a technique of repetition, and without a certain exteriority. No archive without outside"* (AF, 11/26). Now, aside from the implications for the archive (for the concept and for archives themselves), it is clear that Derrida is mobilizing the figure of the death drive on multiple levels, and not just at the metapsychological level at which Freud himself thinks. Derrida is now speaking of how it operates at the level of *the greatest generality*, how something like a death drive pertains to any material trace whatsoever. And indeed, what he says about the archive here is equally true of the trace.

This is crucial to note. Although it might seem that everything Derrida is developing in *Archive Fever* pertains strictly to the themes for which this text has most frequently been mined—historical memory, archivization, archival technology, and so on—it should be clear now that Derrida is here re-elaborating the core logic of the trace and arche-writing examined in chapter 1. Still, how exactly there is a destructive force operative within the trace understood in its greatest generality—and thus, in turn, at the level of life thought as survival—still needs to be elucidated.

This issue is clarified once we look at how Derrida links the figure of the death drive to the logic of iterability. Immediately after the passages just cited, Derrida associates the figure of the death drive with what he describes as a certain intrinsic repeatability necessary for any possible archive. "If there is no archive without consignation in an *external place* which assures the possibility of memorization, of repetition, of reproduction, or of reimpression," he writes, "then we must also remember that repetition itself, the logic of repetition . . . remains, according to Freud, indissociable from the death drive. And thus from destruction" (AF, 11–12/26). "Consequence: right on that which permits and conditions archivization, we will never find anything other than that which exposes to destruction, and in truth menaces with destruction, introducing, *a priori*, forgetfulness and the archiviolithic into the heart of the monument. Into the 'by heart' itself. The archive always works, and *a priori*, against itself" (AF, 12/26–27).[23]

A certain death drive, Derrida thus suggests, inhabits any archive or trace. Why? Because of the absolute necessity of repetition installed within its very structure. In the prosaic sense of the archive, there is no possibility of consignation and recall without a technique of repeatable preservation. In the most expansive deconstructive sense, any archivable trace has to be repeatable from the very outset, from before the time of any "first time," in order to maintain itself. But in both cases, this repeatability is actually made necessary by the possibility of the archivable trace's destruction. The threat of destruction is thus not something that might befall it from the outside, but rather is inscribed within the trace as its own arche-originary condition. This situation is what Derrida seeks to describe in his activation of the radically destructive death drive. In *Archive Fever*, Derrida characterizes it as a kind of internal contradiction within the archive itself: "There would indeed be no archive desire without the radical finitude, without the possibility of a forgetfulness which does not limit itself to repression. Above all . . . beyond or within this simple limit called finiteness or finitude, there is no archive fever without the threat of this death drive, this aggression and destruction drive. This threat is *in-finite*, it sweeps away the entire logic of finitude and the simple factual limits . . . the spatiotemporal conditions of conservation. Let us rather say it abuses them" (AF, 19/38). In this way, "enlisting the in-finite, archive fever verges on radical evil" (AF, 20/39). This is why Derrida can say a bit further on that "Freudian psychoanalysis proposes a new theory of the archive; it takes into account a topic and a death drive without which there would not in effect be any desire or any possibility for the archive" (AF, 29/52).

But the reference to the "in-finite" in this description, to something "beyond or within this simple limit called finiteness or finitude," is key. Once again, at issue here in the description of the archivable trace is not simply its intrinsic exposure to *possible* destruction from the outside. This type of threat is already analytically included in the fact of the trace's essential finitude. It should be clear that Derrida is specifying another threat beyond this one: the one implied by the thought of *"radical* finitude." On this view, by virtue of iterability, the archivable trace has to include, on the inside, the threat of destruction or erasure, and this menace is in fact necessary to its very constitution (since iterability is required for it to sustain itself). What is at issue here is not simple exposure to some outside but the internal condition of the trace. The trace is thus autoimmune: it has to welcome the threat of destruction within itself in order to get going in the first place. Here, an ongoing menace of destruction is always already operative—as the very condition of the trace's living on, its spatiotemporal persistence. Every trace sustains itself originarily *in the wake of* this threat (which has to be operative from the beginning, like repeatability, in order for it to come into being in the first place) and *in the midst of* this threat (insofar as it is implied in the very possibility of its having a here and now), before it is even a question of the threat of erasure that comes from the unpredictable future. In emphasizing that this condition is "in-finite," Derrida calls attention to the fact that this condition is the structural condition of everything that is subject to finitude: it is *not* finite in the sense that it forms the ultra-transcendental condition of the archivable trace, in its essential finitude.

It is this logic that the figure of the death drive crystallizes for Derrida. It speaks powerfully to the essential autoimmunity of the archive, of the trace, and on the horizon, life in general. Derrida in fact emphasizes this point at the very close of *Archive Fever*, when he writes, "The archive is made possible by the death, aggression, and destruction drive, that is to say also by originary finitude and expropriation. But beyond finitude as limit, there is, as we said above, this properly *in-finite* movement of radical destruction without which no archive desire or fever would happen" (AF, 94/146). Thus, Derrida suggests, the death drive is a figure not only of the trace's essential finitude (finitude understood "as limit") but, more radically, of an in-finite opening to destruction which has to be inscribed right away within any entity that is able to sustain itself at all.

The archivable trace, then, as Derrida describes it, is *radically* finite, and radically mortal, in that it locates the threat of absence, destruction, or forgetting at the very heart of every entity or identity. This threat is not an external threat that supervenes on the entity from the outside, but is included in its very constitution. And to the extent that this logic can also be used, as Derrida suggests it can, to think the structure of life, the autoimmunity of life also speaks not just to the necessary, essential exposure of the finite living being to possible death and destruction from the outside, or by means of a contamination or compromising of life that supervenes on it after it has gotten going, but to exposure, on the inside, to this threat. Moreover, to the extent that this exposure is, as we have seen in our discussion of autoimmunity, simultaneously enabling, this exposure to threat on the inside speaks to the very self-destruction that life is originarily. In the later Derrida, the thought of autoimmunity fleshes out the insight that life lives by means of "an economy of death," as we saw Derrida formulating it early on, and which he describes in terms of stricture. Viewed from this perspective, life persists on account of, not despite, an autoimmune self-compromising or self-destructive process. Ultimately, this means, first, that living is always already "living on." But it also means, second, that total death, absolute destruction, consists in the dissolution of what there is to bind, what there is to economize or compromise, a threat, we can now see, that comes from the inside as much as the outside.

In order to follow Derrida's thinking on autoimmunity to the fullest extent, then, we have to envision not just a partial compromising of self-protective processes, such that the entity is barred from closing in on itself absolutely, but also the intrinsic possibility or threat of these processes' absolute dissolution. While the notion of autoimmunity borrowed from the life sciences partially captures this logic, the figure of a certain death drive operative within the autoimmune process is, Derrida seems to have arrived at thinking, a key way of conceptualizing the autoimmunity of life, insofar as it allows us to think the quasi-suicidal dimension of autoimmunity.

Autoimmunity in *Rogues*

It is this trajectory of thought that reemerges in the crucial mobilization of the death drive after *Archive Fever,* the extensive later discussion of autoimmunity found in *Rogues.* The political implications of the deconstructive notion of autoimmunity is not my focus here, but given that *Rogues* is concerned from start to finish with politics, and democracy in particular, it will be difficult to grasp what is at stake in the mobilization of autoimmunity in this text if we do not bear in mind this context.

The first thing to note is that Derrida's explicit project in *Rogues* is to deconstruct, in the name of what he calls "democracy to come," the concept of sovereignty undergirding not only the contemporary notion of the nation-state, but also the concept of the egological, autonomous sovereign individual.[24] The two are linked, Derrida argues, not just conceptually, but in the long tradition of philosophical thought on democracy. Democracy has always been, and must always be, thought in relation to freedom, he suggests, a concept that cannot be thought apart from the notion of "sovereign self-determination": "namely, of the one-self that gives itself its own law, of autofinality, autotely, self-relation as being in view of the self" (R, 10–11). Drawing on the Latin root of the "itself," Derrida designates with the term *ipseity* the principle of the selfsame thus underpinning not only individual and state sovereignty but also freedom. "It is on the basis of freedom that we will have conceived the concept of democracy," Derrida writes, and "there is no freedom without ipseity and, vice versa, no ipseity without freedom—and thus without a certain sovereignty" (R, 22–23). The notion of democracy to come, however, which will in effect amplify the powers of autoimmunity already at work, latently as it were, in the traditional notion of democracy, will then be shown to have the potential to supplant and destabilize this logic.

In the present context, it is perhaps not difficult to see why Derrida explicitly speaks in *Rogues* to the power of psychoanalysis to open up such a project. If Derrida's own interest in psychoanalysis, as we have seen, was first and foremost in its conceptualization of tracing, inscription, and life death, in his discussions of *Nachträglichkeit* he is never far from the thought of the unconscious.

It is not at all surprising, then, to see Derrida indicating repeatedly in *Rogues* and in his 2000 address to the States General of Psychoanalysis, "Psychoanalysis Searches the States of Its Soul," that psychoanalysis forms one of the key sites where the deconstruction of sovereignty is possible. In a discussion of freedom and mastery in *Rogues*, Derrida notes, "What psychoanalysts call more or less complacently the unconscious remains, it seems to me, one of the privileged sources, one of the vitally mortal and mortally vital reserves or resources, for this implacable law of the self-deconstructive conservation of the 'subject' or of egological ipseity" (R, 55/83). It thus becomes clear that in contesting the logic of sovereignty, deconstruction mobilizes a certain logic of the unconscious. He reiterates this point later when he writes: "By speaking in just this way of autoimmunity, I specifically wanted to consider all of these processes of, so to speak, normal or normative perversion quite apart from the authority of representative consciousness, of the I, the self, and ipseity. This was the only way, it seemed to me, of taking into account within politics what psychoanalysis once called the unconscious" (R, 110/155). Even so, Derrida is clear that autoimmunity precedes any psychoanalytic concepts, writing that "without autoimmunity there would be neither psychoanalysis nor what psychoanalysis calls the 'unconscious.' Not to mention, therefore, the 'death drive'" (R, 55/83). This is why, at the very end of "The 'World' of the Enlightenment to Come," Derrida calls explicitly for an Enlightenment to come that "would have to enjoin us to reckon with the logic of the unconscious, and so with the idea, and notice I'm not saying here the doctrine, arising out of a psychoanalytic revolution" (R, 157/215).[25]

Yet beyond a certain logic of the unconscious, the figure of the Freudian death drive provides crucial resources for Derrida's theorization of autoimmunity here, most notably by allowing him to reapproach what we have seen as the automaticity of autoimmunity as it pertains to life itself. We see this clearly when we look at the places where the death drive surfaces in *Rogues*. Speaking of the constitutive autoimmunity of democracy, Derrida describes it at one point as "this strange illogical logic by which a living being can spontaneously destroy, in an autonomous fashion, the very thing within it that is supposed to protect it against the other, to immunize it against the aggressive intrusion of the other" (R, 123/173). But this thought of democracy, he suggests, is only possible on the basis of a certain thinking of autoimmunity at the level of life. The connection is particularly clear in "The 'World' of the Enlightenment to Come":

> Why determine in such an ambiguous fashion the threat or the danger, the default or the failure, the running aground or the grounding, but also the salvation, the rescue, and the safeguard, health, and security—so many diabolically *autoimmune* assurances, virtually capable not only of destroying themselves in suicidal fashion but of turning a certain death drive against the *autos* itself, against the ipseity that any suicide worthy of its name still presupposes? In order to situate the question of life and of the living being, of life and death, of life death, at the heart of my remarks. (R, 123/173)

Moreover, in "Reason of the Strongest," Derrida is clear, discussing the same question, that the deconstruction of ipseity is to be thought even prior to the concept of the state or of the self, "before the separation of *physis* from its others, such as *tekhne*. . . . What applies here to *physis*, to *phuein*, applies also to life, understood before any opposition between life (*bios* or *zoe*) and its others (spirit, culture, the symbolic, the specter, or death)" (R, 109/154–55). Thus, while Derrida does not simply subscribe to Freud's terms, he nonetheless will risk going so far as to declare that there is nothing at all without "this poisoned medicine, this *pharmakon* of an inflexible and cruel autoimmunity that is sometimes called the 'death drive' and that does not limit the living being to its conscious and representative form" (R, 157/215). The deconstructive project is thus to "interrogate in a deconstructive fashion all the limits we thought pertained to life, the being of life and the life of being (and this is almost the entire history of philosophy), between the living and the dead, the living present and its spectral others" (R, 151/209).

Then, underscoring the threatening dimension of the quasi-suicidal autoimmune processes, Derrida pushes this thought further. At stake here is a radical conception of finitude, in-finite finitude as he phrases it. This move allows Derrida to argue that autoimmunity goes beyond defenses turning back on what they are meant to protect. Rather, autoimmunity puts into question the notion that there is some self that is first constituted in its integrity and then secondarily turns back on itself. Hence, he speaks of "the cruel autoimmunity with which sovereignty at once sovereignly affects and cruelly infects itself. Autoimmunity is always, in the same time without duration, cruelty itself, the autoinfection of all autoaffection. It is not some particular thing that is affected in autoimmunity but the self, the *ipse*, the *autos* that finds itself infected. As soon as it needs heteronomy, the event, time and the other" (R, 109/154). Autoimmunity is thus "quasi-suicidal" here in the sense that it highlights how the "self" that is said to attack itself was always already compromised, opened up to its other (see also R, 45/71). It brings forward how, by virtue of the ultra-transcendental structure of the trace, any entity is originarily, automatically, opened up to its other. "A certain death drive," as Derrida put it above, allows him to speak here of how "the interruption of a certain unbinding opens the free space of the relationship to the incalculable singularity of the other" (R, 150/206–7).

Following the figure of the death drive further in these discussions, then, sheds light on an essential feature of autoimmunity. It consistently points to the structure whereby the affirmative character of autoimmunity at the level of life is only possible if there is also, operating always already from the beginning, *an intrinsic, internal threat* of absolute disappearance and destruction. This necessity, however, is easy to miss in considerations of Derridean autoimmunity.

To take one salient example, it is common in discussions of autoimmunity to cite the example Derrida gives in *Rogues* to illustrate the autoimmunity of democracy: the 1992 democratic elections in Algeria, which were suspended in the name of saving democracy from a result that would end it (R, 30–31/53–54). In this example, we see how democracy can produce its own destruction or undoing, but it is easy to read this as a state of affairs democracy might also not produce (indeed, most often does not produce). "A certain suicide of democracy" is only potential here (R, 33/57). But if we take the Algerian election as an example of how democracy produces events *that might turn out to* undo democracy, we overlook the fact that what Derrida is saying here goes much further. His point is not that democracy is autoimmune because it might produce its destruction sometime in the future. His point is that this possible self-destruction *has to be understood as an essential condition of democracy from the very start*. "Democracy has always been suicidal," in Derrida's words (R, 33/57). Yes, this outcome can come at any time from the future, but this is strictly a *consequence* of an essential autoimmunity at work on, and within, democracy in its very constitution. In order to be what it is, democracy has to have always included this internal threat.

The autoimmune threat I am tracing here is even clearer in the other, less commonly cited example Derrida gives in the same chapter of *Rogues*, the example of the autoimmune process seen in the aftermath of September 11 in the United States (R, 39/64). With this example, Derrida has in mind how, after September 11, the United States sought to protect itself by exponentially increasing and expanding antidemocratic measures, various draconian "powers of police investigations and interrogations, without anyone, any democrat, being really able to oppose such measures" (R, 40/64–65). In this process, the largest democracy in the world "must thus come to resemble these enemies, to corrupt itself and threaten itself in order to protect itself against their threats" (R, 40/65). Even beyond this, the attack thematizes an essential autoimmunity at work on the United States as a democracy, insofar as the attack was in large part first made possible by "a culture and a system of law that are largely democratic," such that the United States could "open itself up and expose its greatest vulnerability to immigrants, to, for example, pilots in training" (R, 40/65).

Here, we see something different than a form of autoimmunity that might turn out to be threatening or not. Derrida here describes how the absolutely necessary mobilization of forces of protection produces an internal threat to, or attack on, democracy. This threat does not come from a state of affairs that may or may not come about in some unpredictable future to come but rather is central to democracy's very constitution. This is in fact closer—closer than the example of the Algerian election, as it is often understood—to what Derrida calls "constitutive autoimmunity" (R, 63/95). It is also closer to what Derrida specifies as the dual possibility of threat *and* promise intrinsic to autoimmunity: "not alternatively or by turns promise and/or threat but threat *in* the promise itself" (R, 82/121). In the second example, the threat, the attack on democracy, *is* the promise, the act of protection that ensures its living on. It makes clearly visible the fact that the threat of democracy attacking itself is essential to it, not just as a possibility in the future, but as something that is always already underway from the very beginning. It is part of what constitutes the very promise, or chance, of democracy as such from the get-go. It is this deeper form of duplicity at stake in autoimmunity, I have argued, that the figure of the death drive allows Derrida to articulate, at that point where the model of autoimmunity borrowed from the life sciences—in which an autoimmune process is always a pathology, an essentially aberrant mutation of proper functioning—reaches the limits of its pertinence. It allows Derrida to formulate what he had earlier described as the difficult logic of autoimmunity whereby "protection is itself a threat, an aggression differing from itself, which then twists and tortures us in a spiraling movement" (PM, 59/263).

Survival as Exappropriation

Yet there is another aspect of the autoimmunity of life that matters here: its radically asubjective character. As we have seen, *Rogues* mobilizes a certain logic of the unconscious. In the ongoing conversation with Nancy carried out in "Reason of the Strongest," it is precisely this use of the unconscious—and with it "therefore, the 'death drive,' the cruelty of primary sadism and masochism" (R, 55/83)—that enables Derrida to pose the question of a "non-egological" notion of freedom and, in turn, democracy (R, 55/83). At issue here,

Derrida suggests, is "the spaced divisibility, the hierarchized multiplicity, and the conflict of forces" something like the unconscious "imposes on sovereign identity" (R, 54/82). But if, as we have seen, autoimmunity pertains not just to democracy but, even before it, to life itself, it is necessary to think this automaticity at this deeper level as well. And once we do this, we see that survival, the condition which names the autoimmunity of life, has to be conceptualized as something other than a property and an experience. Anterior to experience, it makes experience possible, but is nonetheless heterogeneous to it. It inscribes in the living being a multiplicity of forces intersecting in a trace structure, a structure which has to be originarily opened up to what, in *Rogues*, Derrida describes as "the absolute exception or singularity of an alterity that is not reappropriable by the ipseity of a sovereign power and a calculable knowledge" (R, 148/203). Survival, then, is the name for the condition of exappropriation constitutive of the living being: it is a function of "the irreducible and nonappropriable différance of the other" (R, 84/123). It is a crucial means of describing not only how, from a Derridean perspective—following Heidegger in a certain way, and up to a certain point—I never have access to "my death" as such, but also how "my life" is equally something I can never have ownership of, always comes by way of the other. Survival, then, describes this dual impossibility.[26]

Derrida develops this thought in a handful of texts, most notably in *Aporias*. There, Derrida shows that what Heidegger theorizes as the nonaccess of *Dasein* to death as such, which Heidegger defines as the possibility of *Dasein*'s impossibility, has certain consequences. Despite what Heidegger wants to say, it makes "death . . . the most improper possibility and the most ex-propriating, the most inauthenticating one" (A, 77/134). Here, "from the most originary inside of its possibility, the proper of *Dasein* becomes from then on contaminated, parasited, and divided by the most improper" (A, 77/134). What's more, earlier in the text, Derrida makes clear that he follows Heidegger's intuition that this problematic has consequences for how I understand my life, for instance as something that belongs to me and that I can therefore decide how to "spend," however short it will have been. If Heidegger privileges death and not life in *Being and Time*, Derrida writes, this is because "it is the originary and underivable character of death, as well as the finitude of the temporality in which death is rooted" that defines the life of a mortal (A, 55/102). It is this character that introduces "the posthumous in the most alive of the present living thing, the rearview mirror of a waiting-for-death [*s'attendre-à-la mort*] at every moment" (A, 55/102). Thus, even when it is not my death but rather "my life" that is at issue, the meaning of this phrase will be fundamentally shaped by the question of death. Yet, to the extent that Derrida then parts ways with Heidegger, asserting that death is fundamentally expropriating, the life of a mortal being for Derrida is that much more forcefully defined by this condition of nonappropriability.

The clearest formulation of what Derrida describes as the intrinsic expropriation of life at stake in the notion of survival, however, is to be found in the first year of the *Death Penalty* seminars. There, building on *Aporias*, Derrida reiterates his claim that Heidegger advances an uncritical conception of death. A certain "pre-comprehension of the meaning of the word 'death' is supposed, more or less explicitly, by all great thinking or philosophies of death (up to Heidegger or Levinas, whatever maybe the differences between them)" (*DP*, 1:237/323), he argues. The issue is that

> [All of these philosophies] must rely, even as they deny it, on so-called common sense, on the alleged objective and familiar knowledge, judged to be indubitable, of what separates a state of death from a state of life . . . that is, of the supposed existence of an objectifiable instant that separates the living from the dying. . . . The simple idea of this limit between life and death organizes all these mediations, whether classic or less classic, even revolutionary, even those of a deconstruction, of a "deconstruction" in Luther's or in Heidegger's sense at least. (*DP*, 1:238/324)

Derrida here describes the way that all of these "great philosophies of death" remain blind to the autoimmunity of life as survival, the structure whereby, as we saw in the crucial passage in *Specters of Marx*, "death is not beyond, outside of life, unless one inscribes the beyond in the inside, in the essence of the living." But here Derrida lays particular emphasis on the fact that these traditional philosophies do so insofar as they remain reliant on an uncritical notion of the *calculability* of death, the "existence of an *objectifiable* instant that separates the living from the dying."

Indeed, what all these philosophies of death miss is that mortal finitude is in fact defined by incalculability, by a certain "principle of indetermination" (*DP*, 1:256/347). This is the case structurally, insofar as "it belongs to life not necessarily to be immortal but to have a future, thus some life before it, some event to come only where death, the instant of death, is not calculable, is not the object of a calculable decision" (*DP*, 1:256/347). Stated somewhat differently, to be a finite mortal is necessarily to live each moment in the face of a future that entails a fundamental indeterminacy with respect to what comes, and especially with respect to what comes in the form of death.

> It is because my life is finite, "ended" in a certain sense, that I keep this relation to incalculability and undecidability as to the instant of

> my death. It is because my life is "finished" in a certain sense, that I do not know, and that I neither can nor want to know, when I am going to die. Only a living being as finite being can have a future, can be exposed to a future, to an incalculable and undecidable future that s/he does not have at his/her disposal like a master and that comes to him or to her from some other, from the heart of the other. (*DP*, 1:256–57/348)

By contrast, "where the anticipation of my death becomes the anticipation of a calculable instant, there is no longer any future, there is thus no longer any event to come, nothing to come" (*DP*, 1:256/347). This would be, in essence, the dream of mastery over finitude and over the future.

The point here is that this condition makes not only "my death" something fundamentally unmasterable that cannot be appropriated, it also makes "my life" something that, precisely, does not and cannot belong to me. On the contrary, life is conceived here as necessarily opened up, on the inside, to alterity—and this is what consequently opens it up to the future. If this is the case, then as a finite being, my life is fundamentally not mine. Rather, what I think of as "my life" in actuality consists, essentially and originarily, in a relation to alterity, to some other. What I, according to common sense, might be tempted to think of as "my life" in fact issues "from some other, from the heart of the other," as Derrida put it in the passage just cited. And as we have seen, in order for my life to sustain itself, in order for me to live on as the survivor that I am, my life must keep and repeat this originary relation to the other. Moreover, as we have seen in our earlier discussions of iterability, it must do so even before it gets underway: this repetition must be arche-originary. This is why Derrida will say, immediately following the passage just cited, "when I say 'my life,' or even my 'living present,' here, I have already named the other in me . . . the other whose heart is more interior to my heart than my heart itself" (*DP*, 1:257/348). Hence, the relation to alterity constitutive of finite life is radically exappropriating.

Consequently, in a small handful of easily overlooked places in *Rogues*, Derrida indicates what is clear in the *Death Penalty* and *The Beast and the Sovereign* seminars: that the task is to think not just this originary, expropriating condition of *survivance*, but also *the various ways it is denied*. Indeed, without some notion of how this condition is sutured over, repressed, or overlooked in the philosophical tradition, in scientific discourse, or at the level of experience, it is hard to imagine why or how deconstruction itself is at all necessary. At one point in *Rogues*, therefore, Derrida notes that *différance* speaks to "the undeniable, and I underscore *undeniable*, experience of the alterity of the other, of heterogeneity, of the singular, the not-same, the different, the dissymmetric, the heteronomous" (R, 38/63). But then he quickly specifies, "I underscore *undeniable* to suggest *only deniable,* the only protective recourse being that of a send-off [*renvoi*] through denial" (R, 38/63).[27] The structure of opening to the other constitutive of *survivance* is here described as an absolutely unconditional ("undeniable") condition, which can always be covered over or denied, but which can never be annulled, except by absolute destruction. Hence, somewhat further on in the same lecture, he describes the autoimmune threat that emanates from an entity's own protective defenses as "just as silent as it is unavowable" (R, 100/143). But there is also an unavowable silence at work in sovereignty, he writes, to the extent that "unavowable silence, denegation: that is the always unapparent essence of sovereignty" (R, 100/143). The dissimulated essence of sovereignty, here, is the disavowal of autoimmunity, in view of a pure, undivided form of life. This in turn reveals an important clue about what deconstruction does: it discloses, or brings forward, the fictional, constructed character of the concepts founded on this denegation.

The key point here, then, following on the discussion of exappropriation, is not only is the notion of "my death" founded on a disavowal, so too is the notion of "my life." On this view, these two visions appear not as truth but as *reactive denials to be deconstructed*; or better, two visions that deconstruct themselves, such that they too are autoimmune, unwittingly seeking the end of mortal life in the attempt to protect it absolutely (mastery over finitude is what is at stake in both). They are autoimmune insofar as absolute life that does not originarily differ or defer itself at all, that does not pass through the heart of the other, as we have seen, would be death: "Without autoimmunity, with absolute immunity, nothing would ever happen or arrive" (R, 152/210).

Negotiating Derrida's Inheritance of Freud

The thought I have now outlined points to the differences between the present account and the one offered by Martin Hägglund. My account owes a debt to Hägglund insofar as his work brings forward the fact that what Derrida called the structure of the trace is an absolutely general condition pertaining to life at large.[28] Further, Hägglund's understanding of survival equally entails an interpretation of binding as key to this concept. Yet in his treatment of this theme in Derrida, Hägglund takes a different approach than the one outlined here, in particular with respect to Derrida's activation of Freud. For his part, Hägglund argues that Derrida goes astray in his apparent endorsement of the notion of the death drive. Hägglund knows full well that Derrida stops short of fully endorsing the psychoanalytic notion of a death drive, but even the fact that Derrida is willing to align the deconstructive thought of autoimmunity with a certain thinking of the death drive is too much for Hägglund. Thus he argues quite forcefully against such an understanding of the death drive, maintaining that it is in fact fundamentally incompatible with the form of radical atheism that he sees following directly from Derrida's thinking.[29]

I have shown, however, that a deeper grasp of Derrida's dealings with Freud allows us to glimpse vital features of Derrida's theorization of life as life death and in turn survival. In particular, it allows us to grasp the specific form of opening to heterogeneity and internal threat at stake in survival that cannot be thought strictly via the temporal dynamics of the trace. Thus Derrida's thinking in this area (what we have seen as his rearticulation of the death drive) contains resources that remain inaccessible in Hägglund's framework and that are crucial for understanding what deconstruction offers today.

To see what Hägglund misses, we can look at his account of why Derrida goes astray in his activation of the Freudian death drive. For Hägglund, the power of deconstruction is that it makes possible a critique not only of metaphysical aspirations for something beyond temporal finitude but also the very idea that something beyond temporal finitude would be desirable in the first place. Deconstruction, on this view, shows that temporal finitude (or, more precisely, the trace structure of time) is not to be understood as a secondary ontological defect or lack of full presence but rather as the ultra-transcendental condition of anything that could be desired at all.[30] Thus, even those forms of thought that claim to put metaphysics into question but do not make this additional move are shown to be outstripped by deconstruction's more radical form of atheism.

This argument then allows Hägglund to critique the foundational notion of desire in Freudian-Lacanian drive theory. In his view, psychoanalytic drive theory is part of what radical atheism puts into question, insofar as drive theory still repeats the fundamental logic of metaphysics, whereby what motivates or drives human action is a desire for, or tendency toward, a state of being that is not subject to time and the vicissitudes of temporal finitude.[31] Whether it is a question of a bodily psychical drive toward the dissolution of all tension or energy in Freud or its corollary in Lacan, psychoanalytic theory is here said to have gone some distance in recognizing that such a state of being is not in fact achievable, but it does not go far enough toward the more radical atheism opened up by deconstruction. Psychoanalysis does not fundamentally put into question the assumption that a state of being resembling something like infinite repose is what we desire, however impossible this would be to attain.

The more properly deconstructive concept of *chronolibido*, he then argues, articulates a truly radical notion of desire insofar as it attempts to think the constitutive difference that makes desire possible in the first place on altogether different grounds. Hägglund thus attempts to think the constitutive difference in the subject that gives rise to desire not in terms of a privative lack in being but rather on the basis of temporal finitude as a positive condition. The constitutive difference in which desire originates is here located in the ultra-transcendental trace structure of time. Hägglund calls this chronolibido insofar as, on this view, the basic desire animating life is traced back to an unconditional "*bond* to temporal life, which is not preceded by any principle or purpose."[32] As Hägglund sketches it, insofar as in temporal succession an entity has the structure not of something that simply is or once was present but rather the structure of a trace of the past retained for a future to come: the movement of desire is here rooted in the fact that nothing at all can rest fully "in and of itself," can be fully present. On this view, Freud is thus right in *Beyond the Pleasure Principle* when he sees that the attainment of pure pleasure would be death, since this would put an end to this constitutive difference and the "binidinal economy" it implies, without which finite life is not even possible. But Freud nonetheless remains firmly within a conventionally atheist metaphysics for Hägglund when he ascribes to life, or the living organism, the desire for the teleological pursuit of such a state in the form of a death drive. This then leads Hägglund to contend that Derrida, when he invokes the concept of the death drive in Freud, is in fact going astray with respect to some of his own most fundamental insights.

The issue, however, is that Hägglund does not fully weigh the reasons Derrida has for mobilizing the death drive. In short, the figure of the death drive allows Derrida to describe the originary condition of autoimmunity as it bears on life. The reason is, as we have seen above, it offers a way for him to think the form of radical destructibility at stake in this logic. Hägglund's framework does not allow him to grasp this destructibility in its fullest scope, however. His conception of survival thus cannot account for the form of radical finitude we have seen at stake there.

As Hägglund characterizes the logic of survival, from the moment life is thought not in terms of a present fullness but an arche-originary process of deferral and delay put into play by the trace structure of time, each and every moment of survival takes on the form of living on in the face of the threat of potential violation and destruction. This threat is implied in the very coming of time as the coming of the unforeseeable other, what or who comes.[33] Tracing is here understood as "the condition for anything to live on in time, but in living it is exposed to erasure, since it is delivered to a future that may transform, corrupt, or delete it."[34] This, for Hägglund, just is the structure of life understood as survival.

The problem is that such exposure to *potential* erasure is insufficient to account for the form of radical finitude at stake in Derridean survival. A more radical threat of destruction or erasure (more radical than what Hägglund calls the "radical finitude of survival"[35]) has to be at work in its very structure, whereby it *is* intrinsically threatened by exposure to heterogeneity, in an active fashion, from the very start. In this way, the logic of Derridean survival entails not just vulnerable exposure of a finite entity to temporal succession and the threat of alteration this entails but, as Derrida puts it in "Freud and the Scene of Writing," a form of death already at work in life via exposure to heterogeneity (WD, 203/302).[36]

At times, Hägglund comes close to this formulation, as when he underscores how no moment of survival can emerge unscathed in the movement of time.[37] Yet the threat implied in survival most often appears in Hägglund's account as what makes life, understood in terms of temporal finitude, possible. The relation to "what does *not* survive" is most often only thought in Hägglund as the necessary condition of further living on that is only exposed to threat insofar as it comes from being open to the future.[38] But this exposure to death has to be thought as simultaneously *making possible and threatening*, potentially absolutely, persistence or living on from the very start. It is this structure that Derrida thinks via the notion of a certain death drive, one that is not simply Freud's, to be sure. If this metaphysical name is at all apt, it is insofar as the form of radical finitude at stake here can be shown to follow not just from a temporal structure but from an understanding of the trace in terms of exposure to heterogeneity in the economy of the same.

We can demonstrate this with reference to Derrida's discussion of "in-finite finitude" in *Archive Fever* examined above. In this passage, Derrida suggests that there would be no archive desire "without radical finitude, without the possibility of a forgetfulness that does not limit itself to repression"—a possibility Derrida aligns with the threat of a "destruction drive" and even a death drive (AF, 19/38). Hägglund reads in this passage an articulation of the logic whereby the threat of destruction has to be implied in each and every moment of living on, but objects to the way Derrida associates this threat with the death drive. This is because, Hägglund argues, the threat of radical destructibility does not derive from some metaphysical death drive but rather is "inherent in finitude in general," in that "the archive would be threatened by destruction even if there were no drive to destroy it: any number of random events can destroy it."[39] But if we return to the passage in *Archive Fever*, we see that something else is at stake in Derrida's formulation here. The point Derrida is trying to make by invoking the death drive is that the deconstructive thought of the trace has to envision a form of destruction that in fact cannot be thought simply on the basis of finitude *tout court*. What he references under the heading of the death drive here, he says, is "beyond or within this simple limit called finiteness or finitude. . . . This threat is *in-finite*, it sweeps away the logic of finitude and the simple factual limits . . . the spatio-temporal conditions of conservation" (AF, 19/38).

Thus the point is not just, as Hägglund glosses it, that to institute a given archive "is necessarily to violate other archives" (other archives somewhere else),[40] but that any and every archive necessarily destroys *some part of what it itself seeks to archive, destroys itself*, given that an archive cannot but condition, and therefore shape through exclusion, the "very institution of the archivable event" (AF, 18/36). Moreover, it is this radical destruction at work in the formation of the entity itself—in this case, the archive—which exceeds the basic condition of finitude and always threatens its very living on, not just the form it takes from one moment to the next (the movement of alteration inherent in temporality). This is also why Derrida emphasizes in *Archive Fever* that the death drive furnishes the figure of a form of destruction that destroys even its own traces, such that what is destroyed is potentially erased without any remainder at all surviving.

Indeed, this thought that the archive necessarily destroys some part of itself is crucial to the pivotal discussion of the "*L'un se garde de l'autre pour se faire violence*" in *Archive Fever* (AF, 78/125). This phrase serves as a kind of supplement to the deconstructive maxim that "*tout autre est tout autre.*" In *Archive Fever*, the phrase emerges out of Derrida's reading of Freud's *Moses and Monotheism* (1939). The "structural justification" (AF, 78/124) for Freud's speculations on Moses, Derrida argues, is that Freud shows how the archive, and on the horizon, any formation of the One—conceived as God or as a unitary nation or people, or as any entity thought to be wholly selfsame and intact in itself—cannot constitute itself without violently repressing the relation to the other in which it originates. But if this is the case, following the logic of iterability, the One simultaneously has to repeat this relation at every moment even as it dissimulates it. This is the dual meaning at work in the reflexive verb *se garde*, which can give rise to the meaning that the One guards itself against the other and the meaning that it keeps, or conserves, the other. As Derrida puts it, "it protects *itself* from the other, but, in the movement of this jealous violence, it comprises in itself, thus guarding it, the self-otherness or self-difference (the difference from within oneself) which makes it the One. The 'One differing, deferring from itself'" (AF, 78/124–25). Formalizing this thought in a way that "crosses psychoanalysis with deconstruction, a certain 'psychoanalysis' with a certain 'deconstruction,'" Derrida speaks of the manner in which the One thus "keeps and erases the archive of this injustice that it is. Of this violence that it does" (AF, 78/125). Thus, the archive as trace erases, or destroys, itself in the very process of continuing to live on.

The logic of survival I am tracing here is in many ways only visible in the wake of Hägglund's engagement with Derrida. Yet my interpretation of Derrida, it should be clear by now, negotiates the question of Derrida's relationship to Freud in a substantially different way. The reason we would do well to think through the even more radical form of finitude we have now seen at stake in Derridean survival is that it is critical to understanding what deconstruction offers today—and not just with respect to the question of life in contemporary Continental thought. It can be demonstrated that the conception of life as survival, entailing radical destructibility within the very structure of "what is most alive in life" (RP, 118/146), is in fact critical to deconstruction's ethical and political dimension. It is now time to take up a discussion of this issue, looking at the normative purchase of deconstruction.

4
Mortality and Normativity

This chapter undertakes a discussion of the ethical and political implications of the logic of life death and survival as it has been articulated to this point. The full scope of its implications are fleshed out in this chapter and the next, but before elaborating the consequences of the thought of survival and mortality, a preliminary issue must be dealt with. To the extent that the ultra-transcendental logic of the trace and *différance,* and in turn the notion of survival itself, are at first glance purely descriptive, the question arises how exactly deconstruction can be said to be normative, if at all, articulating not simply what is but what we *ought* or *should* to do. While Derrida famously advocates for "a new international" in *Specters of Marx* (SM, 35/58), and for the deconstruction of sovereignty and the death penalty in his very late work, he does not fully address how the ultra-transcendental structures just named give rise to this project.

My approach in this chapter to the question of normativity in deconstruction is as follows: first, I describe the issue concerning normativity as it has emerged in recent discussions of Derrida's work and situate the present account in relation to contemporary debates. Staking out a new approach, I then plot a path forward for dealing with the question of normativity informed by the reading of Derrida advanced across the first three chapters of this book. The way to think through deconstruction's normative possibilities, I argue, lies in an understanding of the links between the thinking of survival in texts like *Specters of Marx* and "Faith and Knowledge" and the more explicitly political concerns of Derrida's work from the early 2000s. This approach, I suggest, brings into relief key features of deconstruction's ethical and political stakes.

More specifically, I show that the opening to exteriority and heterogeneity at stake in the notions of life death and survival in Derrida allows deconstruction to effect a critical rethinking of the ground for ethics and politics. As we have seen, the term *survivance* powerfully redeploys the core logic of life death, making possible a notion of radical finitude or mortality. It is this thought in Derrida that is then capable of shaking up both the uncritical precomprehension of life and death informing our inherited ethico-political concepts and the dream of something beyond finitude.

Having laid out how this line of thinking works, in the final section of this chapter, I conclude by showing how the thought of survival and what Derrida will call the "phantasm" of something beyond mortality sheds crucial light on his well-known discussions of justice, the future, and the to-come, concepts that have been the subject of considerable scholarship in recent years but just as much debate. This argument forms the critical ground for the discussion of Derrida's deconstruction of sovereignty, the death penalty, and the theologico-political in chapter 5. In fact, since at stake in this chapter and the following one is, in part, a deconstructive challenge to our inherited concepts of the human and human law (approached, we will see, in Derrida via the definition of "the proper to man"), at issue, on the horizon, will be how to think the question of normativity not only in deconstruction, but in contemporary Continental thought more broadly, given its attempt to think beyond "the human."

The Question of Normativity

We can begin by further elaborating the question of normativity in deconstruction as it has taken shape over the last several years. In fact, following on increased awareness of the marked differences between Derrida and Levinas, much of the recent debate around Derrida's work has centered on the question of whether and how deconstruction is able to provide a basis for making normative claims. The starting point for this debate is the shared agreement among several of Derrida's readers concerning problems in earlier interpretations of Derrida advanced by scholars such as Simon Critchley, Drucilla Cornell, and Richard Beardsworth.[1] Each of these scholars, in their own way, locate in Derrida's thinking of the opening to the other in the 1980s and 1990s a conception of an ethical relation of peace or the possibility of lesser violence.[2] In this interpretation, deconstructive thought leads directly to the normative claim that we ought to cultivate such a relation and helps us in this task. Departing from this interpretation, contemporary readers such as Martin Hägglund, Matthias Fritsch, Samir Haddad, and Marie-Eve Morin have persuasively demonstrated the deep consistency in Derrida's thinking, showing that Derrida's use of core deconstructive notions such as the trace and *différance* in treating ethico-political questions is chiefly descriptive of the aporias underlying ethics and politics.[3] Taking their distance from the earlier readings (by Critchley and Cornell, in particular) in another way, they equally point to the absence of a distinction between ethics and politics in deconstruction—if by politics we are referring to the domain of conditional rules and conventions, considered apart from the relation to a singular other and its unconditional demand for justice.[4] But this move then raises the difficult question of whether the logic of the trace and the thinking of *différance* Derrida situates as the ultra-transcendental source of deconstructive work in general provides sufficient grounds for making any normative claims at all.[5]

For his part, Hägglund points to deconstruction's insistence on a continual opening to an unpredictable future implied in the temporal logic of the trace as incompatible with any secure ethical or political position—particularly with regard to the promise of what Derrida himself, in his early treatment of Levinas, refers to as the possibility of choosing "the lesser violence within an *economy of violence*" (WD, 313n21/136n1).[6] On this view, every ethical and political decision is implicated in "an economy of violence" and there is no ideal of the good that assures any given decision will result in lesser violence, whether it be in our relations to a singular other or to the plurality, insofar as such decisions are always made in the face of an unforeseeable future to come.[7] Here, every response, whether ethical, political, or juridical, necessarily includes with it the possibility of injustice, of greater violence, and this possibility cannot ever be eradicated. While maintaining that reflecting on ethical and political problems is always necessary, this interpretation asserts that deconstruction describes the deep structure of this situation and, in so doing, puts out of play any notion of eradicating violence once and for all, but cannot offer a ground for making normative claims beyond this.[8]

Readers such as Haddad and Fritsch, however, while acknowledging some of the clear tensions between Derrida's thought and Levinas's ethical metaphysics, emphasize the manner in which Derrida's thinking nonetheless includes a normative dimension.[9] For Haddad, this dimension is visible in Derrida's insistence on the fact that we always inherit ethical and political values whether we know it or not, a process which, in the particular way Derrida understands it, necessarily includes choosing a stance in relation to these values. The necessary process of what Derrida calls "choosing one's heritage" (SM, 18/40),[10] on this view, is also one of choosing ethical and political positions. In calling attention to the fact that this process of inheriting is always taking place, deconstruction underscores that such norms and values are not simply given, but chosen, and other choices are always possible. In this way, deconstruction has a normative purchase, even if it does not supply us with specific guidelines for choosing.

For Fritsch, this dimension is to be found in what he reads as the intrinsically normative status of the ultra-transcendental in deconstruction. Concepts such as the trace and *différance*, which describe the necessary openness of any entity to the coming of time and the necessary exposure to alterity, imply, on Fritsch's view, that there is some inherent value in this openness. He then goes on to link this dimension of the basic "infrastructural" (this term coming from Rodolphe Gasché's reading of Derrida[11]) notions to what Derrida at times describes as an originary affirmation of this temporal opening to something other, which can be seen to be operating in Derrida's treatment of any number of ethical and political topics, from the gift to hospitality to democracy. It is on the basis of this ultra-transcendental argument, on this view, that deconstruction is then able to critique inherited discourses, concepts, and institutions. In the same stroke, it demonstrates the impossibility of resting in what Derrida calls "good conscience" in this affirmation.[12] Thus, part of the normative thrust of deconstruction is that it urges us, in the strongest possible terms, to recognize this fact rather than uncritically disavow it.[13]

My argument is that Derrida's discussions of life and survival point to the specific ethical and political purchase of deconstruction, and this brings me closer to Haddad and Fritsch. On the question of whether Derrida's thought contains the resources for making certain normative claims—namely, that it would be *better* to keep conventions and institutions open to the incalculable (even if this is no less violent), and that we *should* do this—I believe the answer is that it does. Moreover, I contend that this follows directly from the ultra-transcendental structures deconstruction posits. The difficulty all commentators who make this claim face, however, is that Derrida does not explicitly address the relation between these ultra-transcendental structures and the ethical and political stakes of deconstruction, and thus some extrapolating work is necessary. While my approach to this work is in certain ways close to Fritsch's, the difference lies in the fact that I contend the best way to do this work is specifically via the thinking of survival found in Derrida and subsequently what he will describe as the "phantasm" or fantasy of something beyond mortal life.

In what follows, I show that the thought of survival in Derrida elaborated across the first three chapters of this book furnishes deconstruction with normative resources in two ways. First, it supplies deconstruction with a new basis, or ground, for critique with respect to what Derrida will show to be the fundamentally theological phantasm of safe and sound life at work in religion and in the still too-theological dominant concepts of the human and human life, the political, and sovereignty. Fleshing out how this line of thinking works in the argument that connects *Specters of Marx* (1993) and "Faith and Knowledge" (1995) to the late seminars (from the early 2000s), I demonstrate how exactly it informs deconstructive critique. In the final section of this chapter, I take up the second way the thought of survival implies normativity: I show that the resources for deconstructive critique in turn imply another, quasi-normative positive purchase.

Survivance and Normativity

To properly grasp how the thought of survival forms the ground for deconstructive critique, I have said, it is necessary to understand the connections between Derrida's thought in the key texts of *Specters of Marx* and "Faith and Knowledge" and the later work, so let us begin by sketching this trajectory.

Now, if, from the beginning, as we have seen, Derrida was thinking the necessary structure of *différance* as what introduces death into life or the living present and fundamentally complicates it, in *Specters of Marx* there is a new element. There, the "beyond present life or its actual being-there" deconstruction tries to think by means of arche-writing and trace is linked to an unconditional demand for justice, justice in our relation to some other and in our relation other others (SM, xviii–xx/17). Deconstruction poses the possibility of justice as necessarily conjoined to something beyond the living present here, because, as "Force of Law" (1990) had made clear, the very idea of justice beyond law, justice as something other than what prevails in the current state of relations, presupposes this opening. Indeed, the very condition of justice is actually, Derrida says at one point, "a *living-on* [*sur-vie*], namely, a trace of which life and death would themselves be but traces and traces of traces, a survival whose possibility in advance comes to dis-join or dis-adjust the identity to itself of the living present as well as of any effectivity" (SM, xx/17–18). The question of justice in our relations to some other and to the plurality of others is here explicitly said to follow from the thought of *survivance*, that is, from the way an interruption is inscribed in life as it is lived in the here and now. If we are always structurally survivors for Derrida, at this point we should hear this statement in another way: we are survivors in the sense that we are always already opened up, in our essential finitude, to a not-freely-chosen relation of responsibility to so many others, facing a call to justice.

The question is how exactly the disadjustment at stake in *survivance* at the "ontological" level gives rise to the disadjustment of the living present that is the source of normativity in Derrida (see SM, 22/44). Now, one way to respond to this question is to say that in the temporal logic of deconstruction, the living present is originarily split and divided, and this is in turn the very condition of justice beyond what presently holds. But this response is not quite satisfactory, insofar as it does not take into account the opening to exteriority in the same, the cleavage or interruption we have seen at play in life death and *survivance*, the logic of which, as we saw, Derrida consistently links in *Specters* to the question of justice and the relation to the other ("the relation to the other, that is to say, the place for justice" [SM, 26/48]).

The better answer is that the originary opening to what is other than life at the level of the living has the simultaneous consequence of opening up life in another precise sense. Life predicated on the economy of death is necessarily rent and open to an irreducible outside, and this opening is the very condition of its persistence. But this also means that the living equally has to be open to heterogeneity inscribed within its apparent selfsameness. More precisely, it has to be open to potential transformation or destruction. Absolute closure would be asphyxiation, whereas absolute openness to heterogeneity (total, aneconomic opening, as opposed to an *economy* of death) would equally be death. This exposure to transformation or destruction would thus be why Derrida is able to link life death and *survivance* to the other, since transformation or violation are what is at stake in exposure to any other. Derrida makes this point in *Rogues*, where he says that "the interruption of a certain unbinding opens the free space of the relationship to the incalculable singularity of the other" (R, 150/206–7).

Consequently, the living being has to be exposed, by virtue of the structure of *survivance* that inscribes a certain heterogeneity in the economy of the same, to everything that is possible in the relation to an other or others, in *survivance* now understood also as "being-with" or "living with" (see SM, xviii/15). The earlier form of exposure we saw operative in survival at the deepest structural level thus opens directly onto exposure to transformation or destruction, and thus to the relation to the other and all the other others. "Being-with," Derrida therefore says in *Specters*, opens up the question of justice that "must carry beyond *present* life, life as *my* life or *our* life. In general" (SM, xix/16).[14] The structure of *survivance* can thus be shown to *include*, within the form of tracing that constitutes it, "the irreducible and nonappropriable differance of the other" (R, 84/123). This is why Derrida can legitimately describe the situation of *survivance* as one that has urgency in the here and now with respect to the question of justice, and not just because every here and now is open to what comes from the unpredictable future.

The phrase "being with" is here understood, in accordance with the necessity across the whole of deconstruction to think beyond a thinking of presence, as pertaining to our relation to others who we do not simply encounter in the mode of full presence. The ground of ethics and politics as the concern for justice, the ground of normativity, is here expanded beyond responsibility to those who are simply alive and present.[15] It is instead shifted in the direction of a thinking of radical finitude as exposure to heterogeneity in the same, thus as exposure not just to ghosts from the past and to those who are not yet born, but also those excluded from "living with" in the here and now. These too are "co-diers," *commourans*, as Derrida would later put it, borrowing the phrase from Montaigne (*BS*, 2:263/363).

Crucially, however, the fact that violence is inherent in any necessary decision remains fully in place here. Thus, this relation is not simply one of peace, but potentially or actually also one of violence, for me and for the other or plurality of others. The structure of mortal finitude Derrida names *survivance* makes it such that the position or place from which we decide is always, originally and structurally, compromised. As we have seen, the structure whereby life is rent by interruption and undoing has the consequence that life has to be open or exposed to potential transformation or destruction in order to live on. Consequently, my life is structurally open to the threat of destruction intrinsically at stake in the relation to some unpredictable other (since the relation to the absolute other and the incalculable necessarily, if it is truly a relation to an undetermined other, carries as much potential threat as it does chance for peace). And this holds too for the other, for the ghost or some other "co-dier."

This is not, however, or at least not originally, because something might come from the future to overturn the conditional norms and calculations I have to employ to respond and thereby change the state of affairs. Instead, we now begin to see, it is because the structure of *survivance* makes it such that the position or place from which I decide is radically unstable. Even though I have to decide, my position as a radically finite being is always stretched open, as it were, in the direction of other "co-diers" and ghosts, in multiple directions; it is never fully stabilized. Always exposed to these others, I can never fully rest in the position from which I negotiate how to live with some singular one or the plurality of others. The question of my responsibilities in this situation therefore has to be continually relaunched. The point is that the necessity to continually negotiate *anew* the call for responsibility is inscribed already in my very life insofar as I am structurally a survivor. And this is, at this point, all that Derrida's framework offers us. In texts such as *The Gift of Death* and *Specters of Marx*, it simply shows the impossibility of resting in good conscience once and for all, seemingly lending credence to the notion that deconstruction cannot make substantive normative claims.

Superlife and Survival

But further developments in "Faith and Knowledge" indicate there is something transformative in the fact that deconstruction allows us to think through, rather than simply disavow, this situation. We see the emergence of this new element in the crucial portions of "Faith and Knowledge" discussed initially in chapter 3.

There, Derrida shows that the thought of finitude spelled out in the deconstructive notions of survival and autoimmunity undercut not only the idea of simple responsibility to those presently living (Derrida's argument in *Specters*), but also the idea of a kind of superlife, a kind of transcendence beyond mere biological life. This notion, Derrida argues in "Faith and Knowledge," is the very notion of the sacred proper to all religion. The holy, the sacred, he shows drawing on Benveniste, is not the profane insofar as it is the absolutely "safe and sound," the unscathed (*FK*, 61/38). He then argues that the driving force behind this theological thought is not the desire for some God immune to everything that might violate it or destroy it, but rather the desire for a form of life immune to such a threat. Religion dreams of "saving the living intact, the unscathed, the safe and sound (*heilig*) that has the right to absolute respect, restraint, modesty" (*FK*, 85/75). Such a form of life beyond mortal life is transcendent, but it is unwittingly autoimmune. In not being subject to mortal finitude, it begins to resemble nothing so much as the not-mortal false life of the automaton or machine ("false" from the perspective of religion). Religious faith is thus "faith in the most living as dead and automatically *sur-viving*, resuscitated in its spectral *phantasma*, the holy, safe and sound, unscathed, immune, sacred" (*FK*, 84/73). This ideal of life is then said to be the result of an "indemnification of a spectrality without limit" (*FK*, 87/78).

Such is, for Derrida, the uncritical desire inhabiting all religion, a desire that he suggests already in this essay (foreshadowing a move to come much later in texts such as *For What Tomorrow, The Animal That Therefore I Am*, and the late seminars) is barely secularized in the history of philosophy. It is in fact carried over into the various philosophical definitions of the human as the one who carries something transcendent and priceless in his or her being, beyond his or her mere biological life, a sacrosanct dignity.[16] This form of absolutely transcendent being, or life beyond mortal finitude (which in the late seminars will appear under the name of "the proper to man"), is defined as a kind of "life more than life," life beyond or above life, superlife.[17]

But the thought of survival and autoimmunity in deconstruction, Derrida argues in "Faith and Knowledge," undercuts this notion. It shows that it is based on an uncritical disavowal of mortal, finite life. It shows that this notion is but a "phantasm," an uncritical notion based on a kind of fantasy, informed not just by disavowal but also by a wish or desire. The deeper thought of autoimmunity and survival provides the ground for deconstruction to contest this phantasm and the theological more broadly, with its vision of a form of life beyond life immune to violation, absolutely safe and sound. It shakes up—as *Of Grammatology* famously describes the work of deconstruction—this uncritical fantasy of something beyond survival and finitude. Specifically, as shown in chapter 3, it does so by showing that the opening to heterogeneity, or internal tension, figured in the thought of survival as autoimmunity is equally at work in religious faith. Belief in a form of unscathed life, in the safe and sound, represses the very condition of its survival, its living on: the opening to heterogeneity and the other in the same figured in temporalization and the trace, and in life thought on the basis of the trace. In order to stay alive, this faith, like everything else, requires the opening "to something other and more than itself: the other, the future, death, freedom, the coming or the love of the other, the space and time of a spectralizing messianicity beyond all messianism" (FK, 87/79).

When we hold this argument in "Faith and Knowledge" alongside the moves made in *Aporias* (1992–93), we begin to grasp the full scope of what Derrida is doing. *Aporias* outlines a critique of what Derrida describes as an uncritical "precomprehension" of death figured in even the most radical modes of thinking finitude in the history of philosophy. Even in Heidegger—who Derrida will consistently say goes a certain distance in deconstructing the traditional notion of death as a border, as mere final terminus of life, its proper endpoint, but does not go far enough. Derrida suggests in several places that Heidegger's notion that only the human has access to death as such, can have an experience of death as its own most proper possibility (glimpsed in the thought that no one can ever die in my place), is itself uncritical at a certain point. Consequently, Derrida argues that what Heidegger cannot think is "*revenance*, spectrality or living-on, surviving, as non-derivable categories or as non-reducible derivations" (A, 61/111). Here Derrida in effect indicates where his later work would go: in the direction of a critique of an uncritical precomprehension of death and of life, thought in terms of the difference between the living being called human and "the animal" in Heidegger (*The Beast and the Sovereign, vol. 2*) and in our inherited concepts more broadly (*The Animal That Therefore I Am* and *The Death Penalty*).

Thus, holding "Faith and Knowledge" and *Aporias* together, we see that the thought of life initially articulated in *Specters of Marx* makes possible deconstructive critique. The logic of life death, and in turn *survivance*, allows Derrida to challenge the vision, the phantasm, of superlife on multiple fronts. On one hand, it allows him, to contest this phantasm as it informs religion. On the other hand, it provides a basis from which to contest the still too-theological inherited concepts informing contemporary political practice. Indeed, the dominant concept of the political, he shows, will always have been predicated on the conception of the human and its transcendent superlife just described.

This second challenge emerges clearly in Derrida's later work. It plays a pivotal role in the 1999–2001 *Death Penalty* seminars—the last in a long series of Derrida's seminars on "Questions of Responsibility"—and in the 2001–3 *The Beast and the Sovereign* seminars, and it is crucial to the line of thinking undertaken in *The Animal That Therefore I Am* and *Rogues*, where we find Derrida arguing that deconstruction is engaged from the beginning in a critical rethinking of "all the limits we thought pertained to life, the being of life and the life of being (and this is almost the entire history of philosophy), between the living and the dead, the living present, and its spectral others" (R, 151/209). The logic of *survivance* in these texts allows Derrida to criticize, from the perspective of an alternate conception of life, what he shows to be a prevailing conception of the human, of the "proper to man," conceived in terms of what raises him or her above mere biological life, the form of living supposedly characteristic of the animal. Again, at stake here is the dream of a kind of superlife beyond life.

Indeed, as the passage from *Rogues* just cited suggests, there are indications that the theme of life serves as a crucial lever for deconstruction throughout Derrida's later work on inherited political concepts and practices, even when it tackles issues that might seem unrelated. Hence, Derrida's comments in the very first section of "The Reason of the Strongest" offer an explicit acknowledgement of this fact. Nearly right away in this essay on the question of "rogue states" (*États voyous*) and democracy, Derrida suggests that "the old word *vie* perhaps remains the enigma of the political around which we endlessly turn" (R, 4/22). Then, having situated what he is going to discuss in relation to a certain fidelity to the to-come and to the future, he concludes by summing up, "It is indeed on the side of chance, that is, the side of the incalculable *perhaps*, and toward the incalculability of another thought of life, of what is living in life, that I would like to venture here under the old and yet still completely new and perhaps unthought name *democracy*" (R, 5/24).

Thus, while somewhat easy to miss, this theme resurfaces in Derrida's critical treatment of the logic of autonomous identity or ipseity at work in the notions of the sovereign self, the sovereignty of the nation-state, and the authority of the people in democracy in *Rogues*. The concept of sovereignty is shown to be in fact predicated on a fundamentally theological, and in turn deconstructible, notion of identity whereby a self, sovereign, or nation-state is thought to be fully unitary, indivisible, and self-identical. These terms are in fact understood, Derrida attempts to show, on the model of the idea of an absolutely sovereign God. In "The University Without Condition," for instance, sovereignty is explicitly recognized as "the heritage of a barely secularized theology" (WA, 207/20). In *Rogues*, the logic of ipseity will be opposed to "another truth of the democratic"— one associated not with sovereignty but with unconditionality and, in turn, a certain democracy to come (R, 14/35). Under this heading, Derrida will speak of "everything that remains incompatible with, even clashes with" ipseity: "namely, the truth of the other, heterogeneity, the heteronomic and the dissymmetric, disseminal multiplicity, the anonymous 'anyone', the 'no matter who', the indeterminate 'each one'" (R, 14–15/35). One of the primary figures of the logic of ipseity to be deconstructed in *Rogues* is therefore the figure of an entity that is entirely autonomous in its potentiality or power, such as that exemplified by Aristotle's Prime Mover. Thus, when Derrida treats Aristotle's philosopheme he will remark, without ever really returning to it, that Aristotle associates the Prime Mover who sets everything in motion with, precisely, "a life, a kind of life, a way of leading life" (R, 15/35). "It is thus a life that exceeds the life of human beings, a life lived by the Prime Mover in a constant, continuous, and unending fashion, something that is for us impossible," he writes (R, 15/35–36).

While Derrida does not take up the deconstruction of sovereignty in *Rogues* with reference to this theme of life, human life, and what, supposedly, exceeds it, it is clear already when we hold these passages together that this deconstructive gesture, whatever it produces as its outcome, bears right away on an inherited notion of life and the human. And it is only a small step further, then, that allows us to say that the critical purchase deconstruction has vis-à-vis sovereignty in its various forms—in opening it up to the thought of the unconditional, as Derrida will call it—stems from this "other thought of life, of what is living in life." The critical lever in deconstruction's contestation of sovereignty as a political concept, then, the one that allows it to show up the blind spot within so many phantasms, here and elsewhere, is its particular thinking of finitude. It is from the perspective of life recast as survival that Derrida is able to say that the phantasm of superlife is an uncritical, yet powerful fantasy producing a kind of truth effect.

Normativity and Critique

We have made some headway, then, on what deconstructive critique, formulated on the basis of the thought of survival, targets. But if, as Derrida suggests in *Rogues* in the passage cited above, a certain thinking of survival drives the deconstruction of the phantasm of sovereignty and those political practices informed by it, how exactly the thought of survival provides the resources for this critique has not yet been fully addressed. We have seen that the thought of survival provides the ground for critique, but how does this critique proceed and how does this thought disrupt a phantasm powerful enough to have dominated our inherited concepts of life, the human, and of the political? These are the crucial questions we now need to explore.

We can begin with how the deconstructive critique under discussion here proceeds. The notion of survival provides the resources and the means to criticize so many concepts based on the notion of superlife, but perhaps above all, in Derrida's late work it makes possible the critique of sovereignty and those forms of political power associated with its logic. The contestation of sovereignty can therefore be illustrative for us. Importantly, as Derrida clarifies in several places, deconstructive critique does not aim to do away with sovereignty altogether—since it is intertwined with the concept of freedom necessary to any possible democracy to come, the political concept Derrida counterposes to sovereignty—but rather at transforming practices, laws, and institutions, in order to open them up to rearticulation and transformation.[18] The thought of survival supplies the resources for deconstructive critique in the precise sense that it exerts a critical, destabilizing force on a notion that is clandestinely theological. It, in essence, undermines, disturbs, or shakes up not only the phantasm at the heart of religion but also our inherited theologico-political framework, wrapped up as it is with the phantasm of a kind of infinite life beyond life. New articulations of the political are then made possible insofar as the existing ones are demonstrated to be not simply given and incontestable but thoroughly fragile or uncritical—in a word, deconstructible.

Yet crucially, the thought of survival performs this shaking up by making the essential fragility of the phantasm of superlife, its fundamental "untenability," appear from the inside, as Derrida puts it in a somewhat different context (*FWT*, 150/243).[19] As should now be somewhat clearer, the form of deconstructive critique Derrida points to proceeds not by positing that affirming life as survival is *better* than not doing so: since it is ultra-transcendental and arche-originary, it is not something we can choose to affirm or not; it precedes any possible choice. Rather it proceeds by using this thought as the basis from which to demonstrate the internal blind spot at the core of the conception of life and the human our inherited theological-political concepts presuppose. Namely, it shows that they must repress or disavow the originary condition of mortality and finitude without which there would be no life whatsoever to protect or affirm. They thus repress their own necessary condition, that which precedes the fantasy of a transcendent form of life beyond life. Viewed from this perspective, our inherited concepts repress the necessary condition whereby life is originally already survival, exposed to exteriority, alterity, and death from the outset, such that the very possibility of "my life" necessarily always and originally passes by way of the heart of the other. While they do not simply go away, they begin to appear as so many reactive phantasms.

Crucially, then, the deconstructive critique of the theologico-political does not operate on the basis of an idea of survival as the sovereign good. Survival is not a good, since it is not something we might choose over anything else. Moreover, positing a sovereign good in this situation would require an idea of absolute justice impervious to what comes or what happens—which Derrida is quite clear in "Force of Law" and elsewhere is impossible—and is to be distinguished, however fragile the distinction might appear, from a certain call to unconditional justice. The ideal of an absolute good is impossible insofar as such an ideal would not be open to transformation in the face of the absolutely unpredictable coming of time and exposure to heterogeneity.

By contrast, deconstructive critique proceeds by bringing forward and underlining the unthought, repressed, or disavowed, but absolutely necessary, constitutive conditions of anything whatsoever. The crucial point, however, is that these conditions fundamentally undercut, undermine, or destabilize the phantasms of superlife and life beyond life taking the form of transcendent dignity, and of an absolutely sovereign entity, self, or power modeled on the idea of God. Stated somewhat differently, once we begin to think this fundamental, ultra-transcendental condition—survival now appearing as a key figure of "the unconditional" which Derrida consistently opposes to sovereignty (see R, xiv/13)—then so many concepts and practices, even if they will not disappear once and for all, begin to appear *as phantasmatic, as phantasms*, and not as truth or fact. The deconstructive thought of survival is here what allows us recognize the difference between the two.

In *Rogues*, Derrida describes in further detail how the procedure of deconstructive contestation or critique I have just described operates. Derrida's declared project, across the two distinct essays which comprise *Rogues*, is to attempt to think, once again, a certain *"democracy to come"*—here, in relation to, or "in the age of," "so-called globalization or *mondialisation*" (R, xii/11). This latter term names in this text, among other things, what is happening in the world at the time of its writing, what Derrida describes quite clearly as a transformation of the field in which the supposedly sovereign nation-state operates, by virtue of shifts in techno-science, international law, capital, and war, and by virtue of the emergence of international terrorism. There is something like a deconstruction already underway, Derrida thus suggests, and the lectures contained in *Rogues* are intended to bring this forward, by means of specific conceptual tools. Chief among these are what Derrida calls "an ultimate lever" (R, xiii, 13): the essential, indispensable distinction between sovereignty and the unconditional. Here, the unconditional is described as the thought of "the experience that lets itself be affected by what or who comes [(ce) qui vient], by what happens or by who happens by, by *the other to come*" (R, xiv/13).

To the extent that the logic of survival can be understood to follow from the constitutive exposure to alterity necessary for any entity whatsoever to "be" in the first place and to persist, even though it is not named here, such a thinking of life is already on the table. Hence its appearance several pages later, in the passages cited above, where that interrogation of the political Derrida undertakes in the essay on "The Reason of the Strongest" is said to bear, in the end, on "the incalculability of another thought of life, of what is living in life." And thus, again, it is this other thought of life, according to Derrida, that is at stake in the notion of democracy to come and what still remains "perhaps unthought" in the concept of democracy we inherit from the tradition (R, 5/24).

The crucial point here is that this thinking of the unconditional has a normative dimension, insofar as it opens onto "a certain unconditional renunciation of sovereignty [that] is required a priori" (R, xiv/13). The unconditional, here, commands or bespeaks a normative renunciation of sovereignty already at the level of what would seem, at first glance, simply a *descriptive* ("constative" to use the Austinian term Derrida prefers) ontological claim about what is (namely, *différance*, the structure of the trace, and thus life as life death and survival). This is, in a nutshell, where Hägglund's account begins and ends. Deconstruction describes the basic conditions of the trace and, in this purely descriptive gesture, puts into question forms of thought that would seek to posit a principle or ideal immune to this condition. And Derrida actually appears to suggest as much on the very next page, when he writes, in one of the book's most frequently cited passages, "No politics, no ethics, and no law can be, as it were, *deduced* [*déduire*] from this thought" (R, xv/14, emphasis in the original).[20]

This means, perhaps first and foremost, that there is no basis here for offering specific ethical and political guidelines. But there are good reasons not to read this statement as suggesting there are no ethical and political implications with respect to deconstruction's basic infrastructures. Rather, everything points in the direction of reading this statement as suggesting there are such normative implications, but that they are not to be *deduced* from these basic infrastructural concepts.[21] And this because the ultra-transcendental, already "prior to" (if this tentative distinction can be granted) the distinction between the ontological and the normative, the "is" and the "ought," is already itself intrinsically normative, as Fritsch has argued. Immediately after the sentence in question, Derrida moves on to specify that while an ethics and politics cannot be deduced from this thought of the unconditional, this nonetheless does not allow one to conclude that "this thought leaves no trace on what is to be done— for example in politics, the ethics, or the law to come" (R, xv/15).[22] And the reason for this has to do with what he has just described on the previous page, the difficult-to-think *"weak force"*—the weak normative force—of unconditionality, which opens any entity or identity up "to what or who *comes* and comes to affect it" (R, xiv/13). This force, by definition, "exceeds the condition of mastery [and thus sovereignty of a self or a supposedly self-identical entity] and the conventionally accepted authority of what is called the 'performative'"; then right away, Derrida specifies, "it thus also exceeds, without contesting its pertinence, the useful distinction between 'constative' and 'performative'" (R, xiv/14). And it is thus the weak normative force of the unconditional, we are justified in saying, that allows deconstruction to go beyond a description of truth or fact, to a certain kind of normative prescription. This prescription consists in a call for the active "renunciation of sovereignty" (R, xiv/13), and for critical vigilance—a term Derrida deploys frequently in these discussions[23]— wherever the phantasm of sovereignty, of the purity of an identity, whether of a self, the state, or God, operates.

Thus, to sum up my first point on the question of normativity, the crucial issue is that the constitutive conditions of mortal finitude named in the concept of life death or survival are the basic conditions for any life or any entity whatsoever. Hence, to bring this structure forward is to bring forward sovereignty's own originary, unconditional condition, which it nonetheless seeks to repress or disavow. The point is that, in underscoring this structure, deconstruction does not have to posit a value or sovereign good beyond mortal finitude and the operations of *différance* and the trace, and yet its conceptualization of this basic infrastructure already has some normative purchase. It allows us to criticize, or renounce, the fantasy of an absolutely inviolable life beyond life at the level of ethics, politics, and law, and with it the phantasm of an absolutely indivisible, self-identical sovereignty.[24]

The Phantasm and Fantasy

Before addressing the further normative purchase of deconstruction, we need to pause on a term we have not properly examined. The term is *phantasm*, and it bears further comment. If, as I have said, deconstruction takes on the phantasm of superlife wherever it operates, we will better understand this critique by understanding just what the phantasm is in Derrida. Grasping this term is particularly pressing in this context, because it seems to mobilize a certain Freudian heritage ("fantasy" is a term Freud frequently uses, after all) even though Derrida adapts this concept to new contexts.

To begin with, when we look back over Derrida's corpus, we see that the term phantasm, first critically deployed in *Specters of Marx* and "Faith and Knowledge," came to occupy an increasingly central place in Derrida's thinking in his very late work. In *Rogues* and in *The Death Penalty* and *The Beast and the Sovereign* seminars, Derrida would have frequent recourse to this term in order to describe the essentially fictional dimension of the fantasy of mastery at work in the notion of sovereignty or, indeed, the death penalty—the fantasy that deconstruction then sets out to contest by showing its untenability. Whether it is the notion of ipseity at the heart of the logic of sovereignty (*Rogues*), the vision of a death given at a specific moment central to the political theology of the death penalty (*The Death Penalty*), or the image of my own death as such (*The Beast and the Sovereign, vol. 2*), the deconstruction of the phantasm, in keeping with the procedure outlined in the discussion above, shows how it in essence deconstructs itself, from the inside, in the very terms in which it is articulated or in which it articulates itself.[25]

Michael Naas has done some important work on this concept, and we now have a fairly firm understanding of the phantasm in Derrida. As Naas has shown, it is a kind of "speculative fiction" that presents itself as an absolute law, or an absolute limit to thought, beyond which thinking and good sense cannot go.[26] The phantasm is a fable of mastery offered in the form of a philosopheme—in the case of sovereignty, the human-animal distinction, and the death penalty—or in the form of a *concept* that is actually a notion: as in the case of the inherited concepts of the self, the nation-state, and God Naas identifies, all of which mobilize the logic of sovereignty. But Naas also identifies two other aspects of the phantasm. First, the phantasm entails a form of repression. It has the appearance of cohering as a concept or logic precisely because the imaginary, fictional character of the wish at its core is repressed or disavowed in its various formulations and the justifications given for it. Second, the phantasm is, at bottom, reactive. The notion of the unitary self in its absolute ipseity, the notion of sovereignty as absolutely undivided and indivisible power, the notion of a death given and as such mastered, the impossible image of my own death which I can only imagine by pretending I am still surviving, all of these evidence an uncritical *reaction* to what deconstruction shows, in its seminal thinking of *différance* and iterability, to be the self-undoing—the constitutive autoimmunity—of any supposedly indivisible element, any entity thought to be immune to contamination by its other. In the present context, the most notable of these would be life thought in opposition to death, which would seem to come only secondarily to infect life from the outside. To the extent that, on the basis of its core thinking of the trace and *différance* deconstruction reveals that the putatively undecomposable logic of the phantasm is in fact founded on a reactionary repression, deconstruction quite simply is, as Naas puts it, the deconstruction of the phantasm.[27] And this will always have been the case, even if it is only designated as such in the later work.

But there is one last dimension of the phantasm as glossed by Naas we should note. Insofar as the phantasm expresses a kind of unthought wish, or desire, for things to be different than they are, it always entails not just an assertion of truth—a claim deconstruction shows, in each case, to be fundamentally fragile, because contested from within—but also passionate attachment, deep investment. Here, Derrida appears to draw on Freud. The phantasm, even if it is fictional, has undeniably real effects because it has a certain captivating power. The phantasm is the crystallization of an affective bond. Because it is charged with affect in this way, the deconstruction of the phantasm, the dissolution of its complex, as it were, does not simply consist in revealing the truth. Rather, going beyond the phantasm entails an active form of working through, as Freud would put it. Relinquishing the phantasm entails overcoming resistance, the resistance posed by our deep attachment to the narrative phantasmatic fiction offers. This would be the ultimate source, for instance, of the theologico-political's captivating power, and thus its longevity, if not its permanency.

It might seem, then, that the deconstruction of the phantasm in Derrida follows the model offered by Freud. This is not quite the case, however, and seeing this reveals something crucial about the phantasm in Derrida. In order to see how he departs from this model, we need to look at Derrida's transformative treatment of the phantasm in Freud in volume 2 of *The Beast and the Sovereign*. In his treatment of Freud there—in a discussion of fantasy in psychoanalysis that, as we will see in a moment, it would be easy to misread—Derrida radically distinguishes the phantasm thought from the perspective of deconstruction from the conception of fantasy in Freud. Thus, while relinquishing the phantasm might very well entail undoing affective bonds, as in Freud, when Derrida demarcates his own thinking from Freud's he in fact shows that something quite different from psychoanalysis is at stake in the deconstruction of the phantasm.

The difference consists in this: taking on the phantasm in deconstruction will *not* entail grasping the more fundamental ground underlying the fiction. This is the very logic of the phantasm itself, after all. It offers the image of something said to be incontestable in all good sense, undecomposable in thought. The phantasm, which is metaphysical, points to some putatively indivisible element that is fundamental to the conceptual scaffolding atop it to the exact extent that this element supposedly cannot be further divided, thereby remaining identical to itself. This is why Derrida will say that even though it might seem that strictly speaking there is "no *logic of the phantasm*"—no logic *to* the phantasm, only a wish or desire—the *logos* as reason, in all its various forms, "itself is precisely *the* phantasm, the very element, the origin and the resource of the phantasm itself, the form and the formation of the phantasm" (*BS*, 2:185/262). Taking on the phantasm, consequently, will require an altogether different logic. Otherwise, deconstruction would simply repeat what it wants to undo. What is this other logic? It is one that follows from recognizing the impossibility of any such indivisible element, from recognizing the nonidentity to itself of everything subject to the trace and *différance* as the structure of the so-called living present. From a deconstructive standpoint, traversing the phantasm thus means, precisely, relinquishing the notion of an absolute ground. It entails thinking not the true ground underneath the fantasy but the groundless ground that shakes up every fantasy of something immune to the originary exposure to heterogeneity, the insertion of the other in the same, at stake in the trace and *différance*.

To the extent that, as Derrida frequently repeated, the ultra-transcendental of *différance* is to be thought as finite (since infinite *différance* would convert back to identity), the deconstruction of the phantasm operates, we have seen, on the basis of a thinking of finitude as mortality or *survivance*. This thought then undoes what deconstruction identifies as the fundamentally theological, phantasmatic vision of a life beyond life, a superlife, untouched by mortality. This "infinitization" (*DP*, 1:258/349)—or "transcendentalization" (*FWT*, 142/229) as Derrida sometimes puts it—of life is at the very heart of *all* the different forms of the phantasm we just cited, from religion to sovereignty to the definition of the human in terms of "the proper to man" to the notion of "*my* death" as something to which I can attest, even when this is said to be the possibility of an impossibility. On this last point, as he makes clear in both *Aporias* and volume 2 of *The Beast and the Sovereign*, Derrida *does* follow Freud in a certain way: this is the reason for Derrida's frequent references to Freud's postulate in the essay on "The Unconscious" (1915) and "Thoughts for the Times on War and Death" (1915) that the unconscious knows nothing about death.[28]

But to see how Derrida ultimately goes beyond the Freud on the phantasm, it is necessary to examine the discussion of Freud in volume 2 of *The Beast and the Sovereign* in further detail. While it might seem that Derrida is simply underscoring certain problems in Freud's theorization of fantasy there, when we look closely at this discussion, we see that Derrida is in fact showing how deconstruction disrupts the desire for ground in the phantasm and in metaphysics more radically than Freud. It does this, he argues, through its thinking of what, if anything, lies beyond the phantasm.

The key is the discussion of fantasy in Freud's metapsychological writings of 1914–15. There Derrida distances his own use of the term phantasm from any other philosophical concept of *phantasma*, and he does so as well with respect to Freud, but for a quite specific reason. There is no "clear, univocal, localizable" (BS, 2:149/218) concept of fantasy in Freud, Derrida points out, and thus deconstruction has no choice but to choose its heritage in this context, to inherit certain threads in Freud which may not be properly Freudian, while discarding others.

The issue is that, like the drive, the notion of fantasy in Freud is a borderline concept. Just as the drive is situated at the border between the psychic and the somatic, fantasy—unconscious, but with undeniably real effects, producing symptoms—is situated, according to Freud, *between* two systems, the unconscious and the system of conscious perception. As Derrida puts it, the phantasm belongs strictly to neither system because it belongs to both at once (BS, 2:150/218–19). The phantasm is unconscious and "incapable of becoming conscious" (SE, 14:190–91), according to Freud, but insofar as it is organized and free from self-contradiction, it draws some of its qualities from the system of consciousness and waking thought. Freedom from contradiction, recall, along with freedom from any form of sequential temporality, is precisely what distinguishes the system "*Ucs.*" from the preconscious and consciousness. The unconscious knows nothing of contradiction, Freud hypothesizes: contradictory impulses and affects exist side by side there, just as different temporal strata are overlaid one on top of another, as in the famous image of the architecture of Rome offered in *Civilization and Its Discontents* (1930). Summing up the situation with fantasy, Freud describes it as belonging "*qualitatively* . . . to the system *Pcs.*, but *factually* to the *Ucs.*" (SE, 14:190–91).

Derrida appears to criticize Freud here for a distinction that makes no sense. The question is how "the same thing" (BS, 2:151/220), the same phantasm or symptom, can have a phenomenal quality, can be part of preconscious-conscious lived experience, while belonging, *in fact*, at bottom, to the absolutely "other place" that is the unconscious. Derrida underlines Freud's "audacity" (BS, 2:151/220) insofar as Freud seems not to realize that what he is saying overflows and challenges the very notion of an opposition between conscious phenomenal experience and unconscious mentation.

But Derrida is not so much criticizing Freud here as much as inheriting from him in a particular way, inheriting a thought that Freud himself does not reflect on explicitly. This thought is a thinking of the phantasm in terms that defy logico-philosophical thought; it is what Derrida calls Freud's "impossible thought, a thought of the impossible or a conception of the inconceivable" (BS, 2:151/220).[29] Even as he is about to distance himself from Freud, Derrida underscores that we need to hold on to this impossible thought "if we want to continue to dare to think what 'phantasm' seems to mean" (BS, 2:151/221). This is the deepest reason Derrida will later say that in thinking the phantasm "the dream, the oneiric, fiction . . . will always be less inappropriate, more relevant, if you prefer, than the authority of wakefulness, and the vigilance of the ego, and the consciousness of so-called philosophical discourse" (BS, 2:185/262–63).

For Derrida, then, Freud's impossible thought is this: the phantasm is *both* a thing rooted in the most real dimension of phenomenal, conscious experience *and* a contradictory thing originating in a certain resolutely uncritical unconscious. And if this is the case, traversing the phantasm cannot consist in the dissolution of the uncritical fiction on the way to what it is properly, actually real. Why? Because the phantasm, on its own, as it were, already partakes of the properly, actually real—not just because it has undeniably real effects, but because it straddles the really real and the fictional. Here, Derrida once again rearticulates Freud for his own purposes. He is using Freud to point to the complex thought we noted a moment ago: that the logic of a fundamental, irreducible ground, without which it is not possible to conceive of the passage through fiction to the real, is the very stuff of the metaphysical phantasm as construed by deconstruction.

Yet if Derrida distinguishes his own thinking from Freud here, it is because this thought that we have just glossed is ultimately not thought through in Freud. Immediately after the discussion of fantasy as a borderline concept, Derrida shows that even as Freud overturns the traditional logic of superficial fiction versus a more fundamental reality, he ultimately falls back into the logic and desire for ground deconstruction seeks to disrupt. Freud ultimately decides that the true ground of the undecidably double phantasm—"undecidably *both* conscious and unconscious" (BS, 2:155/225)—is the unconscious that does not know contradiction. Freud determines in the end that what defines the phantasmatic is its true origin: the fact that it originates in the unconscious, in *Ucs.* "instinctual impulses" (SE, 14:190). Freud decides, in other words, on the fundamental origin and ground of the phantasm, positing that it originates in the system produced and demarcated by repression, the mechanism of psychical censorship. As Derrida points out, Freud makes this move because of the particular understanding of finitude he employs. The necessary finiteness of the space for inscriptions in the psychic apparatus necessitates that retention of instinctual impulses take place in a different system than that of consciousness. "Finitude is . . . a sort of law for this economy," he notes (BS, 2:156/227).

The crucial question, however, is if deconstruction is to be distinguished from psychoanalysis, how does it more effectively shake up the logic at stake in the phantasm, the logic that expresses the desire for ground, but which *also*, we have said, expresses the desire for something beyond mortal life and finitude, a kind of superlife beyond phenomenal life? The answer now comes into view: deconstruction disrupts this logic and this desire by mobilizing an altogether different logic than the one underpinning the phantasm. This, we can now see, is a counter-logic that resists the dream of something beyond phenomenal life *but which does not serve as a ground*, in the same way that the ultra-transcendental thought of the always divisible, in fact always self-dividing, trace does not serve as a proper ground or origin in a new ontology.

The name of this counter-logic is, precisely, *survivance*. The thought of survival as a thinking of life internally opened up to its other inscribes death on the inside of life rather than as what comes to it only belatedly or secondarily. And this thought, Derrida once again says in volume 2 of *The Beast and the Sovereign*, overflows the thought of life *and* death, life versus death.

> Finitude is *survivance*. Survivance in a sense that is neither life nor death pure and simple, a sense that is not thinkable on the basis of the opposition between life and death, a survival that is not . . . *above* life, like something sovereign (*superanus*) can be above everything, a survival that is not more alive, nor indeed less alive, than life, or more or less dead than death . . . . It does not add something extra to life any more than it cuts anything from it, any more than it cuts anything from inevitable death or attenuates its rigor and its necessity. (BS, 2:130–31/193–94)

Thus distinguishing the thought of survival in deconstruction from any other logic of life and death, Derrida writes, "No, the survivance I am speaking of is something other than life death, but *a groundless ground* from which are detached, identified, and opposed what we think we can identify under the name of death or dying, like death properly so-called as opposed to some life properly so-called" (BS, 2:131/194, my emphasis). The difference between Freud and Derrida is to be located here. It consists in the fact that traversing the phantasm in deconstruction entails mobilizing a *groundless thinking of life*, the one traced in the thought of survival and following on everything Derrida thought with respect to the trace, *différance*, and metaphysics from the beginning. The difference between Derrida and Freud, here, has to do with the fact that in deconstruction, unlike in psychoanalysis, the notion of passing through fiction to the true ground is the very stuff of the phantasm itself.

This is why, in the "Provocation" (2001) that prefaces *Without Alibi*, while Derrida echoes his 2000 address to the Estates General of Psychoanalysis in affirming that the most urgent stakes of deconstruction are bound up with the terms sovereignty and resistance, he will only say that if the work of deconstruction produces resistance, it is in accordance with an absolutely nonclassical concept: an enigmatic "equivocal" form of resistance resolutely "without foundation," such that "the foundation is lacking, the ultimate justification is missing" (WA, xxx).[30] If deconstruction thus calls for a renunciation of sovereignty, it does not do so in the mode of a resistance, if by that we mean a counterforce simply *opposed* to sovereignty from some place outside of it (as we cannot but mean, in inheriting the word and concept of resistance from the tradition, as Derrida argues in "Resistances," speaking of Freud and the repetition compulsion[31]). Deconstruction does not resist the phantasm so much as it undermines, disturbs, or shakes it up from within. Rather than resisting the phantasm of sovereignty in the form of an external force, deconstruction proceeds by bringing forward the internal blind spot installed already at the level of its axiomatic logic, one that is in fact already producing, as it were, autodeconstructive effects.

Normativity as Weak Force

Yet, a certain positive form of normativity is actually implied in the seemingly purely negative, critical, destabilizing force of life death or survival as I have outlined it to this point. My argument is that survival, while providing the resources for deconstructive critique, should equally be understood as the positive condition for a certain form of a radical openness with respect to ethical and political decisions.

The first step is identifying the specific form of ethical and political responsibility inscribed in survival itself. Stated succinctly, if my life as a living being is necessarily opened toward exteriority and alterity in order to "be" at all, then, to the extent that I owe my very existence to this opening and this alterity, the condition of survival places me in a relationship of fundamental, heteronomous responsibility to some other or others. Derrida describes this structure in the following terms: "I am in heteronomy. This does not mean that I am not free; on the contrary, it is a *condition of freedom*, so to speak: my freedom springs from the condition of this responsibility which is born of heteronomy in the eyes of the other, in the other's sight. This gaze is spectrality itself."[32] To be sure, as we saw, from a Derridean perspective, *survivance* places me in a relationship of responsibility not merely with respect to some alter ego, but even to that which is not presently living or has never been alive. The key point here, however, is that this relation of responsibility, understood now in terms of absolute heteronomy, is operative already at the level of the ultra-transcendental that precedes the standard distinction between the ontological and the ethical or political, the constative and the performative. This relation of responsibility as heteronomy—in which I am always already called to respond, such that not responding is itself an act I am responsible for—would then be implied in what Derrida describes as my unconditional exposure to heterogeneity.

However, the logic of survival—and the form of responsibility it gives rise to, operating at the ultra-transcendental level—does not, for all that, provide a robust framework for ethical and political action. While we have seen that survival has the power to destabilize, undercut, or shake up inherited modes of thought that disavow the necessity of arche-originary exposure, the "positive" normative force of survival as an originary condition itself has to be understood as a kind of weak force. The reason is that at the same time that the deconstructive thought of survival and the unconditional I have been following here poses a challenge to the logic of sovereignty, for instance—the response to the fact of survival that would seek to immunize life from every threat—it undoes the possibility of specific moral and political guidelines and determinable criteria for what would ultimately be more just. Thinking survival as a constitutive condition affirms *nothing but* the unconditional, necessary exposure to heterogeneity and alterity and, as we will see in a moment, to what comes from the incalculable future, insofar as there can be no entity or life whatsoever immune to this process.

The reason for this lies in the fact that, as we have seen, the thought of survival does not function as a sovereign good. Such a good would be necessary to provide a firm ground for specific criteria for ethical and political decisions. Thus, the form of ethical and political negotiation called for by deconstruction brings with it no promise, no guarantee whatsoever as to the ultimate justness of any given moral and political decision, even with respect to a lesser violence.

As we have seen, rather than disabling all ethical and political action or decision, however, Derrida's thought points to the need for continual negotiation with conflicting, aporetic demands of responsibility wherever it is a question of justice and the good. This point has been duly noted by Derrida's readers. Yet what has at times been missed is that Derrida's work equally points to the necessity of negotiating such demands with a more active awareness of the absolute impossibility of resting in any given decision. Deconstructive thought allows us to say that it would be *better* to think through this impossibility than it would be to repress it. Deconstruction opens here—following the logic of Derrida's thinking of decision, such that one only decides there where a decision assured of its justice or rightness is impossible—not just onto continual vigilance with respect to ethical and political decisions but also onto the necessity of critical "hypervigilance," to use Naas's word, wherever it is a question of ethics and politics.[33]

We can flesh out somewhat further the specific form of affirming unconditional opening I am outlining here with reference to the *Death Penalty* seminars and related texts. There, it is clear that deconstruction will not offer any assurances as to the good. At issue is what Derrida, in *For What Tomorrow*, calls a "hyper-atheological" thinking of life capable of taking on the secretly theological notion of the human and human life (*FWT*, 165/266). In "Psychoanalysis Searches," Derrida specifies that this thinking is to be developed "on the basis of a *sur-vival* that owes nothing to the alibi of some mytho-theological beyond" (WA, 276/83). Crucially, deconstruction is then aligned in this same text with the thought of the *arrivant* or stranger, which is said to "no longer [believe] in the sovereign, neither in sovereign good nor sovereign evil" (WA, 279/87). In short, Derrida here opposes the unconditional and survival to the theologico-political, and on the horizon, religion and the theological itself. And one of the deepest reasons for this is the distance deconstruction takes from what Derrida consistently describes (from "Faith and Knowledge" on, as we have seen) as the fundamentally theological or religious phantasm of an entity or ideal "safe and sound" from, absolutely immune to, contamination and mortal violation.

Derrida describes how deconstruction undermines such an ideal in a key passage in the first year of the *Death Penalty* seminars. It comes at the point at which Derrida has begun to advance what he will call a "deconstruction of death" that will demonstrate that the death penalty, in its desire to master finitude, is never operative where it thinks it is, and thus never functions *as penalty* (see chapter 5). To show that death is not determinable in a given instant—because it is in fact everywhere—is to put the calculability of death presupposed by capital punishment (the calculability of a death that the state must see done and bear witness to), "out of action," Derrida says (*DP*, 1:241/327).[34] This line of argument then prompts a broader reflection on what Derrida calls the "two angels" of deconstruction, its two competing or conflicting calls. On one hand, there is the call to deconstruct "death itself" (*DP*, 1:240/327) in this fashion, out of a desire to save life, to distance oneself from death, and this might even be "the depth of the desire of what is called deconstruction" (*DP*, 1:241/327). On the other hand, there is another voice, which calls for vigilance insofar as it insists, "you will not get off so easily," because things do not end with this first move.

> It is not enough to deconstruct death, as it is necessary to do, and even if it is indeed necessary, it is not enough to deconstruct death, my other angel would continue, in order to assure one's salvation. It is not enough to deconstruct death itself [*Il ne suffit pas de déconstruire la mort même*], as it is necessary to do, in order to survive or take out a life insurance policy. For neither does life come out unscathed by this deconstruction. Nothing comes out unscathed by this deconstruction. ... The question of the death penalty is perhaps that of indemnity. (*DP*, 1:241/327–28, trans. mod.)

Here Derrida spells out the consequences of deconstructing death. In order for the deconstruction of death to work, it has to affirm a radical thought of life as intrinsically exposed to death at an arche-originary level.[35] But then life will never be inviolable; there is no possibility of its ever being absolutely protected. The philosopher-deconstructor cannot deconstruct death and feel that he has saved life, because in the process of taking on and deconstructing death, life has actually been rendered radically unsafe.

With respect to the question of normativity, we can state the consequences this way: Normatively, it is necessary to problematize and critique the phantasm of mastering finitude by means of a power over life and death, one that seems to attest to a kind of superlife beyond mortal finitude. We *ought* to do this, and this follows already from deconstruction's description of what holds at the "ontological" level (speaking more precisely, at the level of what is not actually ontological but ultra-transcendental and arche-originary). But in this very gesture, what is rendered impossible is any form of life immune from violation, and this because deconstruction understands life as originally constituted by this non-immunity, exposure to alterity, violation, death. This is what it means for life not to have come out "unscathed" by the thought of deconstruction. Moreover, what is also rendered impossible is any purely nonviolent, purely life-affirming, ethical and political decision, since life essentially consists here in a broader economy of violence and death and cannot be protected except by asphyxiating it. Even though we have to calculate and make ethical and political decisions, we do not have here any criterion or assurance whatsoever that our ethical and political decisions will be to some degree less violent than others.

This can only mean that the normative purchase of Derridean survival remains, as we have said, that of a *weak force*. There is an absolute necessity at the level of truth, and a certain normative responsibility, at stake in what Derrida will at times describe as an active "originary affirmation" (WA, 276/83) of survival and mortal finitude. But this affirmation cannot provide any criteria for knowing whether a given decision will be just. In fact, it cannot provide any criteria for knowing whether a given decision will not open the possibility of further exposure to destruction, violation, or death—for me, for the other, or for some plurality of others. This is because the opening to irreducible alterity at stake in survival is conjoined to openness to an unpredictable future, as Derrida underscores in the passage above, mobilizing the figure of the *arrivant*. And this openness to a future—of a "subject," of a people, of a species, of a language, of a world—has to include the possibility of further destruction, violation, or death. These are, after all, necessarily components of the absolutely unforeseeable coming of the other as *arrivant* or event, as Derrida often puts it.[36]

Nevertheless, deconstruction does allow us to say that a certain active form of this affirmation is better than the turn away from it. This is what we mean when we say that thinking the unconditional as the exposure to alterity implied in living-dying implies a certain "positive" form of normativity, even if it does not provide specific guidelines for ethical and political action. The ethical or political purchase of deconstruction consists not just in pointing out how the phantasms of mastery, indemnification, and superlife are uncritical, and are always deconstructing themselves from within by virtue of an autoimmune process. It consists *also* in affirming the originary, presubjective opening to heterogeneity that is in fact necessary for there to be any life at all. It actively affirms this situation as a positive condition, instead of disavowing it, and this affirmative gesture *is better* than the alternative.

Why? Because the opening to irreducible alterity at stake in survival is conjoined to openness to an unpredictable future, and this openness to a future is precisely foreclosed in the attempt to deny radical finitude. Or rather, since exposure to alterity and the future is the structural condition for anything that lives, and anything subject to *différance*, it would be better to say that there is always *the attempt* at such foreclosure in its denial. As discussed in chapter 5, this is the process at work in the death penalty, for Derrida. But he also describes this denial of the future in vivid terms in his discussions of terrorism and the event of September 11. In "Autoimmunity: Real and Symbolic Suicides," he explicitly states that, even apart from its cruelty and treatment of women, the form of fanatical terrorism he associates with "the bin Laden effect" attempts to close off the future: "Such actions and such discourse *open onto no future and, in my view, have no future*" (ARSS, 113). This is the case, he continues, because "what is being proposed, at least implicitly, is that all capitalist and modern techno-scientific forces be put in the service of an interpretation, itself dogmatic, of the Islamic revelation of the One" (ARSS, 113). Against this move, which would close down all other possibilities for the future, Derrida says we ought to take the side of the camp that "in principle . . . leaves a perspective open to perfectibility" (ARSS, 114), that is, that leaves open a perspective for new possibilities, which themselves will always be in need of further perfectibility. Thus, following Derrida's line of thinking here, there is a stillborn foreclosure of the future in the denial of survival whether this foreclosure is recognized or not, whether it is conscious or not. There is a negation of the future in the attempt to deny radical finitude—the attempt to protect against threat by remaining within a situation that resembles a repetition of the same.

In this way, the denial of mortality, of radical finitude, boomerangs back on itself. The attempt to protect life absolutely results in the affirmation not of life, which is in fact living on, but of a kind of death, a stasis in which life is closed off to any potential violation or destruction. The reactive denial of radical finitude winds up producing, via an autoimmune process, a state of apparent safety that resembles nothing so much as the death it seeks so desperately to deny. It produces a kind of "death" insofar as death is the end of any possible future to come. The phantasmatic denial of radical finitude winds up affirming a situation in which there is no genuine future. In this way, it rejects still living life, without knowing it, in view of absolutely transcendent life.

Thus, the success of this gesture is only a phantasm. It has no hope whatsoever of succeeding, as Freud would say. This is for two reasons. The first reason is the one we just outlined. It fails because it boomerangs back on itself, in an autoimmune fashion, producing a kind of death in the very effort to protect life absolutely. But secondly, because the structural condition of survival is the condition for anything at all, because the capacity to live on in the face of some future, however minimally, is necessary for any gesture at all to take place, it is equally the condition of the phantasmatic denial. The phantasm can try to cover over this structure, but it cannot do away with it.

The fact of its inevitable failure is, in turn, why the attempt at denying and mastering radical finitude at work in the phantasm must be continually repeated. The phantasm's extraordinary staying power is due not just to passionate attachment but also to the fact that, because it can never succeed once and for all (and this for the deepest structural reasons), the effort to sustain it is always being repeated from the very get-go. The effort to sustain it and keep it going has to be repeated precisely because the phantasm is always being punctured, is always collapsing.

Given everything we have just said, it follows that we *ought to affirm* the greater chance for new possibilities inherent in openness to the future and the event in the genuine sense of this term, possibilities closed off in any situation that is a repetition of the same. This is why Derrida says explicitly in an interview from the 1990s that "the coming of the event is what cannot and *should not* be prevented; it is another name for the future itself" (N, 94/65, my emphasis). He continues: "This does not mean that it is good—good in itself—for everything or anything to arrive; it is not that one should give up trying to prevent certain things from coming to pass (without which there would be no decision, no responsibility, ethics, or politics). But one should only ever oppose events that one thinks will block the future or that bring death with them: events that would put an end to the possibility of the event, to the affirmative opening to the coming of the other" (N, 94/65).

This openness to the future is the only possibility of justice, Derrida then argues, and he goes so far as to say it is better that the future come than not. A bit further on he spells this out explicitly: "[Justice] is the affirmative experience of the coming of the other as other: *it is better for this to arrive than the contrary. . . . The openness to the future is worth more*; that is the axiom of deconstruction, that on the basis of which it has always set itself in motion, and which links it, as with the future itself, to otherness, to the priceless dignity of otherness, that is to say, to justice" (N, 104–5/70, my emphasis).[37] Openness to unforeseeable possibilities and openness to transformation in our institutions, norms, and practices is not necessarily better *in its results* than no transformation, however. Exposure to transformation is, by definition, also openness to the possibility of absolute destruction of whatever or whomever. To be sure, to risk exposure to some incalculable future, as we have seen, equally opens the possibility of what threatens to destroy a finite mortality. And this is strictly unavoidable. Affirming a genuinely unpredictable future to come for a finite mortality brings with it, we have seen, openness to the possibility of even greater violation and the threat of total death. Openness to absolutely unpredictable possibilities coming from the future and openness to transformation is nonetheless better than the reactive denial because affirming this openness is, in fact, the only way of having some future to come, and thus of surviving and living on. It is better than the reactive denial because it is necessary for living on even where it is occluded, and recognizing this truth has a certain "weak" normative force that in turn requires the active affirmation we have just described.

Now, it might be objected that what I have called a certain active affirmation of openness or exposure is, according to the logic of my own argument, always already at work everywhere, even if it is disavowed, and thus what we have in deconstruction is, still, not a normative dimension but simply a description of what is. But a clear distinction between the two levels is precisely what we have now seen Derrida putting into question. What I am describing here as a particular kind of active affirmation of survival and critical vigilance with respect to its necessity, a vigilance without guidelines and without guarantees as to its results, is what deconstruction forces us to think.

It seems clear too that Derrida himself sees a certain "weak" form of normative purchase implied already in the deconstructive description of ultra-transcendental structures. This is what he seems to mean when he says that the thought of the unconditional necessitates that we "prepare" for the coming of the other by being hospitable to it, but in a very particular way. "To be hospitable," Derrida writes, "is to let oneself be overtaken [*surprendre*], *to be ready to not be ready*, if such is possible, to let oneself be overtaken, to not even *let* oneself be overtaken, to be surprised, in a fashion almost violent, violated and raped [*violée*], stolen [*volée*] . . . precisely where one is not ready to receive."[38] Further, since our conditional responses to the call for justice from some other necessarily can have no bearing on the absolutely unpredictable event that comes from the future, beyond every horizon with respect what seems possible in the here and now (the to-come thus described in Derrida as the "impossible"[39]), then "preparing" for the coming of the other will not have substantive content. Rather, the only way to genuinely prepare and be ready for the coming of the other would be to maintain and affirm the form of hyper-vigilance and openness we have now described. This is the form of vigilance that insists on the necessity of continual exposure to chance and threat, such that we never *rest* in any given response to the call for justice, *by actively keeping it from calcifying*.[40]

If this approach cannot provide the grounds for specific ethical and political guidelines for action, or even the promise of a lesser violence, it nonetheless makes possible what Derrida names explicitly in several places a transformation of the ethical, political, and the juridical, out of, driven by, a concern for justice—a transformation that has the chance of something different than mere repetition of the same. Indeed, the opening to the incalculable at stake in survival, to an unpredictable, and thus precarious, future is, in Derrida's thought, a crucial condition of possibility of any possible justice whatsoever. As "Force of Law" makes clear, genuine justice, if it is at all, lies beyond the domain of currently holding conditional rules, laws, and obligations which inevitably do some violence to singularity. Thus, it is essentially, perpetually futural in the specific sense deconstruction lends this term, such that it is understood as absolutely incalculable and unforeseeable. Hence in *Specters of Marx*, Derrida says clearly that the question of justice, both for others who are not yet and no longer, is in fact "turned toward the future, going toward it, also comes from it, proceeds *from* the future" (SM, xix/16). The concern for justice therefore *requires* that there be some further future, and thus requires continual exposure to it. What is called for is a transformation of ethical and political concepts and practices that acknowledges this fact.

Given the notion of survival and exposure to the unpredictable future I have elaborated to this point, this transformation would not be a process that is carried out one time, in a given time and place, but rather would have to be continually reinvented, reencountered, and rearticulated, insofar as it would never be fully closed off from events that come from the future. Just as it would operate in view of a survival that can never be immune from contamination, absolutely safe and sound, the ethical and political transformations thus generated from the form of affirmation I have argued for would themselves never be immune to ongoing critique and contestation.[41]

What we have now outlined as the weak normative force of deconstruction therefore speaks to the need for *radical openness*. The form of radical openness called for by deconstruction requires us to recognize the absolute necessity of continual transformation in whatever conditional rules and guidelines for action we decide upon, by keeping them open to possible alteration. It thus requires us to recognize the necessity of a more primary—in fact, arche-originary—openness to the unforeseeable and the "im-possible." Heeding this demand calls for actively keeping every response to the call to responsibility and the demand for justice from ossifying. This affirmative way of keeping every response from becoming fixed leaves them perpetually open.

We do not know what continual transformation will look like, however, nor can we be sure what this process results in: it is possible that sometimes we calculate that *not* actually transforming a given convention, law, or norm is what would be just. But radical openness requires that this calculation follow from an awareness of the absolute necessity of ongoing renegotiation, rather than from an uncritical belief in our reigning rules and norms to render justice. Finally, radical openness undercuts even the regulative idea of absolute justice, however necessary it might appear as we continually seek to further perfect rules, laws, and norms. Deconstruction shows that it would be better to eschew such a regulative idea, not because it will never be possible in fact—this is embedded in the very definition of the regulative idea—but because we have to, and should, *begin* every ethical and political process of negotiation from the thought of a more primary openness to heterogeneity, and thus, to whatever or whoever comes from the future.

5
Sovereignty, Cruelty, and the Death Penalty

In chapter 4 I argued that the logic of survival supplies deconstruction with a new basis, or ground, for normativity and for critique with respect to what it shows to be the theological phantasm of safe and sound life beyond mortal life. This phantasm is at work in two key areas: in religion and, more clandestinely, in our inherited political concepts, most notably the concept of sovereignty. *Survivance* allows Derrida to criticize, from the perspective of an alternate conception of life or mortal finitude, what he shows to be the vision of something transcendent and immune to heterogeneity and violation underpinning a range of concepts reliant on the logic of sovereignty, from the autonomous, unitary self to the nation-state.[1] As I will show in this chapter, the thought of *survivance* ultimately allows Derrida to contest the inherited concept of the human itself—conceived, like the sovereign and God, in terms of a form of transcendence that exceeds his or her biological life, a transcendence that raises the human above the form of life supposedly characteristic of the animal. But this set of moves equally makes possible a deconstructive critique of contemporary political practices.

This critique extends in multiple directions, we can now begin to see. Putting into question the dream of something absolutely immune to heterogeneity and violation, it would extend not just to borders and to the supposed right of the nation-state to wage war—so many responses to the desire to immunize the nation-state from contamination and threat—but also, most visibly, to the state's sovereign power over the life and death of citizen-subjects. While this allows deconstruction to take on the putatively biopolitical power of the state to decide who to let die or expose to death, the clearest form of power over life and death would be the state's sovereign power to *take life*, the power instantiated in the practice of capital punishment.² Accordingly, the death penalty emerges in Derrida's late work as *the* key instance of the state's sovereign power over life.

Derrida articulated his position on the death penalty in a small handful of texts published in the 1990s and early 2000s, aligning himself explicitly with the abolitionist cause, yet it is only in the 1999–2001 *Death Penalty* seminars that his engagement with the question of capital punishment is fully fleshed out.³ There, Derrida's criticisms of classical abolitionism, and his attempt to formulate a new deconstructive abolitionism, come fully into view. On one hand, he attempts to develop a critique of capital punishment capable of taking on the very principle of the death penalty, not just the various ways it is carried out—something abolitionism in the West, despite its ambitions, has never managed to do. Hence, he consistently reaffirms in the seminars and related texts that deconstruction seeks to contest the death penalty "in a way that is based on principle, that is universal and unconditional" (*FWT*, 137/221). In this way, deconstruction seeks to overcome the flaws in the classical abolitionist arguments concerning cruelty and deterrence, whereby the death penalty is said to be both barbaric and useless: cruel, but also "insufficiently exemplary" (*FWT*, 137/221). On the other hand, we see Derrida in the seminars attempting to go even beyond this and to rethink classical abolitionism in its totality, in order to break what he will ultimately diagnose as a fatal "alliance," operating on multiple fronts, between the classical discourse of abolitionism and the most rigorous arguments *for* the principle of the death penalty, a kind of "symmetry between abolitionism and anti-abolitionism where finally each of them needs the other" (*DP*, 1:259n25/350n1).

Hence, while the first year of the seminars sketches the historical and philosophical framework within which a deconstructive critique of the death penalty can appear, the second year pursues a set of questions aimed primarily at undermining the deep structure of what Derrida consistently cites as the most formidable of the classical philosophical arguments in favor of the principle of the death penalty: Kant's. More specifically, at issue in the second year is the principle of the talion or talionic law installed at the heart of the Kantian argument for the death penalty as an essential feature of human law.

Most importantly, the *Death Penalty* seminars enable us to see how Derrida's treatment of this topic forms a key part of his broader interest, most clearly visible in his very late work, in critiquing the fundamentally theological foundations of our inherited political concepts generally. Crucial to this project, we can now see, is the critique of the theologico-political concept of sovereignty—the notion of an entity immune to all heterogeneity and division, modeled on the idea of God. This notion, Derrida argues consistently across a series of texts, has to be understood not simply as one term among others, but as the key term underpinning not just political discourse in the Christian West, but contemporary political practice as well. Even as the sovereignty of the nation-state is increasingly put into question by the emergence of new forms of international law and large transnational economic entities, he contends, the principle of sovereignty actively informs and underwrites the exercise of state power around the globe. It thus includes everything from the state's power to wage war (see WA, 245/21)—for instance, in the US's unilateral decision to launch a global war on terror in the early 2000s, which forms the backdrop of *Rogues* and Derrida's treatment of the issue of so-called "rogue states" in this text—to the biopolitical administration of the health of populations and to responses to global poverty.

Derrida defines the theologico-political concept of sovereignty in the following way: In its modern form, he argues following Carl Schmitt, sovereignty essentially consists in the exceptional, unshared, and autonomous power of decision belonging to a single subject or entity, the kind of power traditionally attributed to God. Yet, for Derrida, such a notion is ultimately a phantasm—a fictional, but nevertheless powerful, fantasy or idealization of autonomy and power rooted in the merely *apparent* self-identity of the sovereign subject. The phantasm of sovereignty is in fact founded on a repression: the supposedly autonomous sovereign subject necessarily represses the fact of its own internal division. The sovereign entity is divided, Derrida shows across a series of texts in this period, so long as it persists. In order for the sovereign subject or entity to sustain itself, it must be open to heterogeneity, to "the coming of the other" implied in temporalization and living on from one moment to the next (*DP*, 1:256/347). In order to be at all, the sovereign entity must be exposed to something other than itself; it is what it is only to the extent that it is intertwined with a form of alterity.

Wherever the phantasm of sovereignty holds sway, Derrida thus suggests, the fundamental relation to heterogeneity present in its basic structure is repressed. As he often put it, the essentially "performative" dimension of sovereignty—the operation whereby a subject or entity gives itself, or performs, the *appearance* of absolute autonomy—is here occluded or disavowed. For Derrida, "the theological phantasm of sovereignty" is thus the dream of a sovereign subject who, like God, would not be a temporal entity subject to finitude, capable of always remaining self-identical to itself (WA, 244/21).

We begin to see, here, how the critique of the death penalty forms a crucial part of deconstruction's broader contestation of sovereignty. The death penalty traditionally serves as a paradigmatic example of the state's exceptional, sovereign power over life and death. As such, for the deconstruction of the political theology of sovereignty to be effective, it has to take on the death penalty. The question of capital punishment is even the privileged point of entry for the broader critique of the theologico-political itself in Derrida. As he underscores in the first year of the *Death Penalty* seminars, the power over life and death instantiated in the death penalty has to be understood as "the essence of sovereign power, as political but first of all theologico-political power" (*DP*, 1:22/49). Thus, as he puts it just a bit later on, "there is theologico-political wherever there is death penalty [*Il y a théologico-politique partout où il y a peine de mort*]" (*DP*, 1:23/51). The attempt to analyze and penetrate the phantasm of sovereignty, *here understood as the essence of the theological-political*, necessarily passes through a critical analysis of the death penalty.[4]

But what has not been properly understood to this point is how the question of capital punishment provides a crucial point of entry for the deconstructive critique of the theologico-political as such, the nature of this move, and its consequences. In this chapter, building on the previous one, I take up Derrida's late work on the death penalty as a way of demonstrating the full scope of the ethico-political implications of the thought of *survival* elaborated in this book. However, as I will show, because the death penalty serves in Derrida as a particularly crucial practice informed by the powerful yet uncritical logic of sovereignty, this inquiry also allows me to explicate his treatment of inherited political concepts and practices more broadly. In this inquiry, we will see that Freud, and a certain way of inheriting from Freud, will once again provide key resources.[5] While ultimately these resources come back to the thinking of *survivance* Derrida finds in Freud, his mobilization of psychoanalysis in this period also includes a new element: psychoanalysis is said to make possible not only a contestation of sovereignty but also cruelty, through its analysis of what so often appears as the cruel exercise of sovereign power.

Deconstruction and Psychoanalysis, Taking on the Death Penalty

In Derrida's very late work, psychoanalysis becomes a key site where the deconstruction of sovereignty is possible. As we have begun to see, across his writings in this period, Derrida argues that the principle of sovereignty invoked by the modern, secular nation-state in fact has its roots in the fundamentally theological, wholly deconstructible logic of a unitary, autonomous sovereign who, in the end, resembles God. This same logic, I have noted, governs the concept of the individual. Accordingly, he repeatedly indicates that psychoanalysis marks one of the places where the critique of sovereignty is already underway. As Derrida put it in his most sustained treatment of Freud in this period, his 2000 address to the States General of Psychoanalysis ("Psychoanalysis Searches the States of Its Soul: The Impossible Beyond of a Sovereign Cruelty"), the principle of sovereignty ultimately stands for "the autonomy and omnipotence of the subject—individual or state—freedom, egological will, conscious intentionality" (WA, 243–44/19).

The notion of sovereignty therefore includes a whole set of concepts that psychoanalysis, from the very beginning in Freud, puts into question. The thought of the unconscious, Derrida notes here and elsewhere, is after all precisely the thought of what undermines and disrupts "the autonomy and omnipotence of the subject" and "egological will." Viewed from this perspective, psychoanalysis appears as a theory and practice devoted to the idea that there is some thing that undercuts individual sovereignty: another system operative in the psyche that determines human thought and action from a place entirely beyond conscious intentionality. It devotes itself to the idea of the unconscious, then, as that which is fundamentally incompatible with, and entirely inaccessible to, egological will. Hence, in "Psychoanalysis Searches," Derrida locates a critique of sovereignty at the very heart of the psychoanalytic movement. "The first gesture of psychoanalysis," he writes, "will have been to explain this sovereignty, to give an account of its ineluctability while aiming to deconstruct its genealogy" (WA, 244/19–20). The critical analysis of sovereignty thus forms a crucial part of what Derrida, in this period, affirms as psychoanalysis's "revolutionary force" (FWT, 172/280). And from the other side, the deconstruction of sovereignty can itself be understood, we have seen, as one way "of taking into account within politics what psychoanalysis once called the unconscious" (R, 110/155).[6]

We see, then, how psychoanalysis represents one of the key sites where the deconstruction of sovereignty is possible. Yet this is not the only way Derrida mobilizes psychoanalysis in this period. In the *Death Penalty* seminars and elsewhere, he points to another way psychoanalysis enables us to rethink contemporary political practice: in its thinking of cruelty, what he ultimately shows is its conceptualization of a kind of intractable tendency toward cruel destructiveness. This line of thinking in fact plays a key role in the deconstruction of the death penalty. In the seminars, Derrida interrogates the juridical and philosophical discourse around capital punishment in order to examine what so often appears as the cruel exercise of sovereign power; and he calls upon psychoanalysis—and once again, Freud—in order to think through just what this term *cruelty* might mean.

Yet the relation between sovereignty and cruelty in this discussion is not as straightforward as one might suspect. In "Psychoanalysis Searches," Derrida underlines forcefully how the issue is not simply that the exercise of sovereignty begets excessive violence and cruelty. Rather, he suggests, sovereignty and cruelty are bound up with one another in the violent, *reactive* response to the deconstruction in progress of sovereignty already underway. It is thus in "those seismic places where the theological phantasm of sovereignty quakes"—those places where it is becoming unstable—"where the most traumatic, let us say . . . the most cruel events of our day are being produced" (WA, 244–45/21).

More to the point, Derrida turns to Freud in these discussions *precisely because* Freud offers a resolutely nonclassical, "non-progressive" understanding of cruelty. That is, Freud rejects the idea that we will ever get rid of cruelty. The Freud Derrida turns to here is the one who refuses the idea that we will ever make real progress on this front. In the dialogue with Roudinesco from the same year as "Psychoanalysis Searches," consequently, Derrida declares flatly that "there is and will be cruelty, among living beings, among men" (*FWT*, 76/126). In this way, Derrida rejects the position implicit in the classical abolitionist critique of the death penalty as an inherently cruel form of punishment. Here cruelty forms a simple excess whose removal or subtraction would leave the principle of sovereign power itself intact. The deconstruction of the death penalty, for its part, seeks to put the principle of sovereignty itself into question.

What Derrida ultimately finds so useful in Freud in these discussions is what he will describe as a thinking of "endless" cruelty—one that ultimately comes back to the thinking of survival at stake in the deconstructive rearticulation of psychoanalysis traced across the first three chapters of this book, its thinking of life as fundamentally bound up with the possibility of violation and destruction. The thought of *survivance* will then be shown to undercut—to exert a kind of critical force upon—the fundamentally theological conception of human life, law, and "the proper to man" at the heart of the death penalty and sovereignty more generally. It comes to serve as *the* crucial lever in Derrida's treatment of the death penalty, what drives deconstruction in its attempt to formulate a new, more "consistent" abolitionism founded on principle (*FWT*, 142/229; see 149/241). The thought of *survival* will thus be shown to destabilize what Derrida shows is the uncritical phantasm at the core of the political theology of the death penalty, the phantasm of a sovereign mastery over finitude and death. In this way, the deconstruction of the death penalty proceeds—in accordance with the deconstructive strategy outlined in chapter 3—not by assailing the conceptual foundations of the death penalty from the outside (whereby it would be said that the death penalty is not the "best" way to protect human life), but rather by locating and bringing forward conceptual components of its edifice that can be shown to be internally fraught. Ultimately, insofar as Derrida turns to Freud in his discussions of the death penalty in order to operationalize survival, the deconstruction of the death penalty, in its full scope, can perhaps best be understood in the terms of emerging out of Derrida's engagement with Freud in this period.[7]

Endless Cruelty

Before turning to Derrida's activation of Freud in this context, it can be helpful to gloss the basic terms of Derrida's engagement with the death penalty in the seminars. First, the deconstruction of the death penalty carried out in the seminars is intended to break, I have said, what Derrida sees as a fatal "alliance" (*DP*, 1:259n25/350n1) between the classical discourse of abolitionism and the most rigorous arguments for the principle of capital punishment. Crucial to this project is the insight that a new, principled abolitionism must be able to mount a challenge on some ground other than a mere preference for life over death, which Derrida repeatedly shows is insufficient, for the simple reason that it is precisely in the name of life that the proponents of capital punishment (philosophical or otherwise) advocate its necessity. A fundamental interest in life always "risks being shared, in truth, by the supporters of the death penalty," as he puts it, insofar as "'it is in order to protect life, it is in the name of life,' they would say, 'that we urge, in certain cases, the death penalty against those who do not respect life'" (*DP*, 1:255/345–46). Thus, "in order to make the case for abolitionism against this argument, one must demonstrate that the death penalty is not the 'best' means of protecting or affirming the primacy of life" (*DP*, 1:255/346), a claim Derrida shows will always founder on basic, fundamentally undecidable questions concerning its usefulness and efficacy as a deterrent. Hence, Derrida spends quite a bit of time on the inherent slippage between the death penalty as deterrent and as pathological attraction.

Perhaps the most fragile, deconstructible component in the classical discourse of abolitionism for Derrida is its conception of cruelty, and alongside it, the ban, enshrined in the US Constitution and in the international Declaration of Human Rights, on cruel punishment and inhumane treatment. The notion of cruelty as barbaric excess is consistently invoked in the modern discourse of human rights and in the classical humanist arguments against the death penalty, but it is equally crucial, Derrida underscores, to the various efforts aimed at refining and justifying the practice of capital punishment in the modern era. It is in fact central, Derrida shows, to the modern history of the death penalty in Europe and the United States. This history is largely defined, after all, by the development and implementation of ever more "humane" techniques and machines for putting to death, from the "humanitarian" (*DP*, 1:192/268) machine of the guillotine on—a machine whose invention relies, from the very beginning, on the logic of humane death as death without cruelty and with a minimum of bloodshed, what Derrida calls an "anesthesial" logic (*DP*, 1:49/83). This history then runs all the way up to the electric chair, the gas chamber, and lethal injection.[8] The project of attenuating cruelty is thus precisely what abolitionism and the modern apparatus of the death penalty share, where they are once again "in alliance." The humanitarian call to put an end to excessive cruelty is found on both sides.

Indeed, one of Derrida's central arguments in the seminars is that the massive philosophical and juridical discourse devoted to upholding the death penalty has in fact always been indebted to the same logic of progressive advancement informing abolitionism. On this view, both the discourse in favor of the death penalty and the discourse militating against it answer to an archeo-teleological, Enlightenment ideal of progress.[9] Hence the death penalty has a stranglehold on the very notion of progress that would seem to point toward its eclipse.[10] Derrida underscores this fact insofar as he acknowledges that, at the time he is speaking, the practice of capital punishment is by all appearances and measures on the decline in the West and around the globe. In the final session of the second year, for instance, Derrida is explicit that his analysis necessarily approaches "the question of the death penalty" from the position where "at this end of the twentieth century and the beginning of the twenty-first [it] is posed differently," given that there is "a progressive, accelerated abolition of the death penalty on the surface of the earth" (*DP*, 2:261/348). The position of deconstruction in this inquiry is thus undeniably marked, he continues, by the fact that "there is a movement underway, and it is easy to think that it is irreversible" (*DP*, 2:261/348). But even as deconstruction is marked in this way, it is wary of such a view, insofar as if his diagnosis of the fatal alliance between modern abolitionism and the death penalty is correct, it will be necessary to challenge the basic logic of progressive advancement underpinning both.

Yet the deepest reason the abolitionist appeal to the death penalty's inherent cruelty is deconstructible is that, as Derrida demonstrates in the first year of the *Death Penalty* seminars, quite simply, there has never been a rigorous concept of cruelty. Cruelty, rather, has always been the site of a fundamental equivocation or slippage. This is one of Derrida's most explicit themes in "Psychoanalysis Searches," where he highlights the modern history of the death penalty in the United States in particular, most notably the moratorium on executions imposed by the US Supreme Court in 1972. This moratorium would not be lifted, Derrida recalls, until the exercise of capital punishment could be brought into line with the Constitutional ban on cruel and unusual punishment. Recounting this history, he concludes with a question:

Throughout all this history I have just evoked, from the American Constitution to modern international declarations, as in the discourse of common *doxa* for centuries, before and after Sade, it is the obscure word *cruelty* that concentrates all the equivocations. What does "cruel" mean? Do we have, did Freud have a rigorous concept of the cruelty that, like Nietzsche, he spoke of so much (as regards the death drive, the aggression drive, or sadism, etc.)? Where does cruelty begin and end? (WA, 262–63/55–56)

Derrida's aim in raising such questions, however, is not simply to suggest that the classical and contemporary abolitionist arguments against the cruelty of the death penalty remain inadequate. Rather, his aim is to take on the most formidable attempts to think, and justify, the origin and necessity of the death penalty. Crucially, however, he will do so not by simply abandoning the pseudo-concept of cruelty but by attempting to think through, as rigorously as possible, the fundamental equivocation it names.

Thus, if Freudian psychoanalysis has a role to play here, it is because, for Derrida, *only psychoanalysis* attempts to seriously analyze what this word *cruelty* means, beginning with Freud himself. Indeed, in his sociological writings, Freud returned fairly regularly to what he saw as a fundamental tendency toward cruelty and destruction in human beings, one associated in his thinking with the death drive. As Freud conceptualizes it from 1920 on (beginning with *Beyond the Pleasure Principle*), the death drive is first and foremost a drive toward self-destruction, but when it is redirected and turned outward toward external "objects" (another subject can be one such object), it can take the form of a tendency toward aggressive destructiveness (SE, 18:54). This is in fact, Freud suggests, the only way the death drive becomes perceptible. The death drive, he says, operates in absolute silence (see chapter 2); this is how Freud describes the fact that the death drive has no psychical representatives through which somatic excitation coming from the body is given psychical form. Thus, the most visible form the death drive ever takes, Freud suggests in a number of places, is that of a purely "aggressive or destructive drive" (SE, 22:209).

Moreover, despite the marked silence coming from the institution of psychoanalysis on the apparent links between sovereignty and cruelty, Freud himself speaks to just this issue. In fact, in a small handful of places, Freud theorizes that there may be a drive underlying the cruel exercise of sovereign power: a fundamental drive in human beings for mastery or power, what he calls *Bemächtigungstrieb*. In "Psychoanalysis Searches," Derrida glosses it as "a drive for ascendancy, for power, for possession" (WA, 258/47), or alternately, a "drive for power or for sovereign mastery" (WA, 241/14).[11]

As I note in chapter 2, Freud first speculates on the possibility of such a drive fairly early on in *Beyond the Pleasure Principle*, in an easily overlooked passage highlighted by Derrida in "To Speculate" (in a section added to the 1975–76 *Life Death* seminar).[12] At the close of the discussion of the child's game of *fort/da*, Freud hypothesizes that the game provides evidence of a previously unidentified, self-standing drive for mastery operating to some degree independently of the pleasure principle—in this particular instance, a drive directed at mastering and domesticating disturbing psychic material, so that it can be energetically bound and discharged. The possibility of a tendency toward mastery thus offers the very first glimpse of a "beyond of the pleasure principle" in Freud. Yet this hypothesis is left undeveloped in *Beyond the Pleasure Principle*.

In the writings published after 1920, moreover, Freud seems to offer a different account. In his writings on "civilization," war, and violence, he takes special note of the propensity to assert and wield dominance among human beings, and speculates that *Bemächtigungstrieb* is one instance of the ineradicable tendency toward aggressivity and destruction associated with the death drive. On this account, rather than a separate, autonomous drive, we once again have the death drive turned outward, on other subjects. Viewed from this perspective, *Bemächtigungstrieb* is the name for a special drive toward cruel domination, yet one that apparently derives its force from the even more primary tendency named the death drive.

We now begin to see why for Derrida psychoanalysis, having posited an unshakable tendency toward mastery and cruelty in human beings, toward making or letting another suffer, is uniquely positioned to understand the link between sovereignty and cruelty. On one hand, while making or letting another suffer cruelly can entail bloodshed—the word *cruelty* itself, Derrida notes, necessarily invokes a "history of spilled blood (*cruor, crudus, crudelitas*)" (WA, 239/10)—there is another form of cruelty that never entails shedding blood: psychic cruelty. Here psychoanalysis offers powerful resources, enabling us to provide an account of the specifically psychical dimension of cruel violence and forms of suffering that go beyond visible trauma. At the same time, psychoanalysis, having set out to think what in the human subject is absolutely heterogeneous to egological will and conscious intentionality, would offer a key means of thinking the perverse, hidden propensity for making or letting another suffer, "*just for,* if one can still say that, the pleasure of suffering" (WA, 239/10). In *For What Tomorrow*, Derrida points to the importance of just this thought, saying that cruelty "no doubt is essentially psychical" (*FWT*, 142/229). Given this fact, Derrida seems to suggest, only psychoanalysis in the end would be in a position to think the possibility of what, to philosophy, has so often appeared as the most radical evil: pleasure in cruelty, "psychic pleasure in evil for evil's sake" (WA, 238/10). At the very least, even if psychoanalysis were not "the only way that could allow us, if not to know, if not to think even, at least to interrogate what might be meant by this strange and familiar word 'cruelty,' the worst cruelty, suffering *just to* suffer . . . one could no longer anticipate doing so without psychoanalysis" (WA, 239/11).

In "Psychoanalysis Searches," Derrida goes so far as to risk a hypothesis: cruelty might just be the most "irreducible thing in the life of the animate being" (WA, 239/12). Such a hypothesis, he underscores, already appeals in and of itself to psychoanalysis:

> If there is something irreducible in the life of the living being . . . and if this irreducible thing in the life of the animate being is indeed the possibility of cruelty (the drive, if you will, of evil for evil, of a suffering that would play at enjoying the suffering of a making-suffer or a making-oneself-suffer *for the pleasure of it*), then no other discourse— be it theological, metaphysical, genetic, physicalist, cognitivist, and so forth—could open itself up to this hypothesis. They would all be designed to reduce it, exclude it, deprive it of sense. The only discourse that can today claim the thing of psychical suffering as its own affair would indeed be what has been called, for about a century, psychoanalysis. Psychoanalysis would perhaps not be the only possible language or even the only possible treatment regarding this cruelty. . . . But "psychoanalysis" would be the name of that which, without theological or other alibi, would be turned toward what is most *proper* to psychical cruelty. Psychoanalysis, for me . . . would be the name for the "without alibi." The confession of a "without alibi." (WA, 239–40/12–13)

For Derrida, only psychoanalysis is capable of wrestling with this thought of cruelty, refusing to minimize it or banish it from the space of thought as the most radical evil.[13] Indeed, the thought of cruelty might just be psychoanalysis's "ultimate ground" (WA, 239/11) he suggests at one point, its most fundamental insight. And it is precisely in this way that psychoanalysis names the "without alibi": in its refusal to dismiss, or domesticate, the thought of cruelty in living beings. To the contrary, psychoanalysis pushes this thought as far as it will go, opening up a radical thinking of cruelty understood in terms of an absolutely irreducible "*cruel* drive of destruction or annihilation" at the very heart of the human being (WA, 240–41/14). Hence psychoanalysis's refusal of any "theological or humanist alibi" (FWT, 173/281) that would dream of surmounting or eliminating the tendency towards cruelty.

Derrida's interest, however, ultimately lies less in affirming that there is some drive for sovereign mastery operative in human affairs than in what the figure of the *Bemächtigungstrieb* in Freud seems to suggest: an absolutely irreducible tendency toward aggressive, sovereign cruelty.[14] In this way, Derrida suggests, psychoanalysis opens up a thinking of "endless" cruelty. On one hand, cruelty that is absolutely ineradicable is "endless" in a temporal sense: it will never be gotten rid of in some progressive future. Cruelty, this "irreducible thing in the life of the living being," will never be eliminated. "One can staunch bloody cruelty," Derrida writes, "one can put an end to murder by blade, by the guillotine, in the classical or modern theaters of bloody war, but, according to Nietzsche or Freud, a psychic cruelty will always take its place by inventing new resources" (*WA*, 239/10). He then underlines this notion in *For What Tomorrow*, where, as we saw, he states simply that "there is and will be cruelty, among living beings, among men" (*FWT*, 76/126). Yet on the other hand, "endless cruelty" is "without limit," "without opposable term" (*WA*, 239/10) as Derrida puts it. The Freud Derrida turns to in "Psychoanalysis Searches," is above all the Freud who conceptualizes cruelty in precisely this way, the one who thinks, "like the Nietzsche of *Genealogy of Morals*, that cruelty *has no contrary*, that it is tied to the essence of life and the will to power" (*WA*, 271/72, my emphasis).[15]

In the *Death Penalty* seminars Derrida fleshes out the implications of this thought. Such a notion of cruelty, he demonstrates there, in effect begins to shake up the sedimentary discourse around the death penalty, on both sides. This is first of all because, as we have seen, each side is in fact indebted to a progressive, humanitarian ideal of putting an end to barbarity and cruel suffering. The notion of endless cruelty "without opposable term," which takes as seriously as possible the fundamental equivocation at the heart of this concept, is thus shown to have a destabilizing effect on the classical discourse around the death penalty in its totality.[16]

Psychoanalysis, we could now say following Derrida, goes some way in recognizing, reflecting on, or opening up just this slippage, the equivocation at work in any possible thinking of cruelty. Because it posits cruelty as something that is absolutely original, and thus irreducible and ineradicable, it issues one of the most serious challenges to the classical discourse around the death penalty, indebted as it is, on both sides, to a certain set of progressive, Enlightenment ideals. If, as Freud suggests, cruelty has no contrary, "there are only differences in cruelty, differences in modality, quality, intensity, activity, or reactivity within a *same* cruelty" (*WA*, 271/73). And in this way, the rigorous thinking of cruelty found in psychoanalysis, carries a kind of deconstructive force, destabilizing and putting into question the classical discourse on capital punishment.

The Death Penalty and *Survivance*

Yet, beyond this, the notion of endless cruelty Derrida finds in Freud makes possible an even more powerful critique of the death penalty. It in fact opens the way for a new deconstructive abolitionism. As we are about to see, this is because Freud's thinking of cruelty in fact opens onto a particular thinking of *survivance*, one in which destructive cruelty is understood as ultimately inseparable from life, from "the life of the living being" as Derrida puts it in the passage cited above.

Viewed from this perspective, Freud's most revolutionary gesture is the one whereby he thinks the possibility of cruelty and destruction—everything he associates with the radically disruptive force of the death drive—not as trespassing on life from the outside, supervening on it, but rather as absolutely inseparable from it. As we have seen, if the death drive is originary and present in the living being from the very first, the threat of cruel destruction in Freud is inextricable from "what is most alive in life" (*RP*, 118/146). Freud's thinking on the absolutely irreducible presence of a destructive death drive in life emerges here as one of the key ways of conceptualizing the deconstructive thought of survival, the thought of which Derrida suggests ultimately drives deconstruction in its contestation of the death penalty. Indeed, the thought of survival serves as *the* critical lever in the deconstruction of the death penalty. It will ultimately make possible the deconstructive critique of the death penalty *as phantasm*.

Hence, in the penultimate session of the first year of the *Death Penalty* seminars, Derrida suggests that just such a thinking of life forms the ultimate ground of deconstruction in taking on the death penalty. There, drawing together the various threads of the multipronged attack he has to set to work to this point, Derrida addresses clearly and explicitly what motivated his interest in taking on the death penalty, "what interest there was in being an abolitionist, in militating for the abolition of the death penalty" (*DP*, 1:254/345). More specifically, he addresses head-on the question of whether a deconstructive abolitionism "must be as *disinterested* as the supporter of the death penalty in the Kantian logic of the categorical imperative" (*DP*, 1:254/345). And on these questions, Derrida is quite clear: staking out a position directly opposed to Kant's, he confesses an unmistakable interest in, a deep commitment to, life. "I say straight on: yes, I am against the death penalty because I want to save my neck, to save the life I love, what I love to live, what I love living. And when I say 'I,' of course, I mean 'I,' me, but also the 'I,' the 'me,' whoever says 'I' in its place or mine. That is my interest, the ultimate resource of my interest as of *any possible interest* in the end of the death penalty" (*DP*, 1:254–55/345, my emphasis). But because this interest is shared by the supporters of the death penalty—as we have seen, "'it is in order to protect life, it is in the name of life,' they would say, 'that we urge, in certain cases, the death penalty against those who do not respect life'" (*DP*, 1:255/346)—what Derrida has in mind here has to be understood in terms of another figure of interest. A deconstructive abolitionism, like any other, must have a fundamental stake, he insists, it must have some interest, but this interest must be defined otherwise than in terms of the simple interest in *protecting* life: "the abolitionist struggle, in my view, must still be driven; it cannot not be driven, motivated, justified by an interest, but by another interest, by another figure of interest that remains to be defined" (*DP*, 1:255/346).

He then goes on to define as the ultimate source of deconstruction's interest in putting an end to the death penalty a thinking of life as what simply cannot be protected: a thinking of life as survival. Life thought as survival cannot be protected because it is always already threatened and penetrated by death from the very beginning. The critical lever in deconstruction's contestation of the death penalty—the one that allows it to bring out the blind spot within what Derrida will show is the phantasm of mastering death at the heart of the death penalty said to be what is "proper to man"—is its conception of mortal finitude.

This is because the thought of survival fundamentally undercuts the notion of a specifically human form of life beyond life at the core of the political theology of the death penalty, the one contained in what Derrida calls *the* "classic philosopheme of all the great philosophies of right that have favored the death penalty," the philosopheme at the center of the most formidable justifications for the principle of the death penalty (*DP*, 1:116/170, trans. mod.).[17] Derrida's key move is to show that, contrary to what abolitionists such as Hugo would have us believe (see *DP*, 1:194–95/270), the classical philosophical justifications for the death penalty do not entail a devaluation of life—failing to appreciably weigh the true value of the human person in the application of the law, say— but, rather, a deep commitment to the infinite value of human life. As Derrida notes quite often in the first year of the *Death Penalty* seminars, this is precisely what makes the classical philosophical discourse favorable to the death penalty so formidable, from Kant on. At the heart of the longstanding philosophical and political discourse supporting the death penalty, he demonstrates, is not the devaluation of human life but, rather, its hypervaluation—what Derrida describes as a kind of "infinitization" of human finitude—whereby the humanity of the human is said to carry an absolutely priceless, transcendental value that extends beyond his or her mortal finitude (*DP*, 1:258/349). From Kant to Hegel and beyond, in all the "great philosophies of right," Derrida shows, the death penalty is posited precisely as what is "proper to man" insofar as it is understood as the exemplary example of the process whereby "man" puts his biological life on the line in the establishment of the law, risks his life in view of something *more valuable* than mere life (*FWT*, 147/239).

It is this supposed capacity to raise himself above, to transcend and go beyond, his creaturely attachment to biological life, to mere survival or mortality, that lends the human a special dignity and differentiates the properly human realm, subject to the law, from that of the animal. On this view, it is a sign of humankind's enlightenment and its singular access to reason that "man" can raise himself above his attachment to biological life and acknowledge the necessity of the law, and the death penalty, for justice. The ability to recognize the death penalty is here a key part not just of what it means to be an enlightened rational being but to be human (viewed in contradistinction to the animal, which, supposedly lacking access to reason, lacks the capacity to submit its will to the rule of law). This is the ultimate reason Derrida says that "the question of the death penalty could well be the best and most indispensable introduction to the question, what is Enlightenment?" (*DP*, 1:179/252).

In the fourth session of the first year of the *Death Penalty* seminars, Derrida lays out most clearly the kernel of the logic underwriting the death penalty.

> The dignity of man, his sovereignty, the sign that he accedes to universal right and rises above animality is that he rises above biological life, puts his life in play in the law, risks his life and thus affirms his sovereignty as subject or consciousness. A code of law that would refrain from inscribing the death penalty within it would not be a code of law; it would not be a human law, it would not be a law worthy of human dignity. It would not be a law. The very idea of law implies that something is worth more than life [*quelque chose vaut plus que la vie*]. (*DP*, 1:116/170)

What is "worth more than life" here is, precisely, a form of sovereignty proper to the human, its capacity to make the law.[18] It is "worth more" than mere life insofar as, here, the human risks his life for something that outstrips the basic attachment to biological life and mere survival, the form of attachment supposedly characteristic of the animal. The putative willingness to risk his or her life in view of the law is, in turn, what lends the human a special dignity inaccessible to the animal, what raises him or her above the form of living focused only on survival. This is, once again (given how important it is, the point bears repeating), why Derrida theorizes the death penalty not as just one case among others in the field of law but as the very emblem of law in general, as human law. Indeed, insofar as, here, risking life in the establishment of the law opens onto what defines the very humanity of the human, Derrida can justifiably say that the question of the death penalty is perhaps *the* key way of accessing the "proper to man," Derrida's name for the inherited notion of something quintessentially defining the human in contradistinction to the animal (*DP*, 1:1/23).

Crucially, within the logic of this classical philosopheme, the humanity of the human, his or her priceless dignity, is situated entirely beyond his or her biological life; it transcends biological life. The dignity of the human, entirely beyond his or her mortal being, is thus understood as absolutely inviolable, untouched even by death. Hence Derrida can describe the concept of the human (the particular thought of human life) at the base of the death penalty as a fundamentally *theological* concept. It is not explicitly religious, in Kant for example, but it is, as Derrida suggests, theological *in its structure*, insofar as the human's infinite dignity here resembles a kind of infinite life of the spirit. More to the point, drawing on the definition of religion offered in "Faith and Knowledge," the dignity of the human, we can now see, is understood as absolutely safe and sound, located in a realm entirely beyond that of mortal finitude, immune to all possible contamination or destruction. The deconstruction of the death penalty thus consists, in large part, in demonstrating that this idea of life is, like the notion of sovereignty itself, a phantasm—a particularly powerful fantasy or idealization founded on the disavowal of mortality and finitude.

Viewed from this perspective, the logic underwriting the death penalty and classical abolitionism are, at bottom, isomorphic, "welded" together (to borrow the figure of the *"soude"* from *For What Tomorrow*) at a crucial point, beyond their joint mobilization of the logic of progress (*FWT*, 147/239). They are both reliant on the foundational notion of the human as essentially defined in terms of "something worth more than life," something of unimpeachable value transcending mere biological life or survival. This is, in both cases, "man's" intrinsic humanity or dignity, what gives the human a fundamental, inviolable, sovereign *right* to life. It is precisely this quality of the human that is then said to be affirmed when, in certain cases, in order to redress an injury to the community the state puts an end to the biological life of the condemned while respecting and caring for his or her essential humanity, ensuring that the he or she receives a certifiably "humane" execution. The specifically human form of life, here, carries with it a certain inviolability and sanctity and exceeds mortal finitude: it is, ultimately, a form of superlife beyond life.

So long as abolitionism remains bound to what we can now see is an essentially theological notion of a specifically human form of life beyond finitude, it will remain bound to the logic underwriting the death penalty. The principle abolitionism would seek to mobilize against capital punishment will always be found at the core of the classical philosophical arguments *for* the death penalty. While acknowledging the importance of the modern abolitionist movement in the West, we can now say that it is precisely its failure to rid itself of the vision of something beyond life, the vision it *shares* with the death penalty, that ensures that it will always be "in alliance" with the massive tradition of philosophical discourse hospitable to capital punishment, at the deepest structural level—in the form of an unthought, and thus fatal, solidarity.[19]

It is just this notion of a specifically human form of life transcending finitude that deconstruction seeks to contest in taking on the death penalty. Because to truly take it on, we now begin to see, an alternate conception of life is required. What is required is a concept of life premised not on the notion of its absolute sanctity, its infinite immunity, but rather on its intrinsic violability, its internal exposure to death and destruction. To unsettle the death penalty, we now see, what is required is not the infinitization of life but rather a radical thinking of finitude, one that understands exposure to death not as something that befalls life from the outside, and thus as something that can be immunized against, but rather as what is required for life to be what it is in the first place. On this alternate view, life is understood as continually exposed to the possibility of destruction and violation at every moment, and this exposure is inextricable from the very possibility of life, from the very possibility of survival as living on from one moment to the next. In sum, what is necessary is a "hyper-atheological" (*FWT*, 165/226) thinking of life that rejects the move whereby human life is made into an infinite category, a thinking of finite life in terms of survival. What allows deconstruction to contest the death penalty, then, is its rethinking of life in terms of *survivance*.

In taking on the death penalty, however, deconstruction does not simply underscore the fact of mortal finitude, it radicalizes it; hence the "hyper" in "hyper-atheological." Deconstruction shows that mortality consists not in death encroaching on self-identical, self-perpetuating life from the outside, contaminating it secondarily or eating away at it bit by bit. Rather, mortality—understood in terms of originary exposure to the threat of destruction and the threat of an essentially incalculable death—is theorized *as the very condition of any possible life in general*. Openness to destruction is understood here not just as what happens from moment to moment but as arche-originary, as absolutely necessary for life to be what it is. In short, against the notion of infinite life beyond life underwriting the death penalty, against the notion of human life as absolutely inviolable in its infinite dignity, deconstruction deploys a notion of survival as intrinsically exposed to threat. Indeed, this exposure is thought as the *constitutive* condition of survival: as we have seen, with the thought of *survivance*, a certain exposure to heterogeneity, alterity, and "what is other than life"—and thus to both the incalculable and death—is necessary for life to "be" at all in the first place.

In the *Death Penalty* seminars, Derrida articulates this thought in terms of openness to unmasterable otherness, one we saw in previous chapters is implied in temporalization. Speaking of the thinking life (or survival) he will deploy against death penalty, Derrida says, "I can believe in and affirm what is called life, what I call, what an 'I' calls life, only by setting out from and within a 'my life'" which, necessarily and originarily, "passes by way of the heart of the other" (*DP*, 1:255/346). What does it mean that life has to "pass by way of the heart of the other?" Derrida explains it in terms of the continual openness to fundamentally *incalculable* otherness: "Where 'my life,' be it originarily granted by the heart of the other, is 'my life,' it must keep this relation to the coming of the other as coming of the to-come in the opening of the incalculable and the undecideable. 'My life,' and especially my life insofar as it depends on the heart of the other, cannot affirm itself and affirm its preference except over against this" (*DP*, 1:256/347). Here Derrida offers an alternate description of life as *survival*. Life, in order to be at all, in order to "affirm itself," must be constitutively exposed to alterity—including what is other than life, death—and to an unpredictable future to come, to the incalculable. And it can only persist by "keeping this relation," through an iterative process of deferring absolute closure, what I have called asphyxiation.

The Death Penalty as Phantasm of Mastery

Deconstruction's radical thinking of finitude as survival, I have shown, undermines the essential philosopheme at the core of the death penalty. But the thought of survival equally challenges the practice of the death penalty. This is because the fundamentally theological dimension of the death penalty (that is, its fundamentally phantasmatic character) is in fact reflected in its practice. In the crucial final sessions of the first year of the seminars, Derrida shows that the practice of the death penalty is underwritten by the dream of transcending mortal life by mastering death, of "putting an end to finitude" via a sovereign power of decision over the precise moment of death (*DP*, 1:258/349).

The key insight comes when Derrida shows that what the death penalty deprives one of is not life but finitude. This is because "it belongs to life not necessarily to be immortal but to have a future, thus some life before it, some event to come only where death, the instant of death, is not calculable, is not the object of a calculable decision" (*DP*, 1:256/347). In the final session of year one, Derrida puts it this way: "the supreme form of the paradox, its philosophical form, is that what is ended by the possibility of the death penalty is not the infinity of life or immortality, but on the contrary, the finitude of 'my life'" (*DP*, 1:256/347–48). The "infinite perversity" of the death penalty is that it seeks "to put an end to finitude" (*DP*, 1:257n24/349n1). It belongs to finitude, to finite life, in other words, to have a relation to death where death is not calculable, is fundamentally unpredictable. This is what in fact defines my finitude. But this is precisely what the death penalty puts an end to, or at least tries to, by specifying the exact moment of death.

The basic logic of the death penalty as a practice, then, is predicated, we begin to see, on the dream, the phantasm, of going beyond finitude by putting an end to it, of achieving absolute mastery over the time of human life. "The calculating decision, by putting an end to life, seems, paradoxically, to put an end to finitude," Derrida writes; "it masters the future; it protects against the irruption of the other" (*DP*, 1:258/349). Just as the principle of the death penalty is justified on the basis of a vision of life beyond mortal finitude, its practice is motivated by the dream of securing a kind of infinite life by transcending finitude itself. Underpinning the death penalty in its totality, we begin to see, is "the dream of an infinitization and thus of an infinite survival" (*DP*, 1:258/349). Putting an end to finitude seems to secure infinite life, an "infinite survival."[20]

But this vision of infinite survival is but a phantasm. What allows deconstruction to show up the blind spot in this phantasm is, precisely, its thinking of survival, its thinking of the incalculable and the relation to the other as inscribed in the very heart of "my life" (*DP*, 1:256/347). It is on the basis of this thought that the death penalty appears as a deconstructible phantasm, as a stillborn attempt to master death as such. It is from this perspective that Derrida is able to say that the "calculating decision, by putting an end to life, seems, paradoxically, to put an end to finitude; it affirms its power over time; it masters the future; it protects against the irruption of the other. In any case, it *seems* to do that, I say; it only seems to do that, for this calculation, this mastery, this decidability, remain phantasms" (*DP*, 1:258/349). Once life is thought in terms of survival and the opening to the incalculable future, this calculating decision appears as uncritical and impossible, a powerful fantasy producing a kind of truth effect.

Further, it can be demonstrated that the death penalty, as calculable decision with respect to the precise time of death, is not operative in the instant that it thinks it is. The calculable moment of death in fact always remains, structurally, necessarily, fugitive. In the first year of the seminars, Derrida pursues this very demonstration, first, via the philosophical argument whereby "what separates a state of death from a state of life" can be shown to be predicated on a wholly deconstructible precomprehension of death (*DP*, 1:237–38/323–24). It can be demonstrated, on the basis of the thought of the trace as spacing, that the notion of an absolutely determinable instant of death does not hold, and thus the death penalty never succeeds in its own most essential function.[21] As David Wills has suggested, it can perhaps put to death, but it will never function *as penalty* if it cannot deliver, cannot give, the calculable moment of death it seeks to impose.[22] More importantly, if a calculable moment of death is impossible, the death penalty will never make good on its phantasmatic promise of mastering death, and thereby ensuring "an infinite survival."[23]

The Most Freudian Freud

The deconstruction of the deep structure of the death penalty, the deconstruction of the phantasm of mastering death itself, we have now seen, necessarily calls upon a radical thinking of finitude as survival, whereby mortality is inscribed in the very heart of "my life." It is precisely this thinking of finitude, that Derrida finds in Freud in the end, in Freud's thinking of an absolutely indestructible tendency toward cruel aggressivity.

This is what emerges from the reading of Freud offered in "Psychoanalysis Searches." There, Derrida speaks more explicitly than he does in the *Death Penalty* seminars of deconstruction's affirmation of "an unconditional without sovereignty, and thus without cruelty" as intimately intertwined with a certain thinking of a "*sur-vival* that owes nothing to the alibi of some mytho-theological beyond" (WA, 276/83). If there is an alliance in Derrida between deconstruction and psychoanalysis in taking on the death penalty, as Elizabeth Rottenberg has suggested, it emerges most forcefully here, in the manner Freud thinks life in terms echoing the thought of survival.[24]

Crucial here is Derrida's reading of Freud on war and violence in "Why War?" Revisiting Derrida's treatment of Freud in "Psychoanalysis Searches" in light of everything we have seen developed in the *Death Penalty* seminars, what stands out most clearly is Derrida's emphasis on Freud's pessimism and the way he theorizes the life and death in "Why War?" Indeed, Derrida repeatedly underlines Freud's "radical absence of illusion" (WA, 271/72), specifically Freud's insistence on the impossibility of ever doing away with the fundamental tendency toward destruction and cruelty in human beings. Even if we should continually try to counter this tendency, Freud argues, it will never be eradicated; it will always come back, because it is, quite simply, irreducible, inherent in every human being. It can only ever be a question of finding ways of diverting this tendency and the destructiveness of the death drive, he suggests, submitting it as much as possible to "the dictatorship of reason" such that it might be redirected (SE, 22:213). Derrida glosses Freud's remarks this way: "Making very frequent use of the words 'cruelty,' 'aggression drive,' 'hatred drive,' and 'death drive,' he denounces an illusion: that of the eradication of the cruelty drives and the drives for power and sovereignty. What *it is necessary* to cultivate (for it is necessary that an 'it is necessary,' and thus the tie of an ethical, juridical, political obligation, take shape) is a differential transaction, an economy of detour and difference, the strategy, one can even say method . . . of *indirect* progress: an indirect way of combating the cruelty drive" (WA, 271/72).[25]

It is at this point, Derrida underscores, that "Freud's argumentation in 'Why War?' becomes at once more political and, in its logic, more rigorously psychoanalytic" (WA, 269/69). Why? Because at the precise moment Freud suggests that we have a collective obligation to combat the cruelty drive, he hastens to add that the life of the drives, including the cruelty drive associated with the death drive, cannot for all that be hastily submitted to "ethical judgments of good and evil" (SE, 22:209). Life simply cannot do without them. For Freud, the destructive drives, along with Eros or the life drives, are intrinsic to the very possibility of life itself: in Derrida's words, "he knows that there is no life without the competition between the forces of two antagonistic drives" (WA, 273/76). Freud even makes this explicit. "Neither of these instincts," he writes, "is any less essential than the other; the phenomena of life arise from the concurrent or mutually opposing action of both" (SE, 22:209).

According to "the most rigorously psychoanalytic" thinking of the relation between cruelty and life, there is no safeguarding life from the threat of violation and destruction, because life itself is absolutely inextricable from this possibility. The notion of life found in Freud points toward what Derrida calls the only life "that *is worthy* of being lived, without alibi," and thus, "the only one from which to depart . . . for a possible thinking of life" (WA, 276/82–83). Yet Freud himself seems not to grasp the consequences. As Derrida demonstrates, at the very moment Freud emphasizes the unavoidable necessity of learning to live with the destructive drives, he retreats from this thought, suggesting that pacifism such as his own and Einstein's ultimately has its roots in an "organic," "constitutional" preference, in some, for life over death (SE, 22:214–15). Despite Freud's insistence on the fact that there is no possibility of being rid of the destructive drives, without which there is no life at all, Derrida writes, "[He] continues . . . to find in life, in organic life, in the self-protective economy of organic life and thus in one of the poles of the polarity, the roots of the whole ethico-political rationality in whose name he proposes to subjugate or restrict the forces of the drives. It is thus by life, by organic life, that he justifies the right to life (therefore implicitly the condemnation not only of war, but of the death penalty . . .)" (WA, 274/78).[26] At this pivotal moment, Freud attempts to found a pacifist position on what amounts to a preference for one set of drives over another. Yet this is a logic Freud's own thinking will always undercut, since according to the most rigorously psychoanalytic thinking of life and the drives—according to the most rigorously Freudian reading of Freud—there is no life at all without the death and destruction drives, without the threat of destruction and violation.

The notion of life traced in the most rigorously psychoanalytic interpretation of Freud, then, we begin to see, opens onto the thought of *survivance*. Near the end of "Psychoanalysis Searches," Derrida offers a final description of this conception of mortal life:

> An im-possible life, no doubt, a sur-vival, not symbolizable, but the only one that *is worthy* of being lived, without alibi, once and for all, the only one from which to depart (notice I say from which *to depart*) for a possible thinking of life. Of a life that is still worthy of being lived, once and for all. One cannot justify a pacifism, for example, and the *right* to life, in a radical fashion, by setting out from an *economy of life*, or from what Freud alleges . . . under the names of a biological constitution or an idiosyncrasy. This can only be done on the basis of a *sur-vival* that owes nothing to the alibi of some mytho-theological beyond. (WA, 276/82–83)

The critique of the theological phantasm of superlife, and thus the death penalty, that Freud begins to open up entails a commitment to life, but specifically to a notion of life "without theological or humanist alibi," to a "hyper-atheological" thinking of finite life as survival.[27]

Conclusion: The Death Penalty, the Theologico-Political, and the Future

To conclude, let me return to what I said at the outset of this chapter: we need to understand more properly how the deconstruction of the death penalty provides a crucial point of entry for a deconstructive contestation of the theologico-political generally. In so doing, I will demonstrate that the topic of this final chapter, in considering Derrida's engagement with the death penalty on the heels of a broader discussion of normativity in deconstruction, has far greater importance than it might seem. This will shed additional light on the structure of chapters 4 and 5 in this book. Stated succinctly, in turning to the question of the death penalty, this book is doing anything but taking up a mere "case" or "example" of deconstruction's political implications. In fact, the death penalty is no mere case or example for deep philosophical reasons intimately connected to the argument developed across the entirety of this book.

This is because, when we pay close attention to what Derrida is doing in his treatment of the death penalty, we see that it is the key to a deconstruction of our inherited conception of the political in general. The death penalty is not just the exemplary example of sovereignty in action but rather the absolutely necessary point of access to a broader deconstruction of the dominant configuration of the political, now revealed to be fundamentally theological in origin. What we have seen Derrida describe as the essentially theological structure of the death penalty—whereby a vision of superlife beyond life is thought to be what is "proper to man"—is, we now begin to see, a crystallization of the logic at the heart of our inherited conception of the political, *understood as the theologico-political*. The deconstruction of the death penalty is thus what makes possible a strategic deconstruction of the theologico-political in its totality, insofar as the death penalty brings together the theological (the terrain of religion) and the putatively secular concept of the political. It is *the* singular point of their conjunction, and thus a destabilization of the death penalty effects a concomitant destabilization of the political as the theologico-political more generally. This is the structure Derrida is ultimately taking aim at in taking on the death penalty, even if he has an avowed interest in seeking the end of capital punishment in the United States and around the world.

We see this when we look back on the ground we have covered to this point. As discussed in chapter 4, in the crucial essay "Faith and Knowledge" Derrida contends that the notion of something absolutely safe and sound beyond finitude is the very essence of religion and thus of the theological. If this is the case, the mobilization of a notion of superlife beyond finitude we have now seen as absolutely critical to the death penalty is the sign that, with capital punishment, we are in the terrain of the properly theological. We then see how the theological underpins a key form of political practice.

But much more importantly, in analyzing the principle of the death penalty, we see how the theological penetrates the political *in toto*, and thus why it is deconstructible. We see that the political is in fact marked, in its very foundations, by an importation of the theological into its domain—to such an extent that, after the supposed secularization of political concepts in modernity, after the supposed waning of religion, there are in fact not two domains under consideration here but one, the domain of the theologico-political.[28] This is why, in a crucial discussion in the *Death Penalty* seminars, Derrida characterizes the death penalty not as just one example, or case, among others in the field of penal law, but rather as the very "hyphen in the theologico-political [*trait d'union du théoligico-politique*]," the very thing that constitutes their point of contact (*DP*, 1:23/49).[29] Or again, this is why, in *For What Tomorrow*, he describes the death penalty as the very "keystone, or if you prefer, the cement, the weld" holding together the theological (fundamentally indebted to the dream of something beyond finitude) and the political (*FWT*, 148/240).[30]

Indeed, the principle of the death penalty conceived as a key feature of human law is not just any principle. It is, rather, the political principle par excellence, Derrida shows us. As we have seen, the death penalty draws, for its power, on the foundational notion that the human is unique in the capacity to raise itself above survival in submission to the law, the process whereby it puts biological life on the line in view of something worth more than life. On this view, the human is the uniquely political animal because the properly political community is subject to the law, whereas the living-together of "the animal" is pre-political. The key point to emphasize here is it is not enough to say that the death penalty instantiates this humanist idea of the political realm, the realm of law, as what is "proper to man." This humanist idea is *the* idea of the political, the idea of the political we have inherited from the tradition. The death penalty is not an instance of this idea, it is the very thing on the basis of which it is possible to think this idea in the first place.

The death penalty, traditionally, is in fact the only way to think what is "proper to man," the human defined as political being. This is why, in the second year of the seminars, Derrida will say that "the question of the death penalty is none other than the question of the human" (*DP*, 2:210/281). The very property of humanity is always thought in terms of how the human ascends to political life out of mere animal life, and via a kind of sacrifice, the sacrifice of life in view of something worth more than life (in this case, the establishment of the law).[31] Hence Derrida's description in the 1999–2000 seminars of how we are to think of the relation between the theologico-political as such and the death penalty:

> We must not suppose that we already know what "theologico-political" means and that we have then only to apply this general concept to a particular case or phenomenon named "death penalty." No. Perhaps one must do just the reverse. *One must perhaps proceed in the opposite direction, that is, attempt to think the theologico-political in its possibility beginning from the death penalty.* One would then ask oneself: "What is the theologico-political?" And the answer would take shape

thus: the theologico-political is a system, an apparatus [*dispositif*] of sovereignty in which the death penalty is necessarily inscribed. (*DP*, 1:23/50–51, my emphasis)

The theologico-political in its full scope, we thus begin to see, is in fact only possible on the basis of an idea of the death penalty, on the basis of the idea of the human as the one who is willing to sacrifice biological life in the name of something worth more than life.

But this idea is thoroughly theological, insofar as it brings together, crystallizes, the *two* features of religion as Derrida understands it. The first is, as we saw previously, the dream of superlife. The second, which I have not discussed, is the logic of sacrifice just named. This logic is equally at the very core of religion, Derrida showed in "Faith and Knowledge." This second feature of religion is what Derrida calls its "universal sacrificial vocation" (FK, 86/77): its universal activation of a notion of sacrifice whereby "the living" is sacrificeable—riskable and killable—in view of something, again, worth more than life. Here, "Faith and Knowledge" proleptically points the way toward the *Death Penalty* seminars. Religion, Derrida notes in the earlier essay, with its dream of a form of life absolutely immune to contamination and destruction, always calls for absolute respect for life, via the "'Thou shalt not kill' (at least thy neighbour, if not the living in general)" (FK, 86/77).[32] Yet this absolute respect for life is necessarily premised on the notion that human life has some infinite value entirely distinct from the mere fact of its biological existence. Here, "life has absolute value only if it is worth *more than* life. . . . It is sacred, holy, infinitely respectable only in the name of what is worth more than it and what is not restricted to the naturalness of the bio-zoological (sacrificeable)" (FK, 87/78). Derrida then specifies what is worth more than life: "divinity, the sacrosanctness of the law" (FK, 87/78–79).

In religion, then, respect for life is inseparable from a certain idea of the infinite worth of "anthropo-theological life . . . what ought to remain safe (*heilig*, sacred, safe and sound, unscathed, immune)" (FK, 87/79). The infinite worth of specifically human life here originates in its sacredness, its proximity to the divine and the divine's law. Derrida explicitly notes that this idea is taken over in the history of philosophy as the idea of the infinite dignity of human life, citing Kant as the chief example (FK, 87/79). In religion and whatever discourses inherit this logic, consequently, supposedly merely natural animal, or occasionally human, biological life is sacrificeable in view of this transcendence beyond life plain and simple. And indeed, we have just seen Derrida specify already that one of the things worthy of such sacrifice is, precisely, the sanctity of the law. This law might be originally, in religion, divine, but it is only one small, barely "secular" step further to say the sanctity of the law to which the human alone accedes when it raises itself above its attachment to mere survival and acknowledges the need for the dispensation of justice. It is this ascension, according to the putatively secularized philosopheme analyzed earlier, that in turn lends the human being its transcendent dignity (unafforded to "the animal" who does not submit to the law). The fundamentally religious logic of sacrifice, we then begin to see, is absolutely critical to the "speculative scaffolding" (*FWT*, 148/240) of the death penalty, its fusion of the theological and the political.[33]

Thus, when we play close attention to Derrida's analyses in the *Death Penalty* seminars, we see that the death penalty is driven by the same phantasm that animates religion. The death penalty, I have shown, is ultimately driven by the phantasm of transcending finitude; at its core is the uncritical wish that we could put death to death. In the crucial final sessions of the first year, Derrida goes so far as to suggest that this might even be the fundamental phantasm as deconstruction understands it. As we now know, determining the precise end of life fascinates because of "the end of finitude" it seems to offer, because of "the end of this anxiety before the future that the calculating machine procures. The calculating decision, by putting an end to life, seems, paradoxically, to put an end to finitude . . . it masters the future; it protects against the irruption of the other. In any case, it *seems* to do that" (*DP*, 1:258/349). But then Derrida goes one step further, stating that "it would no doubt be possible to show that this is even the origin of phantasm in general. And perhaps of what is called religion" (*DP*, 1:258/349). It is "the force of this effect of phantasmatic truth that will probably remain forever invincible," he continues, ensuring that the death penalty and the abolitionist protest will always survive, even after full and complete abolition (*DP*, 1:258/350).[34] Going further, Derrida then wagers that, as the most durable, possibly irreducible, fundamental phantasm, the dream of infinite survival is in fact the very source of religion. "For this phantasm of infinitization at the heart of finitude, of an infinitization of survival assured by calculation itself and the cutting decision of the death penalty," he writes, "*this phantasm is one with God*, with, if you prefer, the belief in God, the experience of God, the relation to God, *faith or religion*" (*DP*, 1:258–59/350, my emphasis).

Hence, the deconstructive approach to thinking the death penalty—now understood not just as one case of the theological-political among others, but as the very linchpin of its axiomatic logic—undermines, disturbs, or shakes up the political in its totality, insofar as it is thoroughly theological in origin. And this because our inherited understanding of the political is revealed to be predicated on the phantasmatic wish, the impossible desire, to transcend finitude and put death out of play, to exercise a sovereign mastery over death. The form of deconstructive critique I have now laid out shakes up the whole field of the political as traditionally construed by making the failure or essential fragility of the theologico-political logic of the death penalty, its ultimate "untenability," appear from the inside, as Derrida puts it in *For What Tomorrow*, speaking of the death penalty and Kant's philosophy of right (*FWT*, 150/243).[35]

To the extent that, as I have now demonstrated, the death penalty forms the essence of the political as the theologico-political, Derrida and this book—in contesting the death penalty, in taking up what might have at first appeared to be an issue with fairly limited scope—will have opened up the whole field of the political to transformation.[36] This is the project deconstruction should be seen to have been driving at for some time. It is this project, carried out on the basis of an idea of unconditional survival without sovereignty, that already in Derrida's lifetime connects *Rogues* (in which, again, Derrida says clearly that is in view of "another idea of life" that we must think democracy to come) and the *Death Penalty* and *The Beast and the Sovereign* seminars. It is the fundamentally *political* project, moreover, that drives the contestation of the human-animal distinction in Derrida.[37] This project is, as we have seen, not necessarily better in its results: pointing up the impossibility of the reactive phantasm does not necessarily usher in peace or lesser violence. It in fact insists on exposure to the unpredictable future, which may be exposure to absolute destruction. But it does lay bare the necessity of thinking of the political in terms of unconditional exposure to the incalculable that cannot take the form of mere repetition of the same. And given the durability of the phantasm, this deconstruction is always necessary.

The Derridean project of opening up the political to transformation via the critique of superlife and the dream of something beyond finitude, immune to the threat of contamination and destruction, makes possible new forms of deconstructive critique. It makes possible new deconstructive engagements with political concepts and practices well beyond those associated with easily recognizable forms of sovereign power. It opens, as I have said, onto questions concerning the biopolitical management of the health of specific populations alongside the exposure of others to death, the policing of borders, the supposed right of the nation-state to wage war, responses to international terrorism, and beyond. It equally opens onto questions concerning the prevailing humanist conception of rights and the right to life. In this way, the deconstruction of the death penalty gives deconstruction a future, allowing it to be deployed in new contexts and new conjunctures.

It is my hope that this book, in clarifying this deconstructive gesture, contributes to this future by making possible new projects well beyond those we might have originally foreseen following from Derrida's thought. In tracing the thought of survival at stake in Derrida's engagement with Freud, its aim will have been to give deconstruction the chance of living on in this way—not on account of simple deference to Derrida, but on account of what I hope I have now shown deconstruction can do.

Acknowledgments

This book was written over a span of several years, and I have many to thank for the conversations, suggestions, and encouragement essential to its completion. I am indebted to several family members and friends who supported me throughout the time I worked on this book.

Earlier versions of the introduction and chapters 4 and 5 were presented as talks in the Departments of Philosophy and Political Science at the University of Alberta in 2016 and 2018 and benefited greatly from those conversations and the important questions raised by respondents. Two graduate workshops associated with those talks also contributed substantially to the finished work. An earlier version of chapter 1 was workshopped in the French Philosophy Graduate and Faculty Working Group at Fordham University in 2018, and the insightful suggestions and responses of readers in that group were enormously helpful. I thank the group for the invitation. Discussions at two sessions of the Collegium Phaenomenologicum also contributed to this work, one organized by Michael Naas on "Derrida's Seminars" and one organized by Anne O'Byrne on "Critical Phenomenology." I thank both for the generous invitation to participate. I also thank Walter Brogan and Leonard Lawlor for questions on a portion of chapter 4 presented at the Society for Phenomenology and Existential Philosophy in 2019. Initial versions of this research were also presented at the 2018 Derrida Today conference and the annual conference of the Canadian Society for Continental Philosophy in 2018. An earlier version of some of the arguments in chapter 5 were published in "Derrida and the Death Penalty: The Question of Cruelty," *Philosophy Today* 59, no. 2 (2015): 317–36.

I have benefited from a community of scholars who helped me work through ideas central to this book and provided inspiration throughout. Thanks to Mike

Holohan, Jay Worthy, Júlia Diniz, Mauro Senatore, Neal DeRoo, Rick Elmore, Steven Miller, Penelope Deutscher, Geoffrey Bennington, and especially Catherine Kellogg, who not only provided thoughtful suggestions but also critical support for this project.

I owe an enormous debt, both for his philosophical inspiration and for his concrete contributions and comments on the work presented in this book, to Samir Haddad, who I am privileged to call a friend as well as colleague. I am also sincerely grateful for the contributions of Matthias Fritsch, who reviewed the manuscript in detail for Fordham University Press and, long before that, generously shared his work with me, contributing enormously to my own thinking. A second, anonymous reviewer also provided genuinely helpful feedback on the manuscript.

I would also like to thank Teresa de Lauretis and David Hoy in particular for their support of my scholarship in the past and for giving me the tools to do the work of writing this book. In addition, I could not have written this book without the methods and encouragement of Dorothy Duff Brown. At Fordham University Press, Tom Lay's efforts in shepherding this project to publication contributed to it significantly. Charlotte Houser provided support for the research for this project.

Most especially, I thank Marie-Eve Morin, a true light, for her dazzling insights, her support, and her substantial contributions, and my sister, Alison Trumbull, for a lifetime of help and encouragement.

Notes

Introduction

1. Insofar as this book is focused on probing Derrida's relation to Freud on life and death, it does not take up the question of his relation to the French Freudian Jacques Lacan (though it does gesture toward a more detailed treatment of this relation elsewhere), his treatment of the institution of psychoanalysis (for instance, in "Geopsychoanalysis" in *P*, 318–43/327–52), and his homages to the work of Abraham and Torok, psychoanalysts close to him personally ("Me—Psychoanalysis" in *P*, 129–42/145–58 and *"Fors,"* xi–xlviii). With respect to homages to those close to him, see also Derrida's occasional treatments of the work of René Major (for instance, in "Psychoanalysis Searches the States of Its Soul" in WA) and his engagement with a quasi-psychoanalytic conceptuality in the work of Philippe Lacoue-Labarthe (in "Désistance"). See Derrida, "Désistance," trans. Christopher Fynsk, in *Psyche*, 2:196–230/597–638. This overall scheme describing Derrida's relations to Lacan and to Abraham and Torok apart from his relation to Freud is glossed by Maud Ellmann in "Deconstruction and Psychoanalysis," 211–37. For an abbreviated treatment of Derrida and psychoanalysis generally, see also Rottenberg, "Derrida and Psychoanalysis," 304–20.

2. See Bennington, "Derridabase," and *Not Half No End*; Hägglund, *Radical Atheism*, *Dying for Time*, and "The Trace of Time"; Kirby, *Quantum Anthropologies*, and "Grammatology"; and Vitale, *Biodeconstruction*. Vitale, in particular, has offered a treatment of Derrida's engagement with Freud on life and death, but focuses on the relation between this line of inquiry in Derrida and his thinking's relation to the life sciences. This book offers an alternate account of Derrida's dealings with Freud's thinking in its full scope and pursues its implications. See also McCance, *Reproduction of Life Death*.

3. Rottenberg, *For the Love of Psychoanalysis*, 4–5. For a survey of the earlier secondary literature engaging with Derrida and psychoanalysis, consult the notes of this introduction. See, in particular, Bennington, "Derridabase," 133–48; his chapter "Circanalysis (The thing itself)," in *Interrupting Derrida*, 93–109; *Not Half No End*, 1–7 and 47–64; and his chapter "Mosaic Fragment: If Derrida Were an Egyptian," in *Legislations*, 207–26. See also Bergo, "*Mal D'Archive*," 137–54; Forrester, *Seductions of Psychoanalysis*, 221–42; Hägglund, *Dying for Time*, 110–67; Kamuf, *To Follow*, 178–86; Major, "Derrida, lecteur de Freud et de Lacan," 165–78; Mansfield, *The God Who Deconstructs Himself*, 41–67; Marder, *The Mother in the Age of Mechanical Reproduction*, 37–52; Melville, *Philosophy Beside Itself*, 84–114; Rottenberg, "Intimate Relations: Psychoanalysis Deconstruction," 178–95; Royle, *After Derrida*, 61–84; and Wills, *Inanimation* 2, 55–79. Several scholars also try to put deconstruction into conversation with psychoanalysis in order to supplement the one with the other. See Gaon, *Lucid Vigil*; Hurst, *Derrida vis-à-vis Lacan*; Lewis, *Derrida and Lacan*; Major, *Lacan avec Derrida*; and Willet, "Tropics of Desire."

4. I do not treat every aspect of Derrida's engagement with Freud on the question of death in this book, setting one aspect of it aside in tracking how Derrida develops the logic of life death and in turn, survival. The portion I set aside is Derrida's discussion of mourning in Freud in *Memoires: for Paul de Man*. I have two reasons for doing so: it has been treated already at length by other authors and it is actually less prominent than the other Freudian themes in Derrida's very late work, which I wish to elucidate here. For more details on this dimension of Derrida, see, among others, Bennington and Hägglund. See, in particular, Derrida, *Memoires*; Bennington, "Half-life," in *Not Half No End*, 111–19; and Hägglund, "Reading: Freud, Lacan, Derrida," in *Dying for Time*, 110–45. Furthermore, focusing on Derrida's explicit engagements with Freud, this book does not explore each and every text of Derrida's dealing with psychoanalytic themes, many of which do so in a less explicit fashion. See Derrida, *Clang*, the recent retranslation of *Glas*.

5. *Shaking up* here translates Derrida's frequently cited description of the work of deconstruction as "solicitation" (OG, 25/39).

6. It can be helpful here to provide a very brief overview of Derrida's engagement with Freud. It is, to be sure, largely absent from Derrida's first major publication, his introduction to *Edmund Husserl's Origin of Geometry* (1962), the seminal essays "Genesis and Structure," "Force and Signification," and "Violence and Metaphysics," and the pathbreaking work *Voice and Phenomenon* (1967). Yet the critical texts emerging between 1966 and 1968—*Of Grammatology* (1967, though with portions published in 1965–66), "Freud and the Scene of Writing" (1967), and the lecture on "*Différance*" (1968)—consistently indicate their "psychoanalytic import," as Derrida would put it in an early interview (POS, 83/110). Beyond the earliest texts, the engagement with psychoanalysis continues, if somewhat more discreetly, in *Dissemination* (1972), most notably in "Outwork" (D, 25–26/32–33 and 40–41n39/47–48n24), and "The Double Session" (D, 220n32/249n25 and 248n52/279n44). This initial phase of questioning and interrogation in the late

sixties and early seventies then launches a deconstructive working through, or working over, of Freudian concepts that extends across Derrida's entire oeuvre, right up into some of the last texts he wrote. It is worth noting that Derrida's early interest in Freud does not come out of nowhere. Derrida's first essay while studying under Althusser at the École normale supérieure (ENS) for the *agrégation* in 1954–55 was not on Husserl but on the evolution of the notion of the unconscious in Freud and its relation to philosophy. See Peeters, *Derrida*, 71–72.

7. The question of clinical practice in and after Freud, however, is not really one of Derrida's interests. Thus, Derrida's aim is not to produce a new deconstructive form of psychoanalysis. Such a project might be possible—certainly, that Derrida did not seek to do so has not stopped some (such as René Major) from trying to do just this—but it was not Derrida's aim, nor is it the aim of this book.

8. Placing Freud's thinking on the life and death drives in proper context, chapter 2 does not simply treat Freud's *Beyond the Pleasure Principle* on its own, as almost all of the prior discussions of *The Post Card* have. This is the case in McCance's reading of Derrida on *Beyond* in *The Reproduction of Life Death* and Vitale's in *Biodeconstruction*. Wills's *Inanimation* stands as an exception in this regard, but it has a different focus.

1. From Grammatology to Life Death

1. The issue of temporalization is ultimately the key strategic point of entry for Derrida in *Voice and Phenomenon*. It is temporalization that Derrida says "torment[s]" or "contest[s], from the inside, [phenomenology] by means of its own descriptions" (VP, 6/5).

2. Both Hodge, in *Derrida on Time*, and Anderson, in *Derrida: Ethics Under Erasure*, emphasize the "to-come" of futurity, thought in terms of what comes from the future and not in terms of heterogeneity in the here and now, as the key mode of Derrida's thought on temporalization. Hodge sees the *à-venir* as the central thought in Derrida beyond the notion of *différance* itself (18), and she identifies it with a "distinctive mode of thinking futurity" in Derrida (37). Anderson discusses Derrida's conception of alterity and responsibility strictly in terms of a "response to the other to come" that is "a response to the unknown that may or may not 'appear' or happen" (120). She thereby emphasizes in Derrida "the heteronomy of future life and death" (120). This same tendency informs Peng Cheah and Suzanne Guerlac's interpretation in their introduction to *Derrida and the Time of the Political*. They read Derrida's "aporetic" concept of time, and its implications, solely in terms of "an opening onto a future that is not future present, . . . an advent or coming that is structurally imminent to every present reality" (14). While Martin Hägglund's articulation of the trace structure of time—advanced in *Radical Atheism* and *Dying for Time*—does not uniformly emphasize what comes from the future, his understanding of the threat inherent in finitude is always understood in his work in terms of the intrinsic erasability or destructibility of the trace. I will sidestep a

detailed discussion of this aspect of his interpretation here, as a full treatment can be found in chapter 3. Lastly, notable exceptions to the tendency just mentioned can be found in Samir Haddad's *Derrida and the Inheritance of Democracy*, which sets out to revise this tendency explicitly (3–4), and in Matthias Fritsch's *The Promise of Memory*, which seeks to show how Derrida's thought "requires a reelaboration not only of the understanding of the promise for emancipation, but also of the political import of memory" (4). However, both authors are primarily interested in thinking with Derrida on the need for inheriting from the past, thus their precise focus is not on the dynamics of interruption within the here-and-now of the present—and the living present, or life—which forms my focus here.

3. Francesco Vitale has noted some important moments in Derrida's early treatment of Freud but is focused on how Freud's neurophysiological hypotheses relate to Derrida's engagement with the life sciences. Moreover, the account I offer here differs from Vitale's insofar as it *demonstrates* the precise links between Derrida's engagement with the notion of the memory trace in Freud and the logics of life death and arche-writing. See Vitale, *Biodeconstruction*, 3.

4. Morin, "Spacing of Time," 28.

5. The trace is the apt figure because it brings together the specific characteristics just named: it is not fully present (hence continually deferred), defined by iterability, and its identity is constituted in difference (since a minimally identifiable, intelligible mark only has its identity through its relation to other marks).

6. Importantly, in order for all of this to be thought still within the frame of what is finite, the mark or trace as descriptive of the structure of the living present also necessarily has to include destructibility and erasability, and this would also be at stake in temporalization (since a trace that cannot be erased or destroyed is not finite but eternal). The thought of an infinite process of deferral and differentiation, *infinite différance*, operating in any entity would be stasis, full presence, plenitude. Infinite *différance* provides no possibility for the relation to the other in the same necessary to temporalization and, in turn, life, as the rest of the chapter elucidates.

7. Looking retrospectively, Derrida noted in *For What Tomorrow*, "Beginning with *Of Grammatology*, the re-elaboration of a new concept of the trace had to be extended to the entire field of the living, or rather to the life/death relation, beyond the anthropological limits of 'spoken' language (or 'written' language, in the ordinary sense)" (*FWT*, 63/106). In another passage, Derrida affirms, "What is universalizable about differance with regard to differences is that it allows one to think the process of differentiation beyond every kind of limit: whether it is a matter of cultural, national, linguistic, or even human limits. There is differ*a*nce (with an "a") as soon as there is a living trace, a relation of life/death or presence/absence" (*FWT*, 21/43).

8. The thought of the trace thus overflows the notion of life as determined by biology, insofar as the structure of the instituted trace is, as Derrida famously puts it, not more natural than cultural, not more physical than psychic, not more biological than spiritual (OG, 48/70). The trace is, he writes, "absolutely and by rights 'anterior' to all *physiological* problematics concerning the nature of the

engramme, or *metaphysical* problematics concerning the meaning of absolute presence whose trace is thus opened to deciphering" (OG, 65/95).

9. Morin, "Spacing of Time," 29.

10. *Différance* is thus to be understood not just as a consequence of temporization, nor as a consequence of self-differing in space—it designates a thought that is neither simply temporal nor spatial in its essential contours—insofar as it names the "pre-spatial, pre-temporal 'origin' of space and time: the becoming-time of space and the becoming-space of time" (Morin, "Spacing of Time," 29). In "*Différance*," Derrida describes spacing as "the becoming-space of time or the becoming-time of space (*temporization*). . . . It is this constitution of the present, as an 'originary' and irreducibly nonsimple (and therefore, *stricto sensu* nonoriginary) synthesis of marks, or traces of retentions and protentions . . . that I propose to call arche-writing, arche-trace, or *différance*" (M, 13/14). Crucially, he also describes the notion of arche-trace as "being related no less to what is called the future than to what is called the past, and constituting what is called the present by means of this very relation to what it is not: what it absolutely is not. . . . An interval must separate the present from what it is not in order for the present to be itself, but this interval that constitutes it as present must, by the same token, divide the present in and of itself" (M, 13/13).

11. Bennington, *Interrupting Derrida*, 97–102.

12. See Bennington, 101. As Bennington shows, this same schema is at work in the well-known discussion of method in *Of Grammatology* that emerges in midst of Derrida's reading of Rousseau. There, Derrida argues that his deconstructive reading of Rousseau should not be understood as a psychoanalytic reading. The reason is, he specifies, that deconstruction does not attempt to reduce, as psychoanalysis often does, and sometimes in the case of Freud himself (for instance, in his book on da Vinci) the signifier of the written text to a signified (the true meaning of what is symptomatic in Rousseau's life and work). Much more importantly for the purposes of my discussion, however, Derrida then goes further. The work of deconstruction is not psychoanalytic here insofar as it does not employ psychoanalytic concepts as if they are tools simply available for borrowing, he says. They are not tools ready at hand because psychoanalysis forms a key component of the very milieu in which deconstruction finds its footing and its chance of appearing, and therefore it could not be treated simply as a methodology one chooses to employ or not. Moreover, and this is the point Bennington's reading brings out most clearly, Derrida's account of Rousseau's complicity with metaphysics is not psychoanalytic in that, in order for this to be possible, it would be necessary, first, for psychoanalysis to provide an account of how Rousseau's conceptuality stands in relation to the tradition of metaphysics he inherits from, which is after all already there before Rousseau. Indeed, how else would we get a clear picture of how we might use psychoanalysis to analyze the relation between Rousseau's conceptuality and metaphysics? Second, psychoanalysis would then need to delimit which parts of *its own conceptuality* belong to the broader metaphysical tradition and which do not, something psychoanalysis itself has not undertaken. It would be

necessary for psychoanalysis to provide an account of its own position within the history of metaphysics, to "elucidate the law of its own appurtenance to metaphysics and Western culture" (OG, 161/231), something it has not ever done. Thus, we see here Derrida employing, though somewhat less obviously than he does elsewhere, the schema I sketched above. The problem, or complication, in both cases stems not from the fact that psychoanalysis belongs in some way to metaphysics (*every* discourse belongs in some way to metaphysics, on this view, even deconstruction) but rather that it has not yet undertaken the labor of providing an account of its belonging or complicity, and therefore, has not begun to think how it might inhabit metaphysics in a different way than it has to this point.

13. For a treatment of Derrida's discussion of their common inheritance in this piece, see Trumbull, "Deconstruction and Psychoanalysis," 69–91.

14. Freud, *Standard Edition*, 1:295. Hereafter, works by Freud are cited parenthetically in the text as *SE*, followed by the volume and page number.

15. For instance, in *The Interpretation of Dreams*, Freud compares the dream text at various points to the hieroglyph, the rebus, or the pictogram, as opposed to a text written in a phonetic script.

16. In a key sentence Derrida cites, Freud, having noted that if every contact-barrier had the same resistance there would be no way to understand how one pathway is carved out and not another, concludes that "*memory is represented by the differences in facilitations between the psi neurones*" (SE, 1:300).

17. An excellent discussion of this understanding of time as lag can be found in Naas, "When It All Suddenly Clicked," 81–98.

18. Bennington, *Not Half No End*, 58.

19. In the discussion of Rousseau in *Of Grammatology*, Derrida again specifies that the movement of *différance*, while not reducible to a traditional notion of finitude, ought to be understood as fundamentally finite: with respect to life, "Difference began by *broaching* alienation and it ends by leaving reappropriation *breached*. Until death. Death is the movement of differance to the extent that that movement is necessarily finite" (OG, 143/206).

20. See Morin, "Spacing of Time," 31.

21. The full quote refers to "the death drive and the relation to the absolutely other that, to all appearances, interrupts every economy" (M, 19/20), a formulation that cannot be properly understood without delving into the paradoxes of *Beyond the Pleasure Principle*, which I will take up in chapter 2, and thus I have sought to avoid complicating matters further here.

22. Derrida would develop this line of thinking in "Resistances"; see RP, 35/50. See also Derrida, "Let Us Not Forget—Psychoanalysis," 3–8, esp. 5.

23. Any discussion of the complex problem of "temporalization and the so-called 'timelessness' of the unconscious" (WD, 214–15/318), a discussion of the type Hägglund has at times at least begun to initiate in conversation with Adrian Johnston, would have to take into account not just deferred action but also this precise dimension of Freud's thought, such that it would shed further light, despite

Derrida's own apparent unwillingness to follow this particular thread, on the fact that, as he himself put it, "the unconscious is no doubt timeless only from the standpoint of a certain vulgar concept of time" (WD, 215/318). See Johnston, "The true Thing is the (w)hole," 146–68; and Hägglund, "On Chronolibido: A Response to Rabaté and Johnston," 169–81.

2. Interrogating the Death Drive

1. See also WD, 203/302, where Derrida references how the notion of pathbreaking he finds in Freud's *Project for a Scientific Psychology* communicates directly with the later theory of the death drive in *Beyond the Pleasure Principle*.

2. Derrida foreshadows his sustained engagement with Freud in the "Envois" of *The Post Card*, designating Freud, alongside Heidegger, as one of the "great ghosts of the 'great epoch'" (PC, 191/206).

3. Derrida, *Life Death*, originally published as *La vie la mort: Séminaire (1975–1976)*. We can now say that Derrida had begun initially working with certain ideas that would appear in the 1975–76 seminar in the abandoned text of *Le calcul des langues*, dating from around 1973. See Derrida, *Le calcul des langues*, 68–71 and 73–74. Moreover, the editors of *Le calcul des langues* suggest that the brief engagement with *Beyond the Pleasure Principle* found there possibly draws on Derrida's earlier (perhaps 1971–72) seminar entitled "Psychoanalysis in the Text." See Bennington and Chenoweth, "Phalanges," 19. Finally, Derrida returns to Freud briefly in the final session of his 1976–77 seminar, the year after *La vie la mort*. See Derrida, *Theory and Practice*, 118–20. The French edition of *Theory and Practice* incorrectly lists the year as 1975–76.

4. Prior to the publication of the 1975–76 seminar, the line of inquiry I am tracking here—Derrida's engagement specifically with Freud on the life and death drives in this period—has largely been glossed over in the existing readings of *The Post Card*. See Ellmann, "Deconstruction and Psychoanalysis"; Forrester, *Seductions of Psychoanalysis*; Rottenberg, "Derrida and Psychoanalysis"; Royle, *After Derrida*; Weber, "The Debts of Deconstruction"; and Wills, *Matchbook*. The reason is many of Derrida's readers have not held this text alongside his articulation of life death in "Freud and the Scene of Writing." I address the few exceptions below, but special attention is due with respect to Geoffrey Bennington's work in this area. Bennington has tried to outline, in a small handful of places, how Derrida's comments on the death drive redeploy the logic of life death. While I elaborate a new analysis of this material here, this is not because I believe his account is incorrect. Rather, it is simply that Bennington's account is incomplete insofar as he treats this problematic in an abbreviated fashion in works dealing with broader themes in Derrida. Going further in depth on this issue, I argue, allows us to see just how the arche-originary inscription of death within life is to be understood, a dimension of life death, I suggest, a certain thinking of binding brings out most forcefully. See Bennington, "Derridabase," 136–46, and, *Not Half No End*, 47–64.

Particular note is also due to Francesco Vitale's alternate reading of Derrida on Freud in his chapter "Between Life and Death: The Bond" in *Biodeconstruction*. The demonstration I offer in this chapter differs from Vitale's in that I offer a full elaboration of Derrida's treatment of Freud in "To Speculate" that takes into account Derrida's grasp of the full trajectory of Freud's thought and, even more importantly, elaborates the terms of Derrida's engagement with the Freudian notion of the death drive. Lastly, David Wills includes a treatment of life death in *Beyond the Pleasure Principle* and "To Speculate" in his chapter on Freud in *Inanimation*, but his account is oriented toward bringing out a certain thought in Freud, not Derrida: namely, the paradoxical thought of an inorganic element necessary to life itself glimpsed in *Beyond the Pleasure Principle* but not fully developed by Freud; see Wills, *Inanimation*, 59. Derrida helps us see this, according to Wills, insofar as his atypically autobiographical reading of Freud enables us to grasp the latent contradictions in Freud's speculations and the links between his account of the death drive and his speculations on the protozoa in *Beyond the Pleasure Principle*. With its focus on bringing out the themes of the machinic and the inorganic in Freud specifically, this approach differs considerably from the present account of what is at stake in Derrida's reading of Freud.

5. Jacob, *La Logique du vivant*.

6. This nonclassical approach is entirely consistent with, in fact demanded by, Derrida's articulation of writing understood in the most general sense. Indeed, one of his critical points in the early work was that traditional approaches to these terms and many others (time and life, for example) are displaced once we think the trace and writing as originary and not secondary. Thus, certain alternate forms of working are necessary. Stated differently, it might seem that in *La vie la mort* and "To Speculate" Derrida is making a merely formal point about Freud's writing in *Beyond the Pleasure Principle*, but the situation is not so simple insofar as Derrida showed in *Voice and Phenomenon* and *Of Grammatology* that the very idea of "writing" and the iterable mark understood as a purely secondary entity in relation to the primacy of the voice and interior thought is one of the cornerstones of the system of thought he wishes to challenge. Therefore, to challenge this system, Derrida has to take the question of writing in general as seriously as possible, whether in the case of Husserl, Saussure, Nietzsche, or Freud. On this general issue, see *LD*, 26–27/48–49.

7. Only Bennington, to my knowledge, has commented on Derrida's insights into the scene of writing of *Beyond the Pleasure Principle*. See Bennington, "Derridabase," 136–46.

8. See, in particular the works by Bennington and Vitale cited in note 4, as well as McCance, *Reproduction of Life Death*, and Hägglund, *Radical Atheism* and *Dying for Time*. See also Hägglund, "Trace of Time"; Kirby, "Grammatology"; and Senatore, *Germs of Death*.

9. McCance's engagement is with the 1975–76 seminar and her treatment of the notion of life death is restricted to its relation to the life sciences and genetics,

focusing on Derrida's reading of Jacob in the seminar. Life death in Freud is said by McCance to bear only on the movement of Freud's text. See McCance, *Reproduction of Life Death*, 3. Vitale's account is equally focused squarely on Derrida's relation to the life sciences in his elaboration of life death. See Vitale, *Biodeconstruction*, 1–2.

10. Part of two sessions on Nietzsche had been published, alongside "Déclarations d'indépendance," in *Otobiographies*. They had earlier appeared as "Otiobiographies," in *The Ear of the Other*, 1–38. Part of two sessions on Heidegger had been published as "Interpreting Signatures (Nietzsche/Heidegger)."

11. Derrida, "Interpreting Signatures," 257; orig. "Guter Wille zur Macht II: Die Unterschriften interpretieren (Nietzsche/Heidegger)," 73. Derrida revisits this gesture in "Nietzsche and the Machine" (see N, 216–17).

12. Nietzsche deploys masks in keeping with his thinking of life death, according to Derrida. This is because Nietzsche claims that everything is transposed into life on top of the ashes of everything dead and puts down truth and falsehood to the ruse of life, such that life can dissimulate itself and even give rise to a degeneration of life. If this is the case, life can commit a kind of suicide (see LD, 153–54/198). Later, in "Nietzsche and the Machine" (1993), Derrida is much more reluctant to attribute such an identifiable thought of life to Nietzsche: "I cannot bring together anything whatsoever in Nietzsche, whether it concerns life or anything else" (N, 221).

13. This move was telegraphed in the portion of the seminar published in *Otobiographies* (see LD, 27/49–50).

14. For a full, excellent account of Freud's theory of the drives see de Lauretis, *Freud's Drive*.

15. In the *Three Essays*, Freud describes sexuality this way: "The fact of the existence of sexual needs in human beings is expressed in biology by the assumption of a 'sexual instinct,' on the analogy of the instinct of nutrition, that is of hunger. Everyday language possesses no counterpart to the word 'hunger,' but science makes use of the word 'libido' for that purpose" (SE, 7:135).

16. On the virtual aspect of the psyche, see chapter 1.

17. Expanding on the point just made: whereas previously the aims of the ego were considered entirely apart from the phenomenon of psychical conflict and repression, Freud now situates this too *within* the domain of the sexual drives, the representatives of which are subject to repression.

18. Confusingly, in *Beyond the Pleasure Principle* Freud endorses the use of the term "Nirvana principle" to describe the operations of the pleasure principle, a term which more suggests the push to total reduction than to constancy (SE, 18:55–56). This confusion is then amplified by his use of the term to describe the work of the death drive four years later in "The Economic Problem of Masochism" as pushing toward zero (SE, 19:160).

19. By positing this larger trajectory, Freud can view the repetition compulsion, for instance, as giving rise to unpleasure, and thus an *increase* in tension within the apparatus, even as it pursues the ultimate aim of undoing the psychical structures

associated with the ego (which Freud has a concept of even before the second topography) and the binding of the secondary process, the process that allows the living organism sustain living. It would then serve the broader tendency to reduce excitation to absolute zero even as it gives rise to a temporary increase in excitation. It is thus not strictly a contradiction in Freud, as Martin Hägglund has incorrectly argued, that the repetition compulsion, as representative of the death drive, gives rise to more tension rather than less. This is a wrinkle Freud is well aware of, and indeed the notion of the return to the state of inorganic quiescence at the level of the organism is introduced precisely in order to deal with it. As we will soon see, Derrida himself clearly understands Freud's thinking on this point. The Derridean intervention with respect to the death drive lies elsewhere. See Hägglund, *Dying for Time*, 125.

20. Derrida comments at length on this passage in *AF*, 10–13/24–28.

21. At issue here are Freud's comments on the life sciences in the well-known discussion of the recourse to "figurative language" (*Bildersprache*) in psychoanalysis, found at the close of chapter 6 (*SE*, 18:59–60). See Derrida's discussion of this passage, originally absent in the seminar, at *PC*, 382–83/408–9.

22. In the seminar, Derrida argues that the questions of the scene of writing and of "the status of this text (*Beyond*) and of the discourse that is developed within it . . . have—to my knowledge—never been posed" by Freud's readers (*LD*, 277–78/340–41). Throughout this chapter, I prioritize citing the more developed text ("To Speculate") Derrida chose to publish in his lifetime. There are a few occasions, however, in which I cite the didactic formulations of the seminar when they are substantially clearer. Wherever I cite text that appears in both "To Speculate" and *La vie la mort*, I provide page numbers for both. If the citation contains only one reference, then that text is absent in the other. Occasionally, there are similarities but not exact reproductions of wording, and in those cases I refer readers to the similar passage with "see also."

23. Given Freud's broader project and Derrida's gloss on it, it is simply not the case, as Dawne McCance has suggested, that Derrida "has Jacob in mind" when referring to the nonthetic movement of *Beyond the Pleasure Principle* (McCance, *Reproduction of Life Death*, 126).

24. This argument is clear in the overall sweep of the final four sessions of the seminar, but less clear in the passage from *La vie la mort* just referenced. The formulation in "To Speculate" cited above comes closer to the overall argument of the treatment of Freud in the seminar.

25. See *LD*, 254/313: "Everything I describe here [in *Beyond*], in its necessity, does not refer, especially not, to a deliberate, conscious calculation: that is why it is interesting and necessary."

26. Bennington, *Not Half No End*, 58.

27. The published translations of Derrida consistently modify the Strachey translation of Freud: where Strachey has "reel" for *Spule*, the English versions of

The Post Card and *Life Death* have "spool" in place of Derrida's "*bobine*." I have modified Strachey accordingly for consistency.

28. This phrase was added to the passage LD, 246/305.

29. This passage is an expansion on the seminar, in which Derrida does not tie the issue of the game's completion to the mirroring effect he is describing (see the corresponding passage at LD, 253–54/312–13).

30. This insight is the linchpin of Derrida's argument in "To Speculate," which makes it all the more problematic that it has been so frequently overlooked. For instance, David Wills admirably takes up the terms of Derrida's "autobiographical" reading of Freud in this text but does not pursue them in full, focusing instead on how Derrida's insistence on the autobiographical resonance of the tale of the *fort/da* suggests, more broadly, beyond "To Speculate," that we ought to reread Freud's speculations on the protozoa as particularly reflective of his own theoretical investments. See Wills, *Inanimation*, 77–79.

31. This discussion builds on session 11 of *La vie la mort*.

32. Freud explicates this explicitly in "Formulations on the Two Principles of Mental Functioning" (1911). Derrida had in fact underscored this complication in the relation between the two principles, but without developing the thought fully, in both "Freud and the Scene of Writing" (WD, 198/295) and "*Différance*" (M, 18–19/19–20).

33. In a teaching moment in the seminar, Derrida says, "The reality principle is not opposed, as is believed, to the pleasure principle, but instead modifies it, puts it in *différance*, with an *a*" (LD, 230/287).

34. This is also one of the major elements that sets Derrida apart from Laplanche's *Life and Death in Psychoanalysis*. Published in 1970, it was required reading for Derrida's *La vie la mort* seminar.

35. Vitale unfortunately misconstrues Derrida on the exappropriation of the proper death in Freud, chalking it up to the fact that drives "are repressed" (Vitale, *Biodeconstruction*, 146).

36. Of the introduction of the new function of binding, Derrida writes, "This obscurity, which Freud does not insist upon, is due to the fact before the instituted mastery of the PP there is *already* a tendency to binding, a mastering or structuring impulse that foreshadows the PP without being confused with it. It collaborates with the PP without being confused with it. A median, *differing or indifferent* zone (and it is differing only by being indifferent to the oppositional or distinctive difference of the two borders), relates the primary process in its "'purity' (a 'myth' says the *Traumdeutung*) to the 'pure' secondary process entirely subject to the PP" (PC, 351/372–73; see also LD, 268–69/331).

37. Dawne McCance very briefly notes Derrida's observation but does not explain what Derrida means by this or draw out its consequences, instead relating it to the question of Freud's "sovereign mastery" of psychoanalytic knowledge (McCance, *Reproduction of Life Death*, 145).

38. Derrida has a clear didactic exposition of this in LD, 289/354.

39. Emphasizing the resonance of this discussion for binding at the level of the social group or of a community, in the next sentence Derrida suggestively refers to this process as inherent in any "being-together" (PC, 402/429). A note is due on a difficult passage found at this point in *The Post Card*. Following this comment, Derrida argues that the "experience" of stricture at the level of the social group is not determined simply, and in an uncomplicated way, by the relative strength of the force of binding. "A greater stricture," Derrida writes, "can give rise to 'more' pleasure and pain than, in another 'set,' in another nonsystematic adjoining, a lesser stricture" (PC, 402/428–29; see also LD, 293–94/358). Why? Because "the force of stricture, the capacity to *bind itself*, remains in relation to *what there is to bind* (what gives something and gives itself to be bound" (PC, 402/429; see also LD, 293–94/358). A relatively "free" set might be "weakly erotized, weakly hedonized" while a relatively closed set might be strongly erotized or hedonized, and so on. Thus, what begins to come into view here is an account of the general structure of community in general, one that allows us to think the qualitative "experience" of community. But it is one that suggests that any such account of community needs to think through what there is to bind in any given context, the quasi-erotic, not-entirely-conscious affect at play in any community. We can interpret this turn in Derrida's argument as a prefiguration of what he would later call *phantasm*, the expression of an uncritical wish, or a desire, at work in the imagined community of the nation-state. I discuss the phantasm in chapter 4. The key question with respect to community, at this point, would be "what is the structuring phantasm at stake in the binding, or being bound together, of a community?"—bearing in mind that such binding never results in the formation of a unity, this limitation being the inevitable consequence of the structure of exappropriation at play in binding.

40. This has not stopped readers from attempting to put the two (Derrida and Freud) together in some such fashion. See, for example, Willet, "Tropics of Desire."

41. The final session of *La vie la mort* includes only a brief, truncated discussion of this drive for mastery; see LD, 294–95/359–60. Derrida returned to his reading of this drive for power in "'To Do Justice to Freud'" (in RP, 70–118), drawing on an earlier, unpublished presentation from 1985. The final section of "'To Do Justice to Freud'" in large part reproduces this presentation. See Derrida, "Beyond the Power Principle," 7–17.

42. See Derrida's description of the unconscious as "the metaphysical name" for a certain alterity equally at stake in the notion of *différance* in his eponymous lecture (M, 20/21).

43. Vitale misconstrues Derrida's treatment of the motif of mastery in "To Speculate," missing that Derrida does not endorse the concept of a drive for power beyond the death drive, but pushes this notion in an alternative direction (Vitale, *Biodeconstruction*, 162–63).

44. For a description of this thought of the death drive in Derrida and power canceling itself out, see Trumbull, "Power and the 'Drive for Mastery,'" 151–65.

45. For instance, in "Resistances" (1991), Derrida seemingly embraces the death drive in a discussion of the notion of analysis supposedly inaugurated by Freud. But he submits it to a highly figural reading, where it becomes not the name for a silent psychical force but a way of thinking what disturbs every form of analysis, always, in its very operations, from within, by virtue of the very axiomatics of the concept. An analogous move is then deployed in *Archive Fever* (1995), discussed in chapter 3. See also Derrida's much later discussion of Freud's concepts in *For What Tomorrow* (2001), where he could not be clearer that, for him, the whole vocabulary of the unconscious and the drives is part of something like a grand "theoretical fiction" that gives something to be thought but can also be discarded someday: "I would not make the 'unconscious' and the agencies of the second topography into scientific and scientifically assured concepts. I do want to cite them and use the in certain strategically defined situations, but I do not believe in their value or their pertinence beyond this battlefield. Other 'theoretical fictions' are henceforth necessary. . . . One day, the best part of the psychoanalytic legacy will be able to survive without the metapsychology, and perhaps even without any of the concepts I just mentioned" (*FWT*, 174/284).

46. The essay "Le facteur de la verité" dates from 1971 but was published for the first time in *Poétique* in 1975. In *La vie la mort*, Derrida refers his audience to this essay as background for the reading of Freud he undertakes there (*LD*, 220/276). The critique Derrida outlines in "Le facteur de la verité" was in fact underway even earlier. Derrida advanced an initial critique of Lacan in the dialogue published in 1971 as "Positions." There, Derrida fleshes out a stance destined to appear in the "Outwork" of *Dissemination* (1972), where dissemination is explicitly differentiated from a metaphysical thought of castration, or lack, as "a signified, or which mounts to the same, of a transcendental signifier" (*D*, 26/32). Even if Lacan's project is undoubtedly crucial to psychoanalysis after Freud, it remains, Derrida says in "Positions," firmly located within the tradition of metaphysics deconstruction set out to analyze and disrupt (See *POS*, 107–13n44/112–119n33).

47. Derrida returns to the reading of Lacan developed there repeatedly: in "Envoi" (1980) and "Mes chances" (a lecture delivered in 1982, first published in 1988) and then again much later in the two texts found in *Resistances of Psychoanalysis*, "Resistances" (1990) and "For the Love of Lacan" (1991).

48. I provide this demonstration in full in an as yet unpublished manuscript: Trumbull, "Revisiting Derrida's Critique of Lacan, Beyond the Misunderstandings."

49. Johnson, "Frame of Reference," 457–505. Subsequently reprinted in *The Purloined Poe*, 213–51.

50. For an example of how Johnson's interpretation that Derrida advances a prejudicial reading of Lacan set the terms of the debate in the eighties and nineties, see David Pettigrew and François Raffoul's "Editors' Introduction" to *Disseminating Lacan*, 1–22; and Forrester, *Seductions of Psychoanalysis*, 266. Johnson's analysis explicitly and implicitly continues to inform the more recent published accounts of the Derrida-Lacan debate, such as Lorenzo Chiesa's *Subjectivity and Otherness*,

Andrea Hurst's *Derrida vis-à-vis Lacan*, and Charles Shepherdson, "Derrida and Lacan: An Impossible Friendship." This is not to deny that there are outliers. Though almost entirely unknown to English readers, René Major has sought, over the course of several writings, most notably *Lacan avec Derrida*, to forge a new path between Derrida and Lacan by developing a deconstructive psychoanalytical orientation. Lastly, Michael Lewis's *Derrida and Lacan* acknowledges in its broad contours the overall thrust of Derrida's criticisms of Lacan in the 1970s, yet only to then argue that Lacan is able to overcome Derrida's critique by developing a new understanding of how "man" develops out of "animal nature," something Derrida is said to have never thought through—an argument difficult to entertain given that one of the major interventions of deconstruction as it is advanced in the later Derrida is to put into question any easy assurances we might have as to what exactly constitutes "animal nature" and "the proper to man."

51. Lacan attempts in the "Seminar on the Purloined Letter" to outline a notion of the Freudian subject as a "function of the signifier" on the basis of a reading of Poe's short story, and Derrida shows how, in this move, Lacan reduces the literary signifier of Poe's text to a given meaning. Lacan reads the short story, in other words, as a mere illustration of what Freud teaches us. This is a problem insofar as Lacan's whole theory of the subject of the unconscious claims to foreground the play of the signifier—it's asemic functioning, on a level completely divorced from intentionality—and not its meaning. Thus, while Lacan claims to advance a thinking of the signifier that emphasizes pure play and the impossibility of assigning it a fixed meaning, he does so in a demonstration that effectively *reduces* the literary signifier of Poe's short story to a given meaning. See *PC*, 427–28/455–56.

52. Derrida notes its importance in "For the Love of Lacan" (*RP*, 59/77–78).

53. French page numbers refer to the 1998 "augmented" edition of *Psyché*. "Mes chances" was left out of the 1987 edition and does not appear in the 2003 edition.

54. Lacan, *Écrits*, 16–17. See also Lacan, *Écrits 1*, 23–25.

55. See a crucial passage in *"Différance"* where Derrida differentiates deconstruction from negative theology, "even the most negative of negative theologies" (M, 6/6). Preparing the text for publication in *Margins of Philosophy* in 1972, Derrida inserted specific language absent in the original text that spells out that *différance* "reserves and does not expose itself, it exceeds at this precise point and in a systematic way [*de manière réglée*] the order of truth, but without for all that dissimulating itself, as some thing, as a mysterious being, in the occult of a nonknowledge or *in a hole the borders of which would be determinable* (for instance, in a topology of castration)" (M, 6/6, trans. mod., my emphasis). The original text, published in 1968 in the Tel Quel collection *Théorie d'ensemble* does not contain the phrase concerning the hole. See Derrida, *"La Différance,"* 44. See also a similar formulation in *POS*, 113n46/119n34.

56. Here Derrida's critique comes close to Nancy and Lacoue-Labarthe's in *The Title of the Letter*, which he cites (*PC*, 420n4/448n2). See Jean-Luc Nancy and Philippe Lacoue-Labarthe, *Title of the Letter*. Derrida returns to the issue of a new

transcendental foundation in "Envoi" (1980) (*P*, 125/139). "Le facteur de la verité" was first given as a lecture in 1971, and Derrida hosted Nancy and Lacoue-Labarthe at the École normale supérieure (ENS) in 1972 to give a seminar on Lacan's "Instance of the Letter," what would become *The Title of the Letter*, published at the beginning of 1973. See Peeters, *Derrida*, 241.

57. This thought is named most explicitly when Derrida reflects on the debate and underscores that the question of the letter, its divisibility, and its place in Lacan is "indissociable . . . from a thinking of death, from destination as death" (*RP*, 65/84). The context here is the issue of the destination of the letter in Lacan, another name for its place. See also the "Envois" of *The Post Card*, where Derrida writes that the lack of destination is tied to the thought that "it is good, it is not a misfortune, that's life, living life, beaten down, the tragedy, by still surviving life" (*PC*, 33–34/39, trans. mod.).

3. Survival as Autoimmunity

1. See Derrida, "Living On—Borderlines," and "No Apocalypse, Not Now" in *P*, 1:387–409, in particular 403. Derrida's discussion in *Memoires: For Paul de Man* is also concerned with the dynamics of this concept, even if it does not always use the terminology of survival.

2. Derrida had laid the groundwork for this development in his treatment of Heidegger's discourse on death in *Aporias*, delivered as a lecture in 1992 at the Cerisy conference and published the same year as *Specters* (1993). There, probing what he sees as a set of unthought problems within Heidegger's discourse on death, Derrida suggests that Heidegger's notion that only the human has access to death as such is uncritical at a certain point. And this point, Derrida says, concerns precisely the fact that Heidegger cannot think "*revenance*, spectrality or living-on, surviving, as non-derivable categories or as non-reducible derivations" (*A*, 61/111). Derrida goes on to say that this same category of survival is also non-derivable in Freud's discourse on death, the "double Freudian postulate" of the death drive on the one hand and, on the other hand, the absolute unknowability of death at the level of the unconscious, which steadfastly refuses to "[testify] to our mortality, an essential, necessary, or intrinsic mortality" (*A*, 38/74). Derrida sees Heidegger as a particular thinker of finitude early on. See Derrida, *Heidegger*.

3. At one point, Derrida suggests that the question of how to inherit from Marx, and the most living part of his legacy—in the specific sense in which Derrida deploys the term "inherit"—necessarily puts "back on the drawing board the question of life, spirit, or the spectral, of life death beyond the opposition between life and death" (*SM*, 67/94–95).

4. Just about ten years earlier, in the dialogue published as *A Taste for the Secret*, we find Derrida saying much the same thing, insofar as he claims, "I think about nothing but death. . . . I never stop analyzing the phenomenon of 'survival' as the structure of surviving, it's really the only thing that interests me, but precisely

insofar as I do not believe that one lives on post mortem. And at bottom it is what commands everything—what I do, what I am, what I write, what I say" (Derrida and Ferraris, *Taste for the Secret*, 88).

5. Elsewhere in *For What Tomorrow*, Derrida says that "What is universalizable about difference with regard to differ*a*nce is that it allows one to think the process of differentiation beyond every kind of limit: whether it is a matter of cultural, national, linguistic, or even human limits. There is differ*a*nce (with an "a") as soon as there is a living trace, a relation of life/death or presence/absence.... There is differ*a*nce (with an "a") as soon as there is something living [*du vivant*], as soon as there is something of a trace [*de la trace*]" (*FWT*, 21/43). In "Others Are Secret Because They Are Other," we find him elaborating this general proposition in terms of the intrinsic finitude of the trace: "The trace is always the finite trace of a finite being. So it can itself disappear. An ineradicable trace is not a trace. The trace inscribes in itself its own precariousness, its vulnerability of ashes, its mortality.... What I say about the trace and death goes for any 'living thing,' for 'animals' and 'people'" (PM, 159/393–94). See also *The Animal That Therefore I Am*, 104/75.

6. See, for example, BS, 2:130–31/193–94. In *Rogues*, survival is situated squarely at the center of the deconstructive project, most notably with respect to everything it advances on the political, under the heading of what Derrida had, by this point, been calling for some time "democracy to come." While the question of life may not seem essential to thinking democracy, Derrida announces in the preface to "The Reason of the Strongest": "the old word *vie* perhaps remains the enigma of the political around which we endlessly turn" (R, 4/22). He then affirms that it is "toward the incalculability of another thought of life, of what is living in life, that I would like to venture here under the old and yet still completely new and perhaps unthought name *democracy*" (R, 5/24). See also R, 33/57.

7. The exception is Francesco Vitale's chapter "Beyond Life Death: Autoimmunity" in *Biodeconstruction*. My own reading departs from Vitale's by turning back to the Freudian death drive and developing the connection in an altogether different way.

8. Derrida references the notion of an "autoimmune" resistance of psychoanalysis to itself in the preface to *Resistances of Psychoanalysis* (RP, viii/9).

9. While Derrida speaks of "the living ego" here, he is not simply adapting Freudian concepts to a new context, as he makes clear in the discussion of the uncanny in *Specters*. In a discussion of the intersections between Marx's resistance to the specter and Freud's, Derrida distances himself clearly from Freud's position that the uncanny—thought in terms of the return of the repressed—has its grounding in the fundamental metapsychological structures psychoanalysis identifies. Hence Derrida notes that the experience of the specter, a privileged figure for the *arrivant*, the "stranger who is already found within (*das Heimliche-Unheimliche*), more intimate with one than one is oneself," is always repeated, and yet all of this "stems less from a 'repetition automatism' (of the automations that have been turning before us for such a long time) than it gives us to think all *this, altogether other, every other,*

from which the repetition compulsion arises: that every other is altogether other. The impersonal ghostly returning of the 'es spukt' produces an automatism of repetition, no less than it finds its principle of reason there" (SM, 217/273). Thus, even if, as Derrida goes on to suggest, Freud's notion of the uncanny can perhaps put us on the track of the specter, Freud does not think it. This stance on Freud reappears in *Archive Fever*: "as classical metaphysician and as positivist *Aufklärer*, as critical scientist of a past epoch, as a 'scholar' who does not want to speak with phantoms, Freud claims not to believe in death and above all in the virtual existence of the spectral space which he nonetheless takes into account" (AF, 94/146–47). Derrida had telegraphed this reading already in "Mes chances," in a discussion of Freud's comments on superstitions in *The Psychopathology of Everyday Life* (see P, 364–65/373). For another discussion of Freud's complicated relation to the occult, see Jacques Derrida, "Telepathy" (P, 226–61/237–70).

10. See the language of autoimmunity and "inevitability" found in ARSS, 121.
11. Naas, *Derrida from Now On*, 128.
12. Naas, 128.
13. See FK, 61n16/38n12 and 86–87/78–79.
14. I have not included French page numbers for this text because the French publication *Le «concept» du 11 Septembre* (Paris: Galilée, 2004) is not the transcript of Derrida's dialogue with Borradori but rather a translation into French of the English text.
15. See Derrida, "Hostipitality" and *Of Hospitality*, 107–9.
16. Easily overlooked were it not for Geoffrey Bennington's careful reading of this text. See Bennington, *Not Half No End*, 2.
17. Derrida returns to this point, couching it in different terms, in a short interview from 1997 entitled "Paper or Me, You Know . . . (New Speculations on a Luxury of the Poor)." There, he redescribes his reading of Freud's "Note on the Mystic Writing Pad" and says that it is as if, in the "Note," Freud wants go "*beyond a paper principle*" (PM, 48/248). Freud wants to go beyond the paper principle insofar as his model for psychical writing requires, we have seen, a different substrate. It requires the special kind of writing pad that is the mystic pad. Here, Derrida says, "You write without ink, using a pointed pen, and not going through to the wax paper, but only the sheet of the celluloid; hence Freud suggests a return to the tablet of the ancient world" (PM, 49/250). In this way, Derrida suggests, in Freud paper is already disappearing, long before the emergence of computing, say. Indeed, while he is not so naïve as to say nothing new is happening with respect to technologies of writing, the disappearance of paper has always been happening, Derrida argues, insofar as it is due to a structure of "self-immunizing ex-appropriation . . . [that] appears irreducible and timeless" (PM, 59/263). This is the structure, which Derrida explicitly describes here as autoimmune, according to which "Paper protects by exposing, alienating, and first of all by threatening withdrawal, which it is always in one way in the process of. *Protection is itself a threat, an aggression differing from itself*" (PM, 59/263, my emphasis).

18. For a discussion of this difficult passage in "'To Do Justice to Freud,'" see Trumbull, "Power and the 'Drive for Mastery.'"

19. In Jacob, there is no opening to the outside in the program defining the living, the basic model of which is the bacterium. See *LD*, 109/148: "A death coming from the outside (determined here as milieu) is not death. . . . This non-life is a non-death, this non-life is not a death. The non-life that comes from the outside to the bacterium is not a death."

20. As I will discuss in chapters 4 and 5, this logic can be explicitly theological, but it can also be clandestinely theological: putatively humanistic, articulated via a certain notion of Enlightenment.

21. This aggressivity, Freud theorizes, is in fact central to the very formation of "civilization." The moral law of civilization, by which it regulates human relations, he begins to suspect, has its origins not in high ethical ideals but rather in the aggression the subject turns back on itself in the constitution of the superego. Derrida touches on Freud's thinking on the origins of civilization and law toward the end of *Archive Fever* (94/148) and in *The Politics of Friendship* (279/310–11), returning to issues he had discussed previously in "Before the Law" (1985). See Derrida, "Before the Law," 192–94/110–12 and 197–99/115–17.

22. In *Archive Fever*, building off the argument of "Freud and the Scene of Writing," Derrida will claim that what is at stake in psychoanalysis is actually a deconstruction of the traditional concept of the archive. In the archive as traditionally understood, what has been archived and preserved is secure and amenable to recovery and rememoration. Here the archive is thought entirely within the horizon of presence, in terms of the return to presence of what was once present. The very notion of the unconscious, however, undermines this conception of the archive. It poses "the idea of a psychic archive distinct from spontaneous memory, of a *hypomnēsis* distinct from *mnēmē* and from *anamnēsis*" (AF, 19/37); it gives rise to a notion of memory incompatible with any simple act of rememoration or recollection. The repressed in the unconscious is not simply available for recall. As Derrida writes, "a repression also archives that of which it dissimulates or encrypts the archives" (AF, 66/106). Yet, even as Freud's thinking contests the traditional notion of the archive and of memory, Derrida argues, it remains bound to it. Freud seems at times to still think, despite what his own theory suggests, that he might be able to fully reconstruct what lies buried in the unconscious, as Derrida's reading of Freud's reading of Jensen's *Gradiva* at the end of *Archive Fever* makes clear. For Derrida, Freud's discourse on the archive, like his discourse in general, is divided: it challenges the traditional concept of the archive, but it also repeats it.

23. Echoing the remarks in "'To Do Justice to Freud'" cited above, Derrida then underscores that the death drive "even threatens every principality" (AF, 12/27).

24. In a 1999 essay for *L'Humanité*, Derrida says that in deconstruction "it will surely be necessary—it already is—to rework the old concept of *indivisible sovereignty*, whether in relation to the nation-state or the political subject" (PM, 105/327). And then further, "'sovereignty' remains a theological inheritance that has not really been

secularized" (*PM*, 105/327). But he then goes even further, describing it as a fantasy: "Sovereignty has only ever run on fantasy. . . . An omnipotent fantasy, of course, because it is a fantasy of omnipotence" (*PM*, 106/328).

25. See also *"Fichus"* (2001), where Derrida follows up his 2000 address to the Estates General of Psychoanalysis, speaking of the necessity "to insist on the *political* vigilance that must be exercised, without overreaction or injustice, in the reading of Freud" (*PM*, 178/47).

26. Derrida describes this situation frequently with reference to the concrete example of the written trace that I leave behind. In *Learning to Live Finally*, he describes it this way: "I leave a piece of paper behind, I go away, I die: it is impossible to escape this structure, it is the unchanging form of my life. Each time I let something go, each time some trace leaves me, 'proceeds' from me, unable to be reappropriated, I live my death in writing" (*LLF*, 32/33).

27. Speaking of a certain logic of the unconscious in *For What Tomorrow*, Derrida goes so far as to say "a 'subject,' of whatever kind (individual, citizen, state), is instituted only out of this 'fear,' and it always has the force or the protective form of a barrier or a dam. A dam interrupts energy, which it then accumulates and channels" (*FWT*, 179/290).

28. Hägglund, *Radical Atheism*, 2–3. See also Hägglund, "Trace of Time," 36.

29. Hägglund, *Dying for Time*, 186n5.

30. Hägglund, 2.

31. Hägglund, 12.

32. Hägglund, 12.

33. See Hägglund, *Radical Atheism*, 1: "The trace enables the past to be retained, since it is characterized by the ability to remain in spite of temporal succession. The trace is thus the minimal condition for life to resist death in a movement of survival. The trace can only live on, however, by being left for a future that may erase it."

34. Hägglund, *Dying for Time*, 133.

35. Hägglund, *Radical Atheism*, 1.

36. Alteration in temporal succession is how Hägglund most often thinks the negation of full presence. See Hägglund, *Dying for Time*, 3: "The passage of time requires not only that every moment be superseded by another moment, but also that this alteration be at work from the beginning. Every moment must negate itself and pass away *in its very event*. If the moment did not negate itself there would be no time, only a presence forever remaining the same."

37. Hägglund, *Radical Atheism*, 48. See also Hägglund, *Dying for Time*, 15; and Hägglund, *Radical Atheism*, 9. Here, Hägglund writes, "The tracing of time is the minimal protection of life, but it also attacks life from the first inception, since it breaches the integrity of any moment and makes everything susceptible to annihilation." However, as I have argued, in *Radical Atheism*, this annihilation is still almost always thought in terms of the death threat that comes from the unpredictable future.

38. Hägglund, *Dying for Time*, 187n5.

39. Hägglund, 186n5. I will not address at length Hägglund's second reason for objecting to Derrida on this point because it takes us far afield into Hägglund's account of chronolibido. I can offer a brief glimpse here, however. In short, Hägglund develops an account of an affective subject on the basis of what he sees as the unconditional investment in survival Derrida's framework brings forward. This is what motivates him to articulate his second reason for rejecting Derrida's recourse to the death drive: the subjective drive to destroy an archive, he argues, arises not from a drive toward death but a more fundamental investment in survival which furnishes the time and space for the desire for anything at all to take place, including the desire to destroy the archive or to preserve it. It should be clear that in now speaking of a subject's desire to destroy or preserve, we are quite far from what I am discussing in this chapter. For my part, I do not wish to align Derrida's framework with a new notion of libido or desire as does Hägglund, even if I agree that the account of stricture could possibly be put to such ends. If what I have described as survival gives rise to certain subjective *responses*, it would seem more sensible to me, and more Derridean, to describe both positive or negative archive fever (what Hägglund is describing here) as responses that speak to a certain dream of mastery in some subject over the threat of destruction at stake in survival and finitude as thought from the perspective of the trace. This would hold too in the case of suicide, which Hägglund rather counterintuitively theorizes as itself even grounded in the investment in survival, since the act requires some desire being carried out in time and space. But suicide would seem to be much more clearly a phantasmatic response to the basic structure of exappropriation I have shown to be at work in survival. Suicide, a kind of wish fulfillment, would thus be seen as premised on the uncritical fantasy that my life is something at my disposal that I can simply choose to take or not. For Hägglund's account of suicide, see Hägglund, *Dying for Time*, 127–28.

40. Hägglund, 187n5.

4. Mortality and Normativity

1. Critchley, *Ethics of Deconstruction*; Cornell, *Philosophy of the Limit*; and Beardsworth, *Derrida and the Political*.

2. Critchley reads the ethical, affirmative relation to the other as "the goal, or horizon, toward which Derrida's work tends" (Critchley, *Ethics of Deconstruction*, 2). Cornell asserts that deconstruction is driven by an attempt to "enact a nonviolent relation to otherness" (Cornell, *Philosophy of the Limit*, 64). Beardsworth argues for the idea of a lesser violence in the relation to the other as the outcome of the work of deconstruction (Beardsworth, *Derrida and the Political*, 12). For a more recent take on the question of lesser violence in Derrida, see Lawlor, *From Violence to Speaking Out*. This account develops an argument found in Lawlor, *This Is Not Sufficient*, 110–19. See also Samir Haddad's response to *From Violence to Speaking Out*: "Leonard Lawlor's Renewal of Thinking," 393–402.

3. See Fritsch, *Promise of Memory*, 8–9; Hägglund, *Radical Atheism*, 100–106; Haddad, *Derrida and the Inheritance of Democracy*, 73–92; and Morin, "A Mêlée without Sacrifice," 139–43.

4. This is a key part of Derrida's various engagements with Levinas and his treatment of the aporia of responsibility and sacrifice in *The Gift of Death*. Indeed, as Morin writes, "If we understand ethics as having to do with the singular Other and with unconditional demands, and politics as having to do with a plurality of others and hence with general rules, conditional duties and the necessity of institutions, part of the point of Derrida's 'ethics' is to show the impossibility of such a distinction. There is no 'pure' ethics" (Morin, "Spacing of Time," 38n2).

5. Despite its importance, this question has largely been skirted in discussions of Derrida's critique of sovereignty and the death penalty. See, for example, Kelly Oliver's chapter "Death Penalties," in *Technologies of Life and Death*, 188–217; Rottenberg, *For the Love of Psychoanalysis*, 120–76; Wills, "Machinery of Death or Machinic Life," 2–20; and the essays in Oliver and Straub, eds., *Deconstructing the Death Penalty*. The question of normativity has been addressed sporadically in recent attempts to find in Derrida a basis for an "eco-deconstruction" that affirms the preservation of the earth. See Fritsch, Lynes, and Wood, *Eco-Deconstruction*. In the volume, Phillipe Lynes argues that Derrida's activation of general economy in Bataille opens onto a necessary affirmation of the earth, but his account does not deal adequately with the radical openness to whatever comes involved in Derrida's core thought. See Lynes, "Posthuman Promise of the Earth," in *Eco-Deconstruction*, 101–20, especially 113–14. See also Fritsch, "An Eco-Deconstructive Account," in *Eco-Deconstruction*, 279–302. Cary Wolfe's essay in the same volume seeks to address the source of an environmental ethics in deconstruction, but he traces this to Derrida's less developed very late discussions of world, without treating the question of how this relates to core deconstructive concepts. See Wolfe, "Wallace Stevens's Birds, or, Derrida and Ecological Poetics," in *Eco-Deconstruction*, 317–38, especially 333–35.

6. In relation to this issue, see also Derrida's discussion of "transcendental and preethical violence" in Levinas in "Violence and Metaphysics" (WD, 128/188).

7. Hägglund, *Radical Atheism*, 81–82.

8. More to the point, Hägglund argues, openness to what comes is not something I can decide to do or not to do in the first place; it is the absolutely unconditional, ultra-transcendental condition of anything at all. I have to affirm openness to the future, however minimally, even if I do not recognize it, in order to be in the first place, to want or desire anything in the movement of survival from one instant to the next, for Hägglund. Hence, there simply is no possible question of normativity here, insofar as normativity requires as its condition of possibility that I have a choice between doing something and not doing something in the first place.

9. For another fairly recent interpretation that departs from earlier interpretations but pushes the notion of a primary ethical relation in a different direction, see Anderson, *Derrida: Ethics Under Erasure*.

10. See also "The Deconstruction of Actuality" in N, 110–11/73, and Derrida and Stiegler, *Echographies of Television*, 86–87/99–100.

11. See Gasché, *Tain of the Mirror*, 177–78. See also Gasché, *Inventions of Difference*, 11–13.

12. Derrida, *Gift of Death*, 86/82. In *The Gift of Death*, Derrida provides a concrete illustration of this when he speaks of how—even when we think we are resting in good conscience—we participate in a society that "because of the mechanisms of external debt and other similar inequities . . . *puts to* death or (but failing to help someone in distress accounts for only a minor difference) *allows* to die of hunger and disease tens of millions of children (those neighbors or fellow humans that ethics or the discourse of the rights of man refer to) without any moral or legal tribunal ever being considered competent to judge such a sacrifice" (86/82).

13. Deconstruction, as Fritsch puts it, "calls for moral and political decisions to recognize—that is, not to disavow—the ineluctable impossibility of reaching a fully just, hospitable, forgiving, or generously giving decision" (Fritsch, "Deconstructive Aporias," 443). See also Fritsch, *Taking Turns With the Earth*, chap. 5. My own arguments in this chapter and the next owe a debt to this chapter in particular.

14. It is worth noting here that Derrida's framing of "being with" in terms of the relation to some other, even if this also includes a plurality of others, appears to lead him in the direction of a fairly truncated vision of community. In other words, "being with" and "living with" in Derrida is rarely, if ever, thought in terms of living together in a community in which inhabitants have something in common. See, on this issue, his description of "being with" in *The Politics of Friendship*: "Living—that has to be heard with *with* . . . . But every time, it is only one who *lives with* only one: I live, myself, *with* (*suzao*), with each one, each time with only one" (*PF*, 20/38, trans. mod.). For a discussion of this passage and this issue in Derrida, see Morin, "A Mêlée without Sacrifice," 140.

15. In *Specters*, Derrida asks us to envisage, precisely, a form of responsibility or commitment of justice to something other "than the life of a living being," something other than its "actual being-there, its empirical or ontological actuality" (SM, xx/17).

16. Foreshadowing the *Death Penalty* seminars, Kant is Derrida's explicit reference in "Faith and Knowledge" with respect to the notion of human dignity (FK, 87/79).

17. My use of the term *superlife* as a description of what appears to lie beyond finitude owes a debt to Michael Naas's detailed treatment of "Faith and Knowledge" in *Miracle and Machine*. Naas himself prefers the term "surplus life," speaking of "life beyond life, a sur-life, a *sur-vie*, that is, a survival but also a surplus life" (Naas, *Miracle and Machine*, 214).

18. See, for instance, *FWT*, 92/152.

19. In the cited passage, Derrida is speaking of how deconstruction contests the principle of capital punishment in Kant's philosophy of right. This critique is outlined in detail in the second year of the *Death Penalty* seminars.

20. Hägglund cites this very passage as support for his argument on the question of normativity. See Hägglund, *Radical Atheism*, 236n64.

21. For a description of why a simple deduction in this area is impossible, see also WA, 277–78/85–87.

22. Derrida makes the same point concerning the quasi-normative dimension of the relation to the other, that it cannot be "deduced" because it is already at work at the most primary level, in *Advances*: "One must make a place for the other because there is not place without it. What cannot be derived [*Ce qui est indérivable*] from this place is the 'we' of one and the other, one as the other, even when the one guards itself from the other" (Derrida, *Advances*, 49/40). The French carries the connotation of *obviousness*.

23. See, for instance, WA, 204/14.

24. As I discuss in chapter 5, the thought of survival thus enables us to criticize both the fantasy of a pure entity, community, or nation-state immune to contamination and violation, and a certain conception of human life, rights, and dignity.

25. For a discussion of this phantasm of my death in volume 2 of *The Beast and the Sovereign*, see Naas, *End of the World*.

26. Naas, *Derrida From Now On*, 188.

27. Naas, 210.

28. See PC, 363/386 (as well as LD, 239–40/297–99); A, 37–38/72–73; and BS, 2:157–59/227–30. See also "Discussion Between Jacques Derrida, Philippe Lacoue-Labarthe, and Jean-Luc Nancy," in Derrida, *For Strasbourg*, 17–30, especially 28/97.

29. See Derrida's discussion of the "revolutionary force" of the breaches and openings in Freud's thought in FWT, 173/281.

30. To my knowledge, this text has not been published in French, as there is no French equivalent text to the collection *Without Alibi*.

31. On this point, see Derrida's remarks on the impossibility of Freud having "invented" a new concept of analysis and of resistance to analysis: "Who, besides God, has ever *created*, literally 'created,' a concept? Freud had no choice, if he wished to make himself understood, but to inherit from the tradition" (RP, 18–19/33).

32. Derrida and Stiegler, *Echographies*, 122/137.

33. Naas, "An Atheism that (Dieu merci!) Still Leaves Something to Be Desired," 64.

34. The logic here runs more or less along the following lines: "If death is not one"—that is, never singularly locatable, but rather dispersed, however minimally, by the structure of the trace and a disappearing living-on—then "there is . . . nothing clearly identifiable and locatable beneath this word . . . death in the singular [the one necessary to the death penalty] no longer exists" (DP, 1:241/327).

35. At the level of the deconstruction of the death *penalty* (and not death in general), we can put it this way: In order for the deconstruction of death at stake here not to fall back onto the notion of some mythical beyond, it has to continually insist on the absolute impossibility of anything beyond mortality as living-dying. But

if this is the case, life comes out anything but "unscathed," since life is now thought in terms of radical mortality, its essential openness to threat.

36. This is an aspect of Derrida's thought that I think Hägglund has rightly underscored in his treatment of Derrida's frequent references to the chance and the threat that accompany any and every moment of finite life, a structure that follows directly from the thought of spacing, trace, and *différance*. The crucial point here, as Hägglund shows, is not that ethical and political decision-making in this framework aims at a projected ideal of absolute peace but can always fall short in fact; rather it is that the ground on the basis of which such decisions are made is already compromised from the very beginning and offers no promise of a sovereign good.

37. See also the following passage in *Echographies of Television*: "The, shall we say, categorical imperative, the unconditional duty of all negotiation, would be to let the future have a future [*de laisser de l'avenir à l'avenir*], to let or make it come, or, in any case, to leave the possibility of the future open" (85/98).

38. Derrida, "Hostipitality," 360–61.

39. See, in particular, N, 344/498–99.

40. I take this description from Morin, "Spacing of Time," 35, and explain it further below. See also Morin, "A Mêlée Without Sacrifice."

41. This is a point I see Haddad rightly underscoring in his treatment of these issues. See Haddad, *Derrida and the Inheritance of Democracy*, 5.

5. Sovereignty, Cruelty, and the Death Penalty

1. In "The University Without Condition," Derrida makes clear that the concept of sovereignty has to do with "the supposed sovereignty of nation-states" but also undergirds "the concepts of subject, citizen, freedom, responsibility, the people, etc." (WA, 207/20). For a careful and lucid reading of Derrida's treatment of the theologico-political concept of sovereignty, see Naas, *Derrida From Now On*, 81–95.

2. This would hold even if scholars as astute as Penelope Deutscher can legitimately speak of Derrida's occlusion of biopolitics, in Foucault primarily, but also in Agamben. See Deutscher, *Foucault's Futures*, 32–33. See also Deutscher's incisive essay, "'This Death Which Is Not One.'"

3. Derrida's treatment of the death penalty is glossed but not entirely developed in the previously published dialogue with Elisabeth Roudinesco, *For What Tomorrow*, and in his address to the States General of Psychoanalysis from 2000, "Psychoanalysis Searches the States of Its Soul: The Impossible Beyond of a Sovereign Cruelty" (in WA). Beyond these texts, see also "For Mumia Abu-Jamal" and "Globalization, Peace, and Cosmopolitanism," in particular N, 125–29/7–13 and 385–86/19.

4. On the necessity of this passing-through, see Rottenberg, *For the Love of Psychoanalysis*, 125–26.

5. For an alternate reading of these issues, see Naas, "Always the Other Who Decides," 63–86.

6. Yet if deconstruction attempts to take into account what the unconscious does to politics and to the classical notion of sovereignty, this is in part because, as Derrida makes quite clear in "Psychoanalysis Searches," psychoanalysis has, for its part, remained remarkably silent on this topic. Indeed, as Derrida sees it, psychoanalysis in essence fails to take up the critique of sovereignty issuing from its own most fundamental insight. It has never attempted to think through the ramifications of its first gesture, the one whereby it sets out to analyze, and thus begins to deconstruct, the fundamentally fictional character of sovereignty. Consequently, it "has not yet undertaken and thus still less succeeded in thinking, penetrating, and changing the axioms of the ethical, the juridical, and the political" (WA, 244/21).

7. Derrida's recourse to Freud in his writings on the death penalty has received some attention already in work by Elizabeth Rottenberg in particular. For her part, Rottenberg sheds light on why, for Derrida, psychoanalysis might be in a privileged position to address the question of cruelty in the discourse around the death penalty, and she argues forcefully that psychoanalysis offers vital resources to philosophy on this issue. However, the precise work that this notion of endless cruelty performs in Derrida's engagement with the death penalty—the precise way in which it manages to undo the classical arguments for and against capital punishment—is not fully addressed by Rottenberg, nor does she address the link between cruelty in Freud and the thought of survival at the core of the deconstructive critique of capital punishment. These are the issues that are my focus here. See Rottenberg, *For the Love of Psychoanalysis*, 122–36.

8. As Penelope Deutscher has shown, while Derrida recommends rereading Foucault's *Discipline and Punish* "in its entirety" in the first year of the *Death Penalty* seminars (DP, 1:42/74), his actual engagement with Foucault is exceedingly limited, as if he wanted to studiously avoid Foucault. Yet on the matter of the logic of progress underwriting the death penalty, Derrida is much closer to Foucault than he would perhaps like to admit. Though Derrida makes no mention of it, Foucault explicitly references such a progressive logic in *Discipline and Punish*. See Foucault, *Discipline and Punish*, 12–13; and Deutscher, "'This Death Which Is Not One,'" 168–69. On this, and other, overlooked affinities between the two, see Deutscher, *Foucault's Futures*, 21–25 and 32–38.

9. This is one of the reasons, but as we will see not the chief reason, Derrida says in the seminars, "the question of the death penalty could well be the best and most indispensable introduction to the question, what is Enlightenment?" (DP, 1:179/252).

10. It should by now be clear that any attempt to break the fatal "alliance" between modern abolitionism and the philosophical tradition favorable to the principle of the death penalty must have recourse to an altogether different logic. Thus, even as deconstruction aims clearly at putting an end to the death penalty, it must continually underscore that even if there were to be something like total and complete abolition, the death penalty would still live on. "Even when the death penalty will have been abolished, when it will have been purely and simply,

absolutely and unconditionally, abolished on earth, it will survive; there will still be some death penalty," Derrida writes (*DP*, 1:282/380). This is not simply an assessment of what abolitionism should expect but rather a strategic lever for breaking the deadly alliance, operating at a more fundamental level, between abolitionism and the philosophical discourse of the death penalty.

11. Derrida then links the Freudian figure of a drive for power to sovereignty in the first year of the *Beast and the Sovereign* seminars (*BS*, 1:290/388). For a discussion of how Derrida mobilizes the figure of a drive for mastery in his debate with Foucault and how this figure allows him to deconstruct Foucault's conception of power, see Trumbull, "Power and the 'Drive for Mastery.'"

12. See *PC*, 325–27/346–47 and 403–5/430–32.

13. Derrida had in fact telegraphed this move in "Faith and Knowledge," where he speaks of the need to think the *"new cruelty"* in war via psychoanalysis, bringing to bear on it "the question of radical evil and working out the reaction to radical evil that is at the center of Freudian thought" (FK, 89–90/83).

14. Vitale in *Biodeconstruction* unfortunately misreads Derrida's treatment of this issue, insofar as Derrida does not endorse the idea of a drive for power. As I demonstrate below, he does not endorse either the idea of "conjuring away the devastating effects of the cruel drive for power" (163–64).

15. In the first year of the *Death Penalty* seminars, Derrida fleshes out this theme primarily with reference to Nietzsche. However, he wraps up his discussion of Nietzsche by invoking Freud and the thought of a primary sadism, speaking of Freud's "bid to raise the level of originary sadistic cruelty that has no contrary and that means that surpassing cruelty by an apparent non-cruelty would be merely a surpassing *in* cruelty, a surfeit of cruelty" (*DP*, 1:160/226). Freud thus speaks to an aggressivity more cruel than Nietzsche's will to power, more purely destructive.

16. For an account of how this destabilization is carried out with reference to Beccaria and Kant, see Trumbull, "Derrida and the Death Penalty," 317–36.

17. I have modified the English translation to correct an error. The published translation reads "the classic philosopheme of all the great right-wing philosophies [*de toutes les grandes philosophies du droit*] that have favored the death penalty" (*DP*, 1:116/170). But "all the great philosophies of the right that have favored . . . " would be *philosophies de la droite*, which is not what the original has.

18. Dawne McCance engages with this notion of "life worth more than life" but she treats only Derrida's isolation of this humanist logic in Hegel around the time of the 1975–76 seminars and its implications are said to bear only on the question of animal ethics. See McCance, *Reproduction of Life Death*, 7.

19. Fatal in two senses: fatal for the cause of abolitionism but also in that it dictates that abolitionism continues to participate in the "death-dealing" discourse propping up the death penalty (*DP*, 1:254/345).

20. Infinite survival is in fact opposed to *survivance*: it would be living on not for some time but for all time (a form of infinite life).

21. See also Derrida's discussion of the deconstruction of death in the sciences: *DP*, 1:242n19/328–29n2.

22. Wills, "Machinery of Death or Machinic Life," 14–15.

23. For a discussion of this fantasy and the spectacle of the death penalty, see Trumbull, "The All-Seeing Sovereign," 160–79.

24. Rottenberg, *For the Love of Psychoanalysis*, 123.

25. On this illusion, see the concluding section of Freud's letter to Einstein, where Freud writes: "There is no use in trying to get rid of men's aggressive inclinations. . . . The Russian Communists, too, hope to be able to cause human aggressiveness to disappear by guaranteeing the satisfaction of all material needs and by establishing equality in other respects among all the members of the community. That, in my opinion, is an illusion" (*SE*, 22:211–12).

26. See *SE*, 22:213, where Freud speaks explicitly of justifying the idea that "everyone has a right to his own life."

27. Rottenberg, in keeping with the focus of her book, focuses on the contingency in the playing-out of the cruel drive for power whose origin is the death drive. See Rottenberg, *For the Love of Psychoanalysis*, 116. For yet another take on this passage, see Senatore, "This Obscure and Enigmatic Concept," 57–76.

28. Because I am focused on Derrida's critique of the theological dimension of our inherited political concepts, I do not consider here the corollary thought that the religious, in Derrida, might always already have been political. I leave it to others to explore this possibility in "Faith and Knowledge."

29. Others have called attention to Derrida's characterization of the death penalty as what holds together the theological and the political, but no one, to my mind, has *demonstrated* why this is the case in Derrida. See Naas, "Always the Other Who Decides"; Rottenberg, *For the Love of Psychoanalysis*; Howells, "Death Penalty and Its Exceptions"; and Oliver, "Death Penalties," in *Technologies of Life and Death*, 188–217.

30. See also *DP*, 2:248/331: "The death penalty seals the alliance between the theological and the political." In truth, in *For What Tomorrow*, Derrida's formulation is even more complex: there, he refers to the death penalty as the "weld" that holds together the theological, the political, and philosophy (or, more precisely, the tradition of ontological thought in philosophy), insofar as the "speculative scaffolding" that props up the death penalty, via a certain understanding of "the proper to man," sacrifice, and life, is simultaneously philosophical in origin, has its provenance in the classic philosopheme I have been exploring in this chapter (*FWT*, 148/240). This is why, in the same dialogue, Derrida points so emphatically to the "stupefying . . . fact about the history of Western philosophy" that there has never been any philosopher to rigorously and formally contest the death penalty (*FWT*, 145–46/235).

31. In the second year of the seminars, Derrida acknowledges that there are many classical, deconstructible answers to the question "'What is man,' 'What is proper to

man?'" (language, reason, law, politics, modesty, cruelty, death, etc.), but he shows that "the juridco-political apparatus that we call the death penalty" has a relation not only "of essential concatenation, with all the other traits . . . but also a relation of metonymy or synecdoche with the other traits or figures or predicates of what is said to be 'proper to man'" (*DP*, 2:211/283).

32. At the very least, religion in its Abrahamic, monotheistic form does so.

33. See *DP*, 2:240/320–21: "The question of the death penalty remains, in every sense and in the depths of the very enigma of these two words, a sacrificial logic."

34. "Even when the death penalty will have been abolished," he writes a bit later, "when it will have been purely and simply, absolutely and unconditionally, abolished on earth, it will survive; there will still be some death penalty. Other figures will be found for it; other figures will be invented for it, other turns in the condemnation to death" (*DP*, 1:282/380).

35. It shakes up the field of the political in the specific sense discussed in chapter 4. It does not simply demystify and do away with the phantasm at the core of the theologico-political once and for all, but it does transform our relation to it.

36. Stated another way, showing how the death penalty allows a deconstruction of the theologico-political *in toto* neutralizes in advance any potential criticism that, in looking at capital punishment as an instance of sovereign power, Derrida is taking on an issue with less relevance in our contemporary moment, given that this moment is now increasingly thought in specifically biopolitical, or even thanatopolitical, terms.

37. Derrida's contestation of the human-animal distinction has been the subject of considerable attention in the secondary literature, yet the secondary literature has not taken due account of the political project driving Derrida's interest in this area.

Bibliography

Anderson, Nicole. *Derrida: Ethics Under Erasure*. London: Continuum, 2012.
Beardsworth, Richard. *Derrida and the Political*. London: Routledge, 1996.
———. Bennington, Geoffrey. "Derridabase." In *Jacques Derrida*. With Jacques Derrida. Chicago: University of Chicago Press, 1993.
———. *Interrupting Derrida*. London: Routledge, 2000.
———. *Legislations: The Politics of Deconstruction*. London: Verso, 1994.
———. *Not Half No End: Militantly Melancholy Essays in Memory of Jacques Derrida*. Edinburgh: Edinburgh University Press, 2011.
Bennington, Geoffrey, and Katie Chenoweth. "Phalanges." Preface to *Le calcul des langues* by Jacques Derrida, 7–24. Paris: Seuil, 2020.
Bergo, Bettina. "*Mal D'Archive*: Derrida, Freud, and the Beginnings of the Logic of the Trace in 1888." *Derrida Today* 7, no. 2 (2014): 137–54.
Cheah, Pheng, and Suzanne Guerlac, eds. *Derrida and the Time of the Political*. Durham, NC: Duke University Press, 2009.
Chiesa, Lorenzo. *Subjectivity and Otherness: A Philosophical Reading of Lacan*. Cambridge, MA: MIT Press, 2007.
Cornell, Drucilla. *The Philosophy of the Limit*. New York: Routledge, 1992.
Critchley, Simon. *The Ethics of Deconstruction: Derrida and Levinas*. 3rd ed. Edinburgh: Edinburgh University Press, 2014.
de Lauretis, Teresa. *Freud's Drive: Psychoanalysis, Literature, and Film*. London: Palgrave, 2008.
Derrida, Jacques. *Acts of Religion*. Edited by Gil Anidjar. London: Routledge, 2002.
———. *Advances*. Translated by Philippe Lynes. Minneapolis: University of Minnesota Press, 2017. Originally published as "Avances," preface to Serge Margel, *Le Tombeau du dieu artisan*, 7–50. Paris: Minuit, 1995.

———. *The Animal that Therefore I Am*. Translated by David Wills. New York: Fordham University Press, 2008. Originally published as *L'animal que donc je suis*. Paris: Galilée, 2006.

———. *Aporias*. Translated by Thomas Dutoit. Stanford, CA: Stanford University Press, 1993. Originally published as *Apories*. Paris: Galilée, 1996.

———. *Archive Fever: A Freudian Impression*. Translated by Eric Prenowitz. Chicago: University of Chicago Press, 1996. Originally published as *Mal d'Archive: une impression freudienne*. Paris: Galilée, 1995.

———. "As If It Were Possible, 'Within Such Limits' . . . ." Translated by Benjamin Elwood and Elizabeth Rottenberg. In *Negotiations*, 342–70. Originally published as "Comme c'était possible, « within such limits » . . . ," *Revue Internationale de Philosophie* 52, no. 205 (3) (1998): 497–529.

———. "Autoimmunity: Real and Symbolic Suicides—A Dialogue with Jacques Derrida." In *Philosophy in a Time of Terror*, edited by Giovanna Borradori, 85–136. Chicago: University of Chicago Press, 2003. Republished in French in *Le « concept » du 11 Septembre*. Paris: Galilée, 2004.

———. *The Beast and the Sovereign*. Vol. 1. Translated by Geoffrey Bennington. Chicago: University of Chicago Press, 2009. Originally published as *Séminaire: La bête et le souverain, Volume I (2001–2002)*. Paris: Galilée, 2008.

———. *The Beast and the Sovereign*. Vol. 2. Translated by Geoffrey Bennington. Chicago: University of Chicago Press, 2011. Originally published as *Séminaire: La bête et le souverain, Volume II (2002–2003)*. Paris: Galilée, 2010.

———. "Before the Law." Translated by Avital Ronnell and Christine Roulston. In *Acts of Literature*, edited by Derek Attridge, 182–220. New York: Routledge, 1992. Originally published as "Préjugés: Devant la loi." In Derrida, et al., *La faculté de juger*, 87–139. Paris: Minuit, 1985.

———. "Beyond the Power Principle." Translated by Elizabeth Rottenberg. *Undecidable Unconscious* 2, no. 1 (2015): 7–17. Originally published as "Au-delà du principe de pouvoir," *Rue Descartes* 82 (2014): 4–13.

———. *Clang*. Translated by David Wills and Geoffrey Bennington. Minneapolis: University of Minnesota Press, 2021. Originally published as *Glas*. Paris: Galilée, 1974.

———. *The Death Penalty*. Vol. 1. Translated by Peggy Kamuf. Chicago: University of Chicago Press, 2014. Originally published as *Séminaire: La peine de mort, Volume I (1999–2000)*. Paris: Galilée, 2012.

———. *The Death Penalty*. Vol. 2. Translated by Elizabeth Rottenberg. Chicago: University of Chicago Press, 2017. Originally published as *Séminaire: La peine de mort, Volume II (2000–2001)*. Paris: Galilée, 2015.

———. "The Deconstruction of Actuality." Translated by Elizabeth Rottenberg. In *Negotiations*, 85–116. Originally published as "La deconstruction de l'actualité," *Passages* 57 (1993): 60–75. Republished in part as "Artifactualités." In *Échographies de la television: Entretiens filmés*, 11–35. Paris: Galilée, 1886.

———. "Discussion Between Jacques Derrida, Philippe Lacoue-Labarthe, and Jean-Luc Nancy." Translated by Pascale-Anne Brault and Michael Naas. In *For

Strasbourg, 17–30. New York: Fordham University Press, 2014. Originally published as "Dialogue entre Jacques Derrida, Philippe Lacoue-Labarthe, et Jean-Luc Nancy," *Rue Descartes* 52 (2006): 86–99.

———. *Dissemination*. Translated by Barbara Johnson. Chicago: University of Chicago Press, 1981. Originally published as *La Dissémination*. Paris: Seuil, 1972.

———. *Echographies of Television*. With Bernard Stiegler. Translated by Jennifer Bajorek. Cambridge: Polity, 2002. Originally published as *Échographies de la television: Entretiens filmés*. Paris: Galilée, 1996.

———. *Edmund Husserl's Origin of Geometry: An Introduction*. Translated by John P. Leavey, Jr. Lincoln: University of Nebraska Press, 1989. Originally published as *Introduction à l'Origine de la Géometrié de Husserl*. Paris: PUF, 1961.

———. "Faith and Knowledge: The Two Sources of 'Religion' at the Limits of Reason Alone." Translated by Samuel Weber. In *Acts of Religion*, 40–101. Originally published as "Foi et savoir: Les deux sources de la 'religion' aux limites de la simple raison." In *Foi et savior*, 7–100. Paris: Seuil, 2001.

———. "*Fichus*: Frankfurt Address." Translated by Rachel Bowlby. In *Paper Machine*, 164–81. Stanford, CA: Stanford University Press, 2005. Originally published as *Fichus: Discours de Francfort*. Paris: Galilée, 2002.

———. "For Mumia Abu-Jamal." Translated by Elizabeth Rottenberg. In *Negotiations*, 125–29. Originally published as preface to *En direct du couloir de la mort*, by Mumia Abu-Jamal, 7–13. Translated by Jim Cohen. Paris: Découverte, 1996.

———. *For What Tomorrow . . . A Dialogue*. With Elisabeth Roudinesco. Translated by Jeff Fort. Stanford, CA: Stanford University Press, 2004. Originally published as *De quoi demain . . . Dialogue*. Paris: Fayard/Galilée, 2001.

———. "Force of Law: The 'Mystical Foundation of Authority.'" Translated by Mary Quaintance. In *Acts of Religion*, 228–98. Originally published as *Force de loi*." Paris: Galilée, 1994.

———. "*Fors*: The Anglish Words of Nicolas Abraham and Maria Torok." Translated by Barbara Johnson. In *The Wolf Man's Magic Word*, by Nicolas Abraham and Maria Torok, xi–xlviii. Translated by Nicholas Rand. Minneapolis: University of Minnesota Press, 1986. Originally published as "Fors." In *Cryptonomie: Le verbier de l'Homme aux loups*, by Abraham and Torok, 7–73. Paris: Flammarion, 1976.

———. *The Gift of Death*. Translated by David Wills. Chicago: University of Chicago Press, 1995. Originally published as *Donner la mort*. Paris: Galilée, 1999.

———. "Globalization, Peace, and Cosmopolitanism." In *Negotiations*, 371–86. Originally published as "La mondialisation, la paix et la cosmopolitique," *Regards* 54 (2000): 16–19.

———. *Heidegger: The Question of Being and History*. Translated by Geoffrey Bennington. Chicago: University of Chicago Press, 2016. Originally published as *Heidegger: la question de l'Être et l'Histoire*. Paris: Galilée, 2013.

———. "Hostipitality." Translated by Gil Anidjar. In *Acts of Religion*, 356–420.
———. "Interpreting Signatures (Nietzsche/Heidegger): Two Questions." Translated by Diane Michelfelder and Richard E. Palmer. *Philosophy and Literature* 10, no. 2 (1986): 246–62. Originally published as "Guter Wille zur Macht II: Die Unterschriften interpretieren (Nietzsche/Heidegger)." Translated by Friedrich Kittler. In *Text und Interpretation*, edited by Philippe Forget, 62–77. Munich: W. Fink, 1984.
———. "La Différance." In *Théorie d'ensemble* (coll. Tel Quel), 41–66. Paris: Seuil, 1968.
———. *Le calcul des langues: Distyle*. Paris: Seuil, 2020.
———. *Learning to Live Finally: The Last Interview*. Translated by Pascale-Anne Brault and Michael Naas. Hoboken, NJ: Melville House Publishing, 2007. Originally published as *Apprendre à vivre enfin*. Paris: Galilée, 2005.
———. "Let Us Not Forget—Psychoanalysis." Translated by Geoffrey Bennington and Rachel Bowlby. *Oxford Literary Review* 12, no. 1 (1990): 3–8.
———. *Life Death*. Translated by Pascale-Anne Brault and Michael Naas. Chicago: University of Chicago Press, 2020. Originally published as *La vie la mort: Séminaire (1975–1976)*. Paris: Seuil, 2019.
———. *Margins of Philosophy*. Translated by Alan Bass. Chicago: University of Chicago Press, 1982. Originally published as *Marges de la philosophie*. Paris: Minuit, 1972.
———. *Memoires: for Paul de Man*. Translated by Cecile Lindsay, Jonathan Culler, and Eduardo Cadava. New York: Columbia University Press, 1986. Originally published as *Mémoires pour Paul de Man*. Paris: Galilée, 1988.
———. *Negotiations: Interventions and Interviews, 1971–2001*. Edited by Elizabeth Rottenberg. Stanford, CA: Stanford University Press, 2002.
———. "Nietzsche and the Machine." Translated by Richard Beardsworth. In *Negotiations*, 215–56.
———. *Of Grammatology*. Translated by Gayatri Chakravorty Spivak. Baltimore: Johns Hopkins University Press, 1976. Originally published as *De la grammatologie*. Paris: Minuit, 1967.
———. *Of Hospitality: Anne Dufourmantelle Invites Jacques Derrida to Respond*. Translated by Rachel Bowlby. Stanford, CA: Stanford University Press, 2000. Originally published as *De l'hospitalité*. Paris: Calman-Lévy, 1997.
———. "Otobiographies: The Teaching of Nietzsche and the Politics of the Proper Name." Translated by Avital Ronell. In *The Ear of the Other: Otobiography, Transference, Translation*, edited by Christine V. McDonald, 1–38. New York: Schocken Books, 1985. Republished in French in *Otobiographies. L'enseignement de Nietzsche et la politique du nom propre*. Paris: Galilée, 1984.
———. *Paper Machine*. Translated by Rachel Bowlby. Stanford, CA: Stanford University Press, 2005. Originally published as *Papier Machine*. Paris: Galilée, 2001. And as *Fichus: Discours de Francfort*. Paris: Galilée, 2002.
———. *Parages*. Edited by John P. Leavey. Stanford, CA: Stanford University Press, 2010. Originally published as *Parages*. Paris: Galilée, 1986.

———. *The Politics of Friendship*. Translated by George Collins. London: Verso, 2005. Originally published as *Politques de l'amitié*. Paris: Galilée, 1994.
———. *Positions*. Translated by Alan Bass. Chicago: University of Chicago Press, 1981. Originally published as *Positions*. Paris: Minuit, 1972.
———. *The Post Card: From Socrates to Freud and Beyond*. Translated by Alan Bass. Chicago: University of Chicago Press, 1987. Originally published as *La Carte Postale: de Socrate à Freud et au-delà*. Paris: Flammarion, 1980.
———. "Provocation: Forewords." In *Without Alibi*, xv–xxxv.
———. *Psyche: Inventions of the Other*. Vol. 1. Edited by Peggy Kamuf and Elizabeth Rottenberg. Stanford, CA: Stanford University Press, 2007. Originally published as *Psyché: Inventions de l'autre. Édition augmenté*. Paris: Galilée, 1998.
———. *Psyche: Inventions of the Other*. Vol. 2. Edited by Peggy Kamuf and Elizabeth Rottenberg. Stanford, CA: Stanford University Press, 2008. Originally published as *Psyché: Inventions de l'autre: Édition augmenté*. Paris: Galilée, 1998. And as *Psyché: Inventions de l'autre*. Paris: Galilée, 1987.
———. "Psychoanalysis Searches the States of Its Soul: The Impossible Beyond of a Sovereign Cruelty." In *Without Alibi*, 238–80. Originally published as *États d'âme de la psychanalyse*. Paris: Galilée, 2000.
———. *Resistances of Psychoanalysis*. Translated by Peggy Kamuf, Pascale-Anne Brault, and Michael Naas. Stanford, CA: Stanford University Press, 1998. Originally published as *Résistances de la psychanalyse*. Paris: Galilée, 1996.
———. *Rogues: Two Essays on Reason*. Translated by Pascale-Anne Brault and Michael Naas. Stanford, CA: Stanford University Press, 2005. Originally published as *Voyous: Deux essais sur la raison*. Paris: Galilée, 2003.
———. *Specters of Marx: The State of the Debt, the Work of Mourning and the New International*. Translated by Peggy Kamuf. New York: Routledge, 2006. Originally published as *Spectres de Marx*. Paris: Galilée, 1993.
———. *A Taste for the Secret*. With Maurizio Ferraris. Translated by Giacomo Donis. Cambridge: Polity Press, 2001.
———. *Theory and Practice*. Translated by David Wills. Chicago: University of Chicago Press, 2019. Originally published as *Théorie et pratique: Cours de l'ENS-Ulm 1975–1976*. Paris: Galilée, 2017.
———. "The University Without Condition." In *Without Alibi*, 202–37. Originally published as *L'Université sans condition*. Paris: Galilée, 2001.
———. *Voice and Phenomenon: Introduction to the Problem of the Sign in Husserl's Phenomenology*. Translated by Leonard Lawlor. Evanston, IL: Northwestern University Press, 2011. Originally published as *La voix et la phénomène. Introduction au problème du signe dans le phénoménologie du Husserl*. Paris: PUF, 1967.
———. *Without Alibi*. Translated and edited by Peggy Kamuf. Stanford, CA: Stanford University Press, 2002.
———. *Writing and Difference*. Translated by Alan Bass. Chicago: University of Chicago Press, 1978. Originally published as *L'écriture et la différence*. Paris: Seuil, 1967.

Deutscher, Penelope. "'This Death Which Is Not One': Reproductive Biopolitics and the Woman as Exception in *The Death Penalty, Volume 1*." In *Foucault/Derrida Fifty Years Later: The Futures of Genealogy, Deconstruction, and Politics*, edited by P. Deutscher, O. Custer, and S. Haddad, 166–84. New York: Columbia University Press, 2016.

———. *Foucault's Futures: A Critique of Reproductive Reason*. New York: Columbia University Press, 2017.

Ellmann, Maud. "Deconstruction and Psychoanalysis." In *Deconstructions: A User's Guide*, edited by Nicholas Royle, 211–37. New York: Palgrave, 2000.

Forrester, John. *The Seductions of Psychoanalysis: Freud, Lacan, and Derrida*. Cambridge: Cambridge University Press, 1990.

Foucault, Michel. *Discipline and Punish: The Birth of the Prison*. Translated by Alan Sheridan. New York: Vintage, 1995.

Freud, Sigmund. *The Standard Edition of the Complete Psychological Works of Sigmund Freud*. Translated and edited by James Strachey. 24 volumes. London: Hogarth Press, 1953–74.

Fritsch, Matthias. "An Eco-Deconstructive Account of the Emergence of Normativity in 'Nature.'" In Fritsch, Lynes, and Wood, *Eco-Deconstruction*, 279–302.

———. "Deconstructive Aporias: Quasi-transcendental and Normative." *Continental Philosophy Review* 44 (2011): 439–68.

———. *The Promise of Memory: History and Politics in Marx, Benjamin, and Derrida*. Albany: State University of New York Press, 2005.

———. *Taking Turns With the Earth: Phenomenology, Deconstruction, and Intergenerational Justice*. Stanford, CA: Stanford University Press, 2018.

Fritsch, Matthias, Philippe Lynes, and David Wood, eds. *Eco-deconstruction: Derrida and Environmental Philosophy*. New York: Fordham University Press, 2018.

Gaon, Stella. *The Lucid Vigil: Deconstruction, Desire, and the Politics of Critique*. New York: Routledge, 2019.

Gasché, Rodolphe. *Inventions of Difference: On Jacques Derrida*. Cambridge, MA: Harvard University Press, 1994.

———. *The Tain of the Mirror: Derrida and the Philosophy of Reflection*. Cambridge, MA: Harvard University Press, 1986.

Haddad, Samir. *Derrida and the Inheritance of Democracy*. Bloomington: Indiana University Press, 2013.

———. "Leonard Lawlor's Renewal of Thinking." *Southern Journal of Philosophy* 56, no. 3 (2018): 393–402.

Hägglund, Martin. *Dying for Time: Proust, Woolf, Nabokov*. Cambridge, MA: Harvard University Press, 2012.

———. "On Chronolibido: A Response to Rabaté and Johnston." *Derrida Today* 6, no. 2 (2013): 169–81.

———. *Radical Atheism: Derrida and the Time of Life*. Stanford, CA: Stanford University Press, 2008.

———. "The Trace of Time: A Critique of Vitalism." *Derrida Today* 9, no. 1 (2016): 36–46.

Hodge, Joanna. *Derrida on Time*. London: Routledge, 2007.
Howells, Christina. "The Death Penalty and Its Exceptions." In Oliver and Straub, *Deconstructing the Death Penalty*, 87–98.
Hurst, Andrea. *Derrida vis-à-vis Lacan*. New York: Fordham University Press, 2008.
Jacob, François. *La Logique du vivant: Une histoire de l'hérédité*. Paris: Gallimard, 1970.
Johnson, Barbara, "The Frame of Reference: Poe, Lacan, Derrida." *Yale French Studies* 55/56 (1977): 457–505. Reprinted in *The Purloined Poe*, edited by John P. Muller and William J. Richardson, 213–51. Baltimore: Johns Hopkins University Press, 1988.
Johnston, Adrian. "The true Thing is the (w)hole: Freudian-Lacanian Psychoanalysis and Derridean Chronolibidinal Reading—Another Friendly Reply to Martin Hägglund." *Derrida Today* 6, no. 2 (2013): 146–68.
Kamuf, Peggy. *To Follow: The Wake of Jacques Derrida*. Edinburgh: Edinburgh University Press, 2010.
Kirby, Vicki. "Grammatology: A Vital Science." *Derrida Today* 9, no. 1 (2016): 47–67.
———. *Quantum Anthropologies: Life at Large*. Durham, NC: Duke University Press, 2011.
Lacan, Jacques. *Écrits: The First Complete Edition in English*. Translated by Bruce Fink. New York: Norton, 2006.
———. *Écrits 1*. Paris: Seuil, 1999.
Laplanche, Jean. *Life and Death in Psychoanalysis*. Translated by Jeffrey Mehlman. Baltimore: Johns Hopkins University Press, 1985.
Lawlor, Leonard. *From Violence to Speaking Out: Apocalypse and Expression in Foucault, Derrida, and Deleuze*. Edinburgh: Edinburgh University Press, 2016.
———. *This Is Not Sufficient: An Essay on Animality and Human Nature in Derrida*. New York: Columbia University Press, 2007.
Lewis, Michael. *Derrida and Lacan: Another Writing*. Edinburgh: Edinburgh University Press, 2008.
Lynes, Phillipe. "The Posthuman Promise of the Earth." In Fritsch, Lynes, and Wood, *Eco-deconstruction*, 101–20.
Major, René. "Derrida, lecteur de Freud et de Lacan." *Études françaises* 38, nos. 1–2 (2002): 165–78.
———. *Lacan avec Derrida: Analyse Désistentielle*. Paris: Mentha, 1991.
Mansfield, Nick. *The God Who Deconstructs Himself: Sovereignty and Subjectivity Between Freud, Bataille, and Derrida*. New York: Fordham University Press, 2010.
Marder, Elissa. *The Mother in the Age of Mechanical Reproduction*. New York: Fordham University Press, 2012.
McCance, Dawne. *The Reproduction of Life Death: Derrida's* La vie la mort. New York: Fordham University Press, 2019.
Melville, Stephen. *Philosophy Beside Itself*. Minneapolis: University of Minnesota Press, 1986.

Morin, Marie-Eve. "A Mêlée without Sacrifice: Nancy's Ontology of Offering against Derrida's Politics of Sacrifice." *Philosophy Today*, SPEP Supplement 50 (2006): 139–43.

———. "The Spacing of Time and the Place of Hospitality: Living Together According to Bruno Latour and Jacques Derrida." *Parallax* 21, no. 1 (2015): 26–41.

Naas, Michael. "Always the Other Who Decides: On Sovereignty, Psychoanalysis, and the Death Penalty." In Oliver and Straub, *Deconstructing the Death Penalty*, 63–86.

———. "An Atheism that (Dieu merci!) Still Leaves Something to Be Desired." *New Centennial Review* 9, no. 1 (2009): 45–68.

———. *Derrida from Now On*. New York: Fordham University Press, 2008.

———. *The End of the World and Other Teachable Moments: Jacques Derrida's Final Seminar*. New York: Fordham University Press, 2015.

———. *Miracle and Machine: Jacques Derrida and the Two Sources of Religion, Science, and the Media*. New York: Fordham University Press, 2012.

———. "When It All Suddenly Clicked: Deconstruction after Psychoanalysis after Photography." *Mosaic: An Interdisciplinary Journal of the Arts* 44, no. 3 (2011): 81–98.

Nancy, Jean-Luc, and Philippe Lacoue-Labarthe. *The Title of the Letter: A Reading of Lacan*. Translated by David Pettigrew and François Raffoul. Albany: State University of New York Press, 1992.

Oliver, Kelly. *Technologies of Life and Death*. New York: Fordham University Press, 2013.

Oliver, Kelly, and Stephanie M. Straub, eds. *Deconstructing the Death Penalty: Derrida's Seminars and the New Abolitionism*. New York: Fordham University Press, 2018.

Peeters, Benoît. *Derrida: A Biography*. Translated by Andrew Brown. Cambridge: Polity, 2013.

Pettigrew, David, and François Raffoul, eds. *Disseminating Lacan*. Albany: State University of New York Press, 1996.

Rottenberg, Elizabeth. "Derrida and Psychoanalysis." In *A Companion to Derrida*, edited by Zeynep Direk and Leonard Lawlor, 304–20. Malden, MA: Wiley Blackwell, 2014.

———. *For the Love of Psychoanalysis: The Play of Chance in Freud and Derrida*. New York: Fordham University Press, 2019.

———. "Intimate Relations: Psychoanalysis Deconstruction." *Derrida Today* 11, no. 2 (2018): 178–95.

Royle, Nicholas. *After Derrida*. Manchester: Manchester University Press, 1995.

Senatore, Mauro. *Germs of Death: The Problem of Genesis in Jacques Derrida*. Albany: State University of New York Press, 2018.

———. "'This Obscure and Enigmatic Concept': Philosophy of Cruelty in Nietzsche, Freud, and Beyond." *Itinera* 15 (2018): 57–76.

Shepherdson, Charles. "Derrida and Lacan: An Impossible Friendship." *Differences* 20, no. 1 (2009): 40–86.

Trumbull, Robert. "The All-Seeing Sovereign: Blindness and Vision in Derrida's Death Penalty Seminars." *Symposium* 20, no. 2 (2016): 160–79.
———. "Deconstruction and Psychoanalysis: 'A Problematic Proximity.'" *Derrida Today* 5, no. 1 (2012): 69–91.
———. "Derrida and the Death Penalty: The Question of Cruelty," *Philosophy Today* 59, no. 2 (2015): 317–36.
———. "Power and the 'Drive for Mastery': Derrida's Freud and the Debate with Foucault." In *Foucault/Derrida Fifty Years Later: The Futures of Genealogy, Deconstruction, and Politics*, edited by P. Deutscher, O. Custer, and S. Haddad, 151–65. New York: Columbia University Press, 2016.
———. "Revisiting Derrida's Critique of Lacan, Beyond the Misunderstandings." Unpublished manuscript.
Vitale, Francesco. *Biodeconstruction: Jacques Derrida and the Life Sciences*. Translated by Mauro Senatore. Albany: State University of New York Press, 2018.
Weber, Samuel. "The Debts of Deconstruction and Other, Related Assumptions." In *Taking Chances: Derrida, Psychoanalysis, and Literature*, edited by J. H. Smith and W. Kerrigan, 33–65. Baltimore: Johns Hopkins University Press, 1984.
Willet, Cynthia. "Tropics of Desire: Freud and Derrida." *Research in Phenomenology* 22, no. 1 (1992): 138–51.
Wills, David. *Inanimation: Theories of Inorganic Life*. Minneapolis: University of Minnesota Press, 2016.
———. "Machinery of Death or Machinic Life." *Derrida Today* 7, no. 1 (2014): 2–20.
———. *Matchbook: Essays in Deconstruction*. Stanford, CA: Stanford University Press, 2005.
Wolfe, Cary. "Wallace Stevens's Birds, or, Derrida and Ecological Poetics." In Fritsch, Lynes, and Wood, *Eco-deconstruction*, 317–38.

Index

Abolition (of the death penalty), 128, 134, 152, 181–82n10, 184n34
Abolitionism, 128, 132–35, 138–40, 142–43, 152, 181–82n10, 182n19
Abraham, Nicolas, 157n1
Agamben, Giorgio, 180n2
Agrégation, 159n6
Algeria, 86–87
Althusser, Louis, 159n6
Anderson, Nicole, 159n2, 177n9
Animal, animality, 14, 43, 74, 105–6, 112, 127, 141–42, 150–53, 170n50, 172n5, 182n18, 184n37
Arche-writing, arche-trace, 2, 6–7, 11–12, 14–16, 19, 27, 29, 30, 67, 80, 101, 160n3, 160n6–7, 161n10
Archive, 79–82, 94–96, 174n22, 176n39
Aristotle, 107
Austin, John L., 110
Autobiography, 6–7, 37, 39–41, 49, 52, 164n4, 167n30
Autoimmunity, 3, 7–8, 71–78, 81–89, 91–93, 104–5, 112, 122–23, 172n7–8, 173n10, 173n17

Bataille, Georges, 177n5
Beardsworth, Richard, 98, 176n1–2
Beccaria, Cesare, 182n16
Bennington, Geoffrey, 3, 11, 17, 28, 37, 50, 157n2, 158n3–4, 161n11–12, 162n18, 163n3–4, 164n7–8, 166n26, 173n16
Bergo, Bettina, 158n3
Binding, 7, 38, 44, 47, 58–60, 62–64, 67, 82, 91, 93, 136, 163–64n4, 165–66n19, 167n36, 168n39. See also stricture

Biology, 6, 19, 21, 36, 39, 40–42, 49, 74, 137, 160n8, 165n15, 183n21. See also life sciences
Biopolitical philosophy, 1, 180n2
Biopolitics, 9, 127, 129, 153, 180n2, 184n36. See also thanatopolitics

Canguilhem, Georges, 36
Cheah, Pheng, 159n2
Chenoweth, Katie, 163n3
Chiesa, Lorenzo, 169n50
Community, 5, 77–78, 142, 168n39, 178n14, 179n24, 183n25
Cornell, Drucilla, 98–99, 176n1–2
Critchley, Simon, 98–99, 176n1–2
Cruelty, 85, 122, 128, 130–39, 146–47, 181n7, 182n13–15, 183n27, 183–84n31

da Vinci, Leonardo, 161n12
Death, 1–2, 12, 14–16, 27–31, 33–34, 35–37, 39, 41, 46–48, 54–61, 63–64, 67, 69–70, 74–78, 85, 88–91, 94, 98, 101–2, 105–6, 109, 112–14, 117, 120–24, 127, 129–30, 132–34, 140, 142–47, 152–53, 158n4, 162n19, 162n21, 163n4, 171n57, 171n2, 171–72n4, 173n9, 174n19, 175n26, 175n33, 178n12, 179n25, 179n34–35, 183n21
Death drive, 7, 35–36, 41, 44, 46–48, 50–51, 53–57, 59–61, 63–65, 135–36, 139, 146–48, 159n8, 162n20, 163n1, 163–64n4, 165n18, 165–66n19, 163–64n4, 168n43, 169n45, 171n2, 172n7, 174n23, 176n39, 183n27
Death penalty, 9, 97–98, 112, 120–22, 127–35, 138–46, 148–53, 177n5, 178n19, 179n34–35, 180n3, 181n7–9, 181–82n10, 182n16–17, 182n19,

195

Death penalty *(continued)*
   183n23, 183n29–30, 183–84n31, 184n33–34, 184n36
de Lauretis, Teresa, 165n14
Democracy, 3, 7, 71, 83–84, 86–88, 100, 106–7, 110, 172n6
Democracy to come, 83, 107–10, 153, 172n6
Derrida, Jacques, works by: Advances, 179n22; *The Animal That Therefore I Am*, 65, 69, 104–6, 172n5; A, 88–89, 105, 114, 171n2, 179n28; AF, 24, 78–83, 94–96, 166n20, 169n45, 173n9, 174n21–23; ARSS, 72, 74–75, 122–23, 173n10, 173n14; BS, vol. 1, 2, 11, 65, 70, 90, 101, 104, 106, 112, 153, 182n11; BS, vol. 2, 2, 11, 65, 70, 90, 101, 103–5, 106, 112–17, 153, 172n6, 179n25, 179n28; "Before the Law," 174n21; "Beyond the Power Principle," 168n41; *Clang*, 158n4; DP, vol. 1, 2, 11, 70, 89–90, 101, 104–6, 112, 120, 114, 120–21, 128–30, 133–34, 138–42, 144–46, 150–53, 178n16, 179n34, 181n8–9, 181–82n10, 182n15, 182n17–19, 183n21, 184n34; DP, vol. 2, 2, 11, 70, 90, 101, 104–6, 112, 120, 128, 133–34, 138, 144, 146, 150–53, 178n16, 178n19, 183n30, 183–84n31, 184n33; "Désistance," 157n1; D, 158n6, 169n46; *Ear of the Other*, 165n10, 165n13; *Echographies of Television*, 118, 178n10, 179n32, 180n37; *Edmund Husserl's Origin of Geometry*, 158n6; FK, 72, 74, 77–78, 97, 101, 104–5, 112, 120, 142, 149, 151, 173n13, 178n16–17, 182n13, 183n28; "Fichus," 175n25; For Strasbourg, 179n28; FWT, 69–70, 77, 104, 108, 114, 120, 128, 131–32, 136, 138, 140–43, 150, 153, 160n7, 169n45, 172n5, 175n27, 178n18, 179n29, 180n3, 183n30; "Force of Law," 68, 101, 109, 125; "Fors," 157n1; *Gift of Death*, 100, 103, 177n4, 178n12; Heidegger, 171n2; "Hostipitality," 125, 173n15, 180n38; "Interpreting Signatures," 41, 165n10–11; LLF, 11, 69–70, 175n26; "Let Us Not Forget—Psychoanalysis," 162n22; *Le calcul de langues*, 163n3; LD, 2–3, 35–39, 40–41, 49–58, 60–63, 67, 71, 136, 163n3, 164n6–7, 164–65n9, 165n12–13, 166n22–25, 166–67n27, 167n28–29, 167n31, 167n33–34, 167n36, 168n38–39, 168n41, 169n46, 174n19, 179n28, 182n18; "Living On—Borderlines," 68, 171n1; MP, 16, 30–31, 35, 158n6, 161n10, 162n21, 167n32, 170n55; *Memoires*, 158n4, 171n1; N, 124–25, 128, 165n11–12, 178n10, 180n39, 180n3; OG, 2, 6, 11–12, 14–18, 70, 105, 158n5, 160n7, 160–61n8, 161–62n12, 162n19, 164n6; *Of Hospitality*, 173n15; PM, 87, 172n5, 173n17, 174–75n24; POS, 158n6, 169n46, 170n55; PF, 72–73, 174n21, 178n14; PC, 3, 6–7, 35–39, 41, 49–58, 60–67, 71, 136, 159n8, 163n2, 163–64n4, 164n6–7, 166n21–24, 166–67n27, 167n30–31, 167n36, 168n39, 168n43, 169n46, 170n51, 170–71n56, 171n57, 179n28, 182n12; P, 66, 68, 157n1, 169n47, 170n53, 170–71n56, 173n9; RP, 18, 36, 66–67, 73, 76, 79, 96, 118, 139, 162n13, 162n22, 168n41, 169n45, 169n47, 170n52, 171n57, 172n8, 174n18, 174n23, 179n31; R, 11, 70, 72, 74, 78, 83–88, 90–91, 102, 106–12, 129, 131, 153, 172n6; SM, 68–69, 72–74, 76–78, 89, 97, 99, 101–3, 105, 112, 125, 171n2–3, 172–73n9, 178n15; *Taste for the Secret*, 171–72n4; *Theory and Practice*, 163n3; VP, 6, 11–13, 15–16, 158n6, 159n1, 164n6; WA, 69, 84, 107, 118, 120, 122, 128–32, 134–38, 146–48, 157n1, 175n25, 179n21, 179n30, 180n3, 181n6; WD, 3, 6, 12, 15–19, 22–24, 26–29, 32–36, 38, 75, 79, 94, 99, 158n6, 162n16, 162–63n23, 163n1, 163n4, 167n32, 174n22, 177n6, 179n23, 180n1
Derrida studies, 2, 11–12, 16, 20, 37, 72
Destruction, destructibility, 3, 8, 20, 22, 54–55, 61, 66, 72–76, 78–86, 91, 93–96, 102–4, 122–24, 131–32, 135–37, 139, 142–43, 146–48, 151, 153, 159–60n2, 160n6, 175n37, 176n39
Deutscher, Penelope, 11, 180n2, 181n8. See also threat
Différance, 2, 13–16, 25–26, 29–31, 35, 38, 50, 54, 55–58, 61–65, 68–70, 73, 88, 90–91, 97, 99–102, 110–14, 117, 122, 159n2, 160n6–7, 161n10, 162n19, 167n33, 168n42, 170n55, 172n5, 180n36
Drive (Trieb), 42–45, 47, 62–63, 72, 92, 115, 165n14, 167n35
Drive for mastery, 51, 59, 63–64, 76, 135–38, 147, 168n41, 168n43–44, 174n18, 182n11, 182n14, 183n27

École Normale Supérieure (ENS), 36, 159n6, 171n56
Economy of death, 2–3, 6, 15, 20, 27–31, 33, 35, 41, 67, 69, 75, 82, 102, 162n21
Einstein, Albert, 147
Ellmann, Maud, 157n1, 163n4
Energy, energetics, 20–21, 23–28, 30–32, 38, 42–48, 54–55, 59–60, 62, 92, 136, 175n27
Enlightenment, 84, 134, 138, 141, 174n20, 181n9
Eros, life drives. See Freud, Sigmund; theory of life and death drives
Ethics, ethical relation, 3, 5, 8, 71, 96–100, 103, 110–11, 118–22, 124–26, 130, 147, 176n2, 177n4–5, 177n9, 178n12–13, 180n36, 181n6, 182n18
Exappropriation, 58, 60, 62–64, 71, 82, 88–91, 167n35, 168n39, 173n17, 176n39
Exteriority, 6, 15–16, 30, 80, 98, 102, 109, 118

Ferraris, Maurizio, 172n4
Finitude, 6–8, 12, 29, 31, 33, 38, 62, 70–71, 77, 81–82, 85, 88–96, 98, 101, 103–5, 107–8, 111, 114, 116–17, 120–24, 127, 129, 132, 140, 142–46, 148–50, 152–53, 159–60n2, 160n6, 162n19, 171n2, 172n5, 176n39, 178n17, 180n36
Forrester, John, 158n3, 163n4, 169n50
Foucault, Michel, 76, 180n2, 181n8, 182n11
Freud, Sigmund, works by: *Beyond the Pleasure Principle*, 6–7, 20, 22, 32, 36–37, 39, 41–42, 44–64, 75, 78–79, 93, 135–36, 159n8, 162n21, 163n1, 163–64n4, 164n6–7, 165n18, 165–66n19, 166n21–23, 166n25, 166–67n27, 167n29–30, 167n33; *Civilization and Its Discontents*, 48, 78–79, 115, 136; "The Economic Problem of Masochism," 165n18; *The Ego and the Id*, 43, 48; "Formulations on the Two Principles of Mental Functioning," 54, 167n32; *Delusions and Dreams in Jensen's Gradiva*, 174n22; "Instincts and Their Vicissitudes," 42; *The Interpretation of Dreams*, 19–22, 24, 42, 162n15, 165n16, 167n36; *Leonardo da Vinci and a Memory of His Childhood*, 161n12; *Moses and Monotheism*, 95; "On Narcissism," 42–44, 165n17; "The Psycho-analytic View of Psychogenic Disturbance of Vision," 43; "A Note Upon the 'Mystic Writing Pad,'" 19–22, 32–33, 75, 173n17; *Project for a New Scientific Psychology*, 19–27, 42, 162n14, 162n16, 163n1; *The Psychopathology of Everyday Life*, 173n9; *Studies on Hysteria*, 22–23; "Thoughts for the Times on War and Death," 114; *Three Essays on the Theory of Sexuality*, 42–43, 165n15; "The Unconscious," 14–17; "Why War?," 135, 146–47, 183n25–26; theory of life and death drives, 3, 6–7, 35–37, 41–42, 44–48, 57–59, 61–62, 64, 78, 147–48, 159n8, 163n1, 163–64n4, 166n23. See also binding, death drive, drive, drive for mastery, energy, memory trace, *Nachträglichkeit*, neurology, pathbreaking, pleasure principle, reality principle, repetition compulsion, representatives (psychical), resistance, unconscious
Fritsch, Matthias, 98–100, 110, 160n2, 177n3, 177n5, 178n13
Future, futurity, 1, 8–9, 12–13, 16, 27, 29, 30, 71, 78, 82, 86–87, 89–90, 93–94, 98–99, 102–3, 105–6, 119, 122–26, 138, 144–45, 152–54, 159–60n2, 175n33, 175n37, 177n8, 180n37

Gaon, Stella, 158n3
Gasché, Rodolphe, 100, 178n11
God, 95, 104, 107, 109, 111–12, 127–30, 152, 179n31
Guerlac, Suzanne, 159n2

Haddad, Samir, 98–100, 160n2, 176n2, 177n3, 180n41
Hägglund, Martin, 3, 8, 11, 38, 72, 91–96, 98–99, 110, 157n2, 158n3–4, 159–60n2, 162–63n21, 164n8, 165n19, 175n28–38, 176n39–40, 177n3, 177n7–8, 179n20, 180n36
Hegel, G. W. F., 36, 39, 140–41, 182n18
Heidegger, Martin, 2, 4–6, 14, 30, 39–41, 88–89, 105, 163n2, 165n10, 171n2
Hodge, Joanna, 159n2
Hospitality, 74, 100, 125, 173n15, 178n13
Howells, Christina, 183n29
Hugo, Victor, 140
Human (concept of), 1, 98, 100, 104–8, 112, 114, 120, 127–28, 132, 137, 140–43, 150–53, 172n5, 178n16, 179n24, 183–84n31, 184n37
Hurst, Andrea, 158n3, 170n50
Husserl, Edmund, 4–6, 11–13, 15–16, 23–24, 27, 158–59n6, 164n6

Inheriting, inheritance, 17–18, 34, 72, 78, 99, 110, 115, 118, 150–51, 161–62n12, 162n13, 171n3, 174–75n24, 179n31
Ipseity, 83–85, 88, 106–7, 112
Iterability, 13–14, 26–27, 29, 73, 78, 80–81, 90, 95, 112, 144, 160n5

Jacob, François, 6, 36–37, 39, 41, 57, 77–78, 164n5, 165n9, 166n23, 174n19
Jensen, Wilhelm, 174n22
Johnson, Barbara, 65–66, 169n49, 169–70n50
Johnston, Adrian, 162–63n21

Kamuf, Peggy, 158n3
Kant, Immanuel, 128, 139, 140–42, 151, 153, 178n16, 178n19, 182n16
Kirby, Vicki, 3, 157n2, 164n8

Lacan, Jacques, 7, 38, 65–67, 92, 157n1, 169n46–48, 169–70n50, 170n51, 170n54, 170–71n56, 171n57
Lacoue-Labarthe, Philippe, 157n1, 170–71n56, 179n28
Laplanche, Jean, 167n34
Language, 1, 19, 30–31, 70, 73, 122, 137, 160n7, 170n51, 172n5, 183–84n31
Lawlor, Leonard, 176n2
Levinas, Emmanuel, 4–5, 89, 98–99, 177n4, 177n6
Lewis, Michael, 170n50
Life, living being, 1–3, 6–9, 11–12, 14–16, 18, 20, 24–25, 27–34, 35–50, 53–58, 60–65, 67, 68–80, 82–91, 93–94, 96, 98, 100–111, 113, 117–23, 127, 129–30, 132–33, 137–53, 160n6–8, 162n19, 163–64n4, 164n6, 165n12, 166n19, 171n57, 171n3, 172n5–6, 174n19, 175n26,

Life, living being (continued)
175n33, 175n37, 178n15, 178n17, 179–80n35, 180n36, 182n18, 183n26, 183n30; life and death (in opposition), 2, 8, 36–39, 50, 53, 55–56, 61, 69–70, 85, 98, 112–13, 117, 157n1–2, 160n7, 171n3, 172n5

Life death (la vie la mort), 2–4, 6–7, 11–12, 16, 19, 24, 29, 30–32, 34, 35–39, 41, 49–50, 53–58, 62–65, 67, 68–69, 71–72, 74, 83, 85, 92, 97–98, 102, 105, 110–11, 117–18, 122, 158n4, 160n3, 163–64n4, 164–65n9, 165n12, 171n3, 179–80n35

Life sciences, 2–4, 36–37, 48, 72, 76–77, 83, 87, 137, 157n2, 160n3, 164–65n9, 166n21. See also biology

Living on. See survival

Luther, Martin, 89

Lynes, Philippe, 177n5

Major, René, 157n1, 158n3, 159n7, 170n50
Mansfield, Nick, 158n3
Marder, Elissa, 158n3
Marx, Karl, 4, 171n3, 172n9
McCance, Dawne, 3, 37, 157n2, 159n8, 164n8, 164–65n9, 166n23, 167n37, 182n18
Melville, Stephen, 158n3
Memory, memory trace, 4–5, 19–26, 28, 33, 79–80, 160n2–3, 162n16, 174n22
Metaphysics, 4–5, 14, 17–20, 23–24, 30, 32, 34, 36, 39–40, 49–50, 63–65, 67, 77, 92–94, 99, 113–17, 137, 160–61n8, 161–62n12, 168n42, 169n46
Metapsychology, 5, 34, 42–43, 48, 52, 63–64, 80, 169n45
Montaigne, Michel de, 103
Morin, Marie-Eve, 13, 16, 98, 160n4, 161n9–10, 162n20, 177n3–4, 178n14, 180n40
Mortality, 12, 29, 38, 65, 70, 77–78, 82, 88–89, 91, 97–98, 100, 103–4, 108, 111, 114, 117, 121–24, 127, 140–46, 148. See also finitude
Mourning, 158n4

Naas, Michael, 11, 73, 112–13, 120, 162n17, 173n11–12, 178n17, 179n25–27, 179n33, 180n1, 180n5, 183n29
Nachträglichkeit, 4, 19–20, 23–24, 27, 30, 84
Nancy, Jean-Luc, 87, 170–71n56, 179n28
Nation-state, 83, 95, 106, 109, 112, 127, 129–30, 153, 168n39, 174n24, 179n24, 180n1
Neurology, neurophysiology, 19–21, 34, 160n3, 162n16
Nietzsche, Friedrich, 2–3, 6, 30, 36, 39–41, 50, 135, 138, 164n6, 165n10–12, 182n15
Normativity, 3, 8–9, 96, 97–103, 106–11, 118–26, 127, 148–49, 177n5, 177n8, 178n13, 179n20, 179n22, 180n36

Oliver, Kelly, 177n5, 183n29
Ontology, 1, 12–13, 92, 101, 110, 117, 119, 121, 178n15

Pathbreaking (*frayage*), 20, 22–26, 28, 30–31, 162n16, 163n1
Peeters, Benoît, 159n6, 171n56
Pettigrew, David, 169n50
Phantasm, 8, 98, 100, 105–9, 111–18, 121, 123, 127, 129–30, 132, 139–40, 144–46, 152–53, 168n39, 176n39, 179n25, 184n35
Plato, 4, 17
Pleasure principle, 25, 44–45, 47–57, 59–61, 63, 76, 136, 165n18, 167n32–33, 167n36
Poe, Edgar Allan, 170n51
Politics, the political, 3, 5, 8–9, 68, 71, 74, 83–84, 96–100, 103, 106–8, 110–11, 118–22, 124–32, 140, 147, 149–50, 152–53, 172n6, 174n24, 175n25, 177n4, 178n13, 180n36, 181n6, 183n28–30, 184n31, 184n35, 184n37. See also theologico-political
Power. See drive for mastery
Presence, 13, 15–18, 22–24, 26, 29, 31, 65, 67, 79, 92, 102–3, 160n6–7, 161n8, 172n5, 175n36
"Proper to man," 98, 104, 106, 114, 132, 140–42, 149–50, 170n50, 183n30, 183–84n31
Psychoanalysis, 3, 7, 16–17, 19, 24, 31, 36, 42, 52, 65, 71, 77, 79, 81, 83–84, 91–92, 95, 113, 117–18, 130–32, 135–38, 146–48, 157n1, 158n3–4, 159n7, 163n3, 172n8, 181n6–7, 182n13; and metaphysics, 17–18, 23–24, 35, 49, 161–62n12

Raffoul, François, 169n50
Reality principle, 25, 54–55, 57, 76, 167n32–33
Religion, 5, 7, 42, 71, 77, 100, 104–6, 108, 114, 120, 142, 149, 151–52, 184n32
Repetition compulsion, 44–45, 51, 56, 59, 63–65, 76, 118, 165–66n19, 172–73n9
Representatives (psychical), 43, 48, 79, 135, 165n17
Resistance, 21–22, 24, 26, 28, 30–31, 35–36, 74, 79, 113, 117–18, 162n16, 172n9, 179n31
Rottenberg, Elizabeth, 3, 146, 157n1, 158n3, 163n4, 177n5, 180n4, 181n7, 183n24, 183n27, 183n29
Rousseau, Jean-Jacques, 161n12, 162n19
Royle, Nicholas, 158n3, 163n4

Sacrifice, 77–78, 150–52, 177n4, 178n12, 183n30, 184n33. See also religion
Sade, Marquis de, 135
Saussure, Ferdinand de, 164n6
Schmitt, Carl, 129
Senatore, Mauro, 164n8, 183n27
September 11, 74, 86, 122

INDEX

Shaking up, solicitation, 3–4, 8–9, 18, 98, 105, 108, 114, 118–19, 138, 152, 158n5, 184n35
Shepherdson, Charles, 170n50
Sovereignty, 3, 9, 74, 83–85, 88, 91, 97–98, 100, 106–12, 114, 117–20, 127–32, 135–38, 141–42, 144, 146–47, 149, 151, 153, 174–75n24, 177n5, 180n1, 181n6, 182n11, 184n36
Spacing (*espacement*), 16, 23–24, 30, 32, 146, 161n10, 180n36
Straub, Stephanie M., 177n5
Stricture, 7, 54, 58, 61–65, 67, 82, 168n39, 176n39
Suicide, 74–76, 83, 85–86, 165n12, 176n39
Superlife, 8, 104–9, 111, 114, 117, 121–22, 127, 140, 142–43, 148–49, 151, 153, 178n17
Survival (*survivance*), 2–4, 7–9, 12, 34, 36–38, 68–73, 75–78, 80, 82, 87–98, 100–12, 114, 117–25, 127, 129–30, 132–33, 139–46, 148, 150–54, 158n4, 171n57, 171n1–2, 171–72n4, 172n6, 175n33, 176n39, 177n8, 178n17, 179n24, 179n34, 181n7, 182n18, 182n20

Tel Quel, 170n55
Temporalization, temporization, 8, 11–13, 15–16, 27, 30, 32, 105, 129, 144, 159n1, 160n6, 161n10, 162–63n22, 175n36–37
Thanatopolitics, 184n36. See also biopolitics
Theologico-political, 3, 9, 98, 108–9, 112–13, 120, 128–30, 140, 148–53, 180n1, 182n30, 183n28–29, 184n35–36
Theology, the theological, 8–9, 77, 100, 104–8, 112, 114, 120, 127–30, 132, 137, 140, 142, 144, 146, 148–53, 174n20, 174–75n24, 183n28–29, 182n30. See also religion
Threat, 28–30, 36, 71, 74–78, 80–83, 85–87, 91–94, 103–4, 119, 123–25, 127, 140, 143, 159–60n2, 175n37, 176n39, 180n35. See also destruction, destructibility
To-come (*l'àvenir*), 8, 16, 93, 98–99, 106, 110–11, 124, 144, 159–60n2, 177n5, 180n37
Torok, Maria, 157n1
Trace, 2, 5–6, 11, 13–16, 18–19, 23–24, 27, 29, 31–33, 64, 67, 69–71, 79–83, 86, 88, 91–97, 99–102, 105, 110–11, 113–14, 117, 146, 160n5–7, 160–61n8, 161n10, 164n6, 172n5, 175n26, 175n33, 175n37, 176n39, 179n34, 180n36
Trumbull, Robert, 162n13, 168n44, 169n48, 174n18, 182n11, 182n16, 183n23

Ultra-transcendental, 2, 14–15, 27, 65, 67, 82, 86, 92–93, 97, 99–100, 108–10, 114, 117, 119, 121, 125, 177n8
Unconscious, 4–5, 19, 21, 23, 25, 42, 45, 50, 59, 61–62, 66, 84, 87–88, 114–16, 131, 159n6, 162–63n21, 168n42, 169n45, 170n51, 171n2, 174n22, 175n27, 181n6

Violence, 95–96, 98–100, 103, 119, 121, 125, 132, 136, 146, 153, 176n2, 177n6
Vitale, Francesco, 3, 157n2, 159n8, 160n3, 164n4, 164n8, 165n9, 167n35, 168n43, 172n7, 182n14

Weber, Samuel, 163n4
Willet, Cynthia, 158n3, 168n40
Wills, David, 146, 158n3, 159n8, 163–64n4, 167n30, 177n5, 183n22
Wolfe, Cary, 177n5
Wood, David, 177n5
Writing, 1, 4, 7, 14, 17–22, 32–34, 37, 39–41, 49, 52–53, 68, 70, 75, 79, 160n7, 164n6, 173n17, 175n26

Robert Trumbull teaches philosophy at Seattle University.

www.ingramcontent.com/pod-product-compliance
Lightning Source LLC
Chambersburg PA
CBHW032035290426
44110CB00012B/817